You cannot learn the martial arts overnight.
With all the obstacles,
It will take you your entire lifetime.

The Complete Master's Kick
Library of Congress Catalog Card Number: 88-092048
ISBN 0-929015-01-0

Copyright 1988 © by Master Hee Il Cho.
Published in the United States of America by Master Hee Il Cho.
All rights reserved. No part of this book may be reproduced in any manner without written permission of
Master Hee Il Cho, 10587 Pico Blvd., Los Angeles, CA., 90064.

A man who goes fishing in the deep sea respects the sea greatly. It is vast and powerful, and demands that the man feel humbled.

A man who goes fishing in a still pond feels superior to the pond. In it, he sees no danger and therefore finds it soft and powerless.

Life is as the sea; deep and mysterious with strong currents that demand respect.

Be as the fisherman before the sea - respect life and be humble before it. Only then will you be able to fish its depths.

About The Olympics...

Many martial artists have felt threatened by the inclusion of Tae Kwon Do as a demonstration sport in the 1988 Olympics games from Seoul. They have felt that, if Tae Kwon Do is not their style, then their style will somehow fall from grace. Such is not the case.

The mere fact that the world will be watching, interested, in this new event will bring honor not just to Tae Kwon Do, but to all schools of martial arts. All styles will benefit, because the personal achievement of Olympic competition transcends the competing sport. The Olympics are not a threat but a milestone, and I can only hope that Tae Kwon Do will become a permanent addition to the Olympic list of events.

I would like to congratulate all Olympic competitors, not only those who are participating in Tae Kwon Do. An Olympic athlete embodies the aims to achieve for all martial artists, and as such they deserve and have my utmost respect.

Dedication

DEDICATION

    I dedicate these books to all martial artists around the world who work to improve themselves mentally, physically, and spiritually through their martial arts training.

    As members of the same family of martial artists, we are all traveling in the same direction, regardless of schools and styles.

    Though the arts which we love may be different and have different names, they share the same spirit. Our hearts are as one.

What is life?

Life is a dream,
    but if you only dream
        then your life is nothing.

Make your dreams realities.

Table of Contents

MASTER'S KICK

```
COPYRIGHT..........................................3-6
DEDICATION........................................7-34
INTRODUCTION.....................................35-72
PHILOSOPHY OF MASTER HEE IL CHO..................73-86

FRONT RISING KICK................................87-96
PUSHING KICK....................................97-108
CRESCENT KICK (INSIDE TO OUTSIDE)..............109-120
AXE KICK.......................................121-130
TWISTING KICK..................................131-142
FRONT SNAP KICK................................143-152
SIDE KICK......................................153-166
HOOK KICK (FRONT LEG, MOVING IN)...............164-178
LOW SIDE KICK..................................179-186
45 DEGREE ROUNDHOUSE KICK......................187-194
FRONT INWARD HOOK KICK.........................195-204
CRESCENT KICK (OUTSIDE TO INSIDE)..............205-214
ROUND HOUSE KICK...............................215-224
BACK SPINNING CRESCENT KICK....................225-236
BACK TURNING KICK..............................237-246
BACK SPINNING HOOK KICK........................247-258
BACK SPINNING KICK.............................259-270

MASTER CHO'S PHOTO ALBUM.......................271-288
```

Preface

This book is intended to fill the void in the Martial Arts literature which has been discovered by all serious students and instructors as well as others interested in the sport. Although this book is written as if we are talking to the student who intends to study the subject seriously and hopes to achieve proficiency of a higher level, we do not wish to discourage those who are interested only in using these techniques as an interesting and stimulating form of exercise or as a diversion. Such people may put into the Martial Arts as much as they wish and take from it what they want but only in direct proportion to what they have put in.

Acknowledgements

While it is impossible to acknowledge everyone who has, in some way, contributed to the completeion of these publications, we must recognize those most directly involved.

Special recognition must be given to Jeff Schechter. Because of his involvement in nearly every phase of manuscript preparation, he may almost be considered the second author.

I would also like to single out the following people for their help in various ways during the writing of this book:

>   Kuy Ha Cho   David Goldner
>   In Kyu Cho   Eddie Ikuta
>   Steven O'Dell   Steven Krashen
>   Mario Veltri   Sung Woong Kim
>   David Carter   Marcello Real
>   Randy Goldstein   Jerry Isdale
>   Max Schachenmann   Kihyon Kim
>   Bobby Burns

...and all the members of the Action International Martial Arts Association

Each day is a chance to develop new ideas.
    To make new plans.
        To gain new wisdoms to understand life.

Understand this,
    and then you can understand the
        preciousness of life.

To begin a new life, begin a new day.

Master Kuy Ha Cho, Vice President of the A.I.M.A.A.

 CHO'S TAE KWON DO CENTER

Master Hee Il Cho
11304 1/2 Pico Blvd.
West Los Angeles, CA 90064

Master Cho:

I have just finished reviewing the final proofs of your new books. I am amazed at the amount of information and detail you have included in these volumes. I know that you have worked very hard for more than two years to complete these volumes and the end product shows the time that went into, and commitment to the quality of the books. You have completed what has to be the most thorough, authoritative and easy to understand reference books. When you look at the eleven books that you have completed, it is obvious that you have accomplished what no other martial artist has ever attempted before. You have left a record of your knowledge for all martial artists to benefit from in the future. You have accomplished this without promoting any specific martial arts style and have provided the instructor as well as the student an opportunity to learn and improve their skills.

I am very proud to be associated with these publications. I am confident that when these publications are available to the martial arts community, they will become the most authoritative training guides available.

Regards,

Kuy Ha Cho

To My Mother:
    She is a person whose heart is bigger than a mountain,
        And wider than the ocean.
She has taught me to believe in myself,
        As strongly as she believes in herself.

TO MY WIFE, MIHYUN

I'd like to thank you, my beloved wife, for helping me a great deal with my life. Without your good spirits and support I could not have achieved all that I have. You are so patient, and your deep love for me has guided me to my success. I will always thank you for that.

I would like to express
    my heartfelt appreciation
        and thank you to

    Jeff Schechter,
        without whose contribution
            and assistance

    the creation of this book
        would never have been possible.

                Hee U Cho

All Ireland Tae Kwon·Do Association

NATIONAL SECRETARY,
17 VICAR STREET,
BARRACK STREET,
CORK,
IRELAND.

TEL:021 964648

**All Ireland Tae Kwon Do Association Chairman,
Mr. Adrian Walsh**

Master Hee Il Cho
Cho's Tae Kwon Do Centers
11304 1/2 Pico Boulevard
Los Angeles, California 90064

Dear Master Cho:

I want to take this opportunity on behalf of the All Ireland Tae Kwon Do Association to thank you for your recent visit to Ireland in connection with our annual testing.

For more than six years, as our head instructor, our association has continued to grow and it is with great pride that we associate ourselves with you. It has been through your efforts, direction, and training that our association has grown into one of the largest in the nation. As our head instructor, we are extremely proud of the high reputation and standing you maintain in England, Ireland, and Europe in the martial arts community. Your dedication to the martial arts and training as well as the many books that you have published is a credit to you and all of those who associate with you.

Thank you again for your leadership and association with the All Ireland Tae Kwon Do Association. We look forward to your speedy return to Ireland.

Very truly yours,

Adrian Walsh
Chairman
All Ireland Tae Kwon Do
Association

Mr. Philip Ameris, Action International Martial Arts Association Technical Directors

Seek to extend yourself
To the furthest extent of life's
Endless horizons.

Jason Cho, age 8

MASTER CHO SHARES HIS KNOWLEDGE

WITH MARTIAL ARTISTS ALL AROUND THE WORLD.

Master In Kyu Cho, Chairman of the A.I.M.A.A.

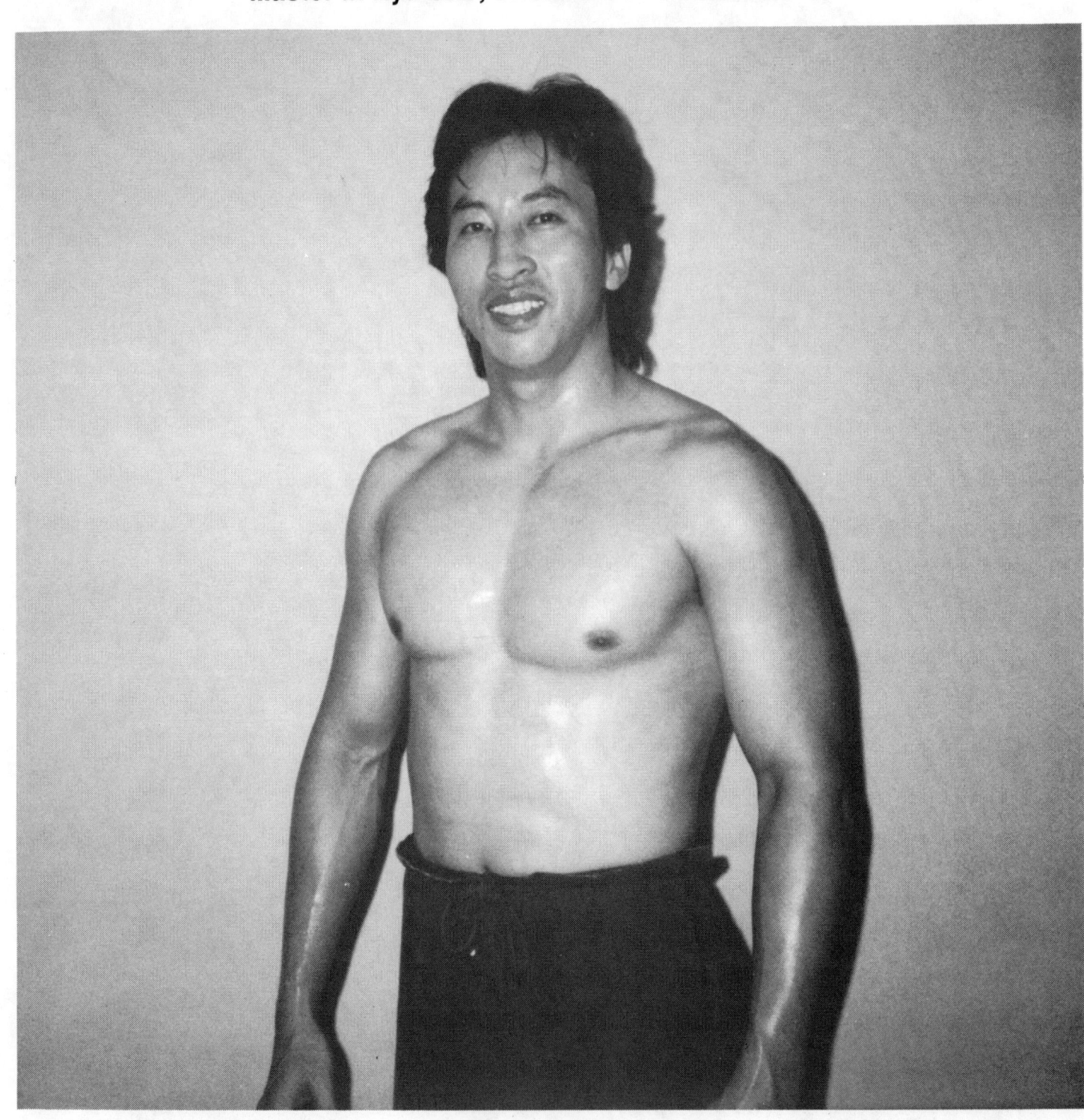

 CHO'S TAE KWON DO CENTER

Hee Il Cho
11304 1/2 Pico Blvd.
West Los Angeles, Ca 90064

My dear brother:

After reviewing the proofs of the books, I can see now that it is in the final stages and when completed will be a major addition to the books you have already published.

I know from first hand experience that you have dedicated your life to the martial arts and these books are your legacy to those who wish to enrich themselves as you and the many thousand students who have trained under you have. For me, your inspiration, dedication and guidance have provided me with the foundation for my own personal development. Training with you these many years is a real honor as I know of no other individual who has dedicated his life to the martial arts as you have and whose dedication and inspiration is felt in each and every person who has trained with you. I know you realize how much I appreciate all that you have done for me. I look forward to following in your footsteps and working by your side in the future.

Yours very truly,

In Kyu Cho

MASTER HEE IL CHO
A Biography

No other martial artist in the world has been invited to speak and demonstrate more that Master Hee Il Cho. An eighth-degree black belt in the Korean art of Taekwon Do, Master Cho is **known** throughout the world as one of the leading practitioners and innovators in the martial arts. His noteriety has led to more cover articles than any other martial artist in history.

Master Cho was born in Korea at the beginning of that country's bleakest hour. As a child he knew little other than the suffering and hunger brought about by war. The ability to survive was hard won. These childhood experiences helped mold his strong spirit.

Master Cho began studying Kang Soo Do at the age of ten after being severely beaten by a gang of youths at a local fair. He received his black belt at age thirteen, at which time he and his family moved to Inchon, near Seoul. Here, Master Cho began to study Taekwon Do, an art that would provide a lifetime of mental and physical development.

At the age of twenty one and already a fourth degree black belt, Master Cho was chosen to teach self-defence to the Korean Army. After his military service, Master Cho traveled to India and Germany where he taught servicemen the art of weaponless combat. Traveling with a demonstration team in 1969, Master Cho came to the United States and decided to stay.

After a brief time in Chicago, Master Cho settled and started teaching in South Bend, Indiana. Initially, times were hard but the indomitable spirit developed through the years of training allowed Master Cho to persevere. Eventually, He moved to Rhode Island and open a string of seven schools from 1972 through 1975.

Longing for warmth after a lifetime of bitterly remembered winters, Master Cho moved to Southern California in 1975. His school and reputation grew, and with it he recognized the need for a new organization; one based on the principles of Taekwon Do, but which would be for all martial arts diciplines. He founded the Action International Martial Arts Association which now enjoys worldwide membership of individuals and over a hundred schools. Through AIMAA, Master Cho hopes to reach all martial artists, regardless of the system they are studying and encourage in them them the true spirit of the martial arts.

Besides AIMAA, Master Cho is also the head instructor of both the England and Ireland Taekwon Do Associations. He visits and conducts seminars in Europe and other parts of the world on a regular basis.

As a tournament competitor, Master Cho has won more than twenty five championships around the world. He is the author of several successful martial arts books; "Man of Contrasts," a book of his techniques, philosophies and insights, "The Complete Taekwon Do Hung", a detailed three volume set which illustrates the various patterns practiced in Taekwon Do, "The Complete Martial Artist, Vols 1 and 2," a comprehensive exploration of the skills and training needed to for total mind, spirit and body fitness. To this impressive list of titles, Master Cho has recently completed five more books: "The Complete Master's Kick," "The Complete Master's Jumping Kick," "The Complete One Step and Three Step Sparring," "The Complete Tae Geuk Hyung of W.T.F," "The Complete Black Belt Hyung of W.T.F."

In addition to his written works, Master Cho has produced a series of over 31 instructional video tapes, the largest and most complete martial arts video library ever created by one person, including a video tape for Sybervision Inc. entitled "Defend Yourself."

While many masters of his caliber are content with writing and working behind a desk, Master Cho continues to work out and teach regularly at the AIMAA Headquarters, actively passing on his enthusiasm to his students.

As the title of Master Cho's first book so accurately states, Master Cho is a "Man of Contrasts." He has seen both devastating ugliness and inspirational beauty. He brings an understanding of both forces, light and dark to his growing legion of followers. He is what every student deserves; a cool breeze in the desert of false masters, an inspirational instructor and the complete martial artist.

> Life is full of changes
> Don't Resist
> Try Flowing

MASTER CHO SHARES HIS KNOWLEDGE

WITH MARTIAL ARTISTS ALL AROUND THE WORLD.

INTRODUCTION

I first met Master Hee Il Cho on the evening of April 11, 1984. It was my first night in Los Angeles after having driven cross country from New York. I was a high yellow belt, having studied for 6 months with Grandmaster Suh Chong Kang in Brooklyn. Before leaving New York I informed my instructor that I would be moving to Los Angeles and would need a new school, and I was told that the only school I should take class at was Master Cho's. Being loyal to my teacher, I looked up Master Cho's studio as soon as I arrived in California.

My first exposure to Master Cho and his teaching techniques was altogether intimidating. By coincidence I happened to walk into his school while he was teaching an advanced class, and where I was used to doing techniques like the Front Rising Kick slowly and only a few in either direction, I sat and watched in amazement as Master Cho led his students in doing five or six kicks in both directions - at full speed, over and over again until maybe fifty kicks were thrown. And then he started them throwing Inside to Outside Crescent Kicks. And then Outside to Inside Crescent Kicks. I had never seen a workout which was as hard or as thorough as the one I was now watching, and I immediately thought to myself that, in spite of my teacher's insistence, I should look for a different school. I did too; looking at several in the area, but eventually decided that if I was going to be serious about training, then I should train with the best. That meant Master Cho. His accomplishments as a martial artist were as numerous as they were varied; eighth degree black belt with 35 years of experience, on the covers of over 25 American and European magazines, winner of over 25 National and International Championships, author of 6 books, producer of 20 instructional video tapes, President of the Action International Martial Arts Association (A.I.M.A.A.), Republic of Ireland Tae Kwon Do Association (A.I.T.A.), and the Tae Kwon Do Association of Great Britain (T.A.G.B.). - and as soon as I decided not to be lazy, I realized how fortunate I was to have the opportunity to train with him.

My first weeks with Master Cho were the most difficult. I thought that I was a big shot, having done very well at my other school in my belt level. At the last tournament I was in in New York, I placed first in Breaking, first in Form and second in Sparring, but at Master Cho's do-jang I felt like the beginner I really was. Even Master Cho's students reflected his dedication to excellence in the martial arts.

Here were students at exactly my belt level who were already working on throwing jump-spinning kicks, a Master Cho trademark. I felt completely un-coordinated, and needless to say, very humbled. That's when my training really began.

Master Cho was very patient with me, and his no-nonsense approach to Tae Kwon Do was soon paying off. I learned that speed and strength are not as much inherited as they are earned, and the only way to earn them was through hard work and a clear approach to what it is you are hoping to achieve. You must have a clear goal in mind, chart a course that will take you to that goal, and then stick to the path which you have laid out for yourself. That is the way to accomplishment.

Master Cho has never taught a technique starting with the result and working backwards towards what the basics of the technique are, and it is with this same approach to Tae Kwon Do that Master Cho now presents this book, to the martial arts community. It is a nuts and bolts approach to <u>completely</u> understanding the mechanism of how to kick.

Each chapter covers a different kick, and the chapters themselves are broken into various sections:

- First - a brief description of the kick is given, citing the kick's historical, technical, and/or practical roots.

- Second - a step-by-step depiction, using both words and images, of how to properly throw the kick. All actions are broken down into their simplest components, described in detail to help facilitate learning the technique.

- Third - a discussion of what the most common mistakes are when attempting to execute the particular kick.

- Fourth - Master Cho's recommendations for the number of repetitions needed to master the kick - both at the beginners and the advanced level, followed by when the appropriate time to breathe is during the execution of the technique.

- Fifth and Sixth - weight lifting and stretching exercises picked by Master Cho to help increase the speed and power of the appropriate muscles for each kicking technique.

The beauty of *The Complete Master's Kick* is that Master Cho has designed each chapter to be a stand alone entry. A student doesn't need to read the entire book in order to benefit from the knowledge packed into its pages. If you wish to learn the 45 Degree Roundhouse Kick, all you need to do is to turn to that chapter and <u>everything</u> you need to know is right there, one thing after the other. No references are made to other sections, so you don't have to do any hunting for the information you need. Because of this, there is a certain amount of repetition, especially in the sections which describe the weight lifting and stretching techniques, however Master Cho has gone out of his way to include as many different exercises as possible; you will find three or four different ways of accomplishing the same stretch. Everything you need is given to you. All you need to add is your own self- determination.

Two years of planning, photographing, research, interviews with doctors and physical therapists, demonstrating and revising have gone into making   **The Complete Master's Kick** the most comprehensive volume ever assembled on the subject of the martial arts kick.   its approach to kicking is completely modern and reflects years of experience and modification rather than a rigid adherence to outdated methods which fail to incorporate the latest understanding of body mechanics and Kinesics. It is Master Cho's hope that every martial artist who chooses to use this **The Complete Master's Kick** does so with the same integrity and enthusiasm with which it was

prepared. The "art" in the martial arts comes from self-motivation, and a thirst for personal excellence.   "The Complete Master's Kick."
is another tool for you to use to quench that thirst.

The path of the martial artist is never paved, though with help it can be well-lit. As Master Cho says in his first book, "Man of Contrasts":

> "The task is difficult; there are many despairs that will taunt you and require much patience of you. But, if you are willing to make the effort and commit yourself, the rewards are limitless, more than you can really imagine. This I promise you."

Jeff Schechter

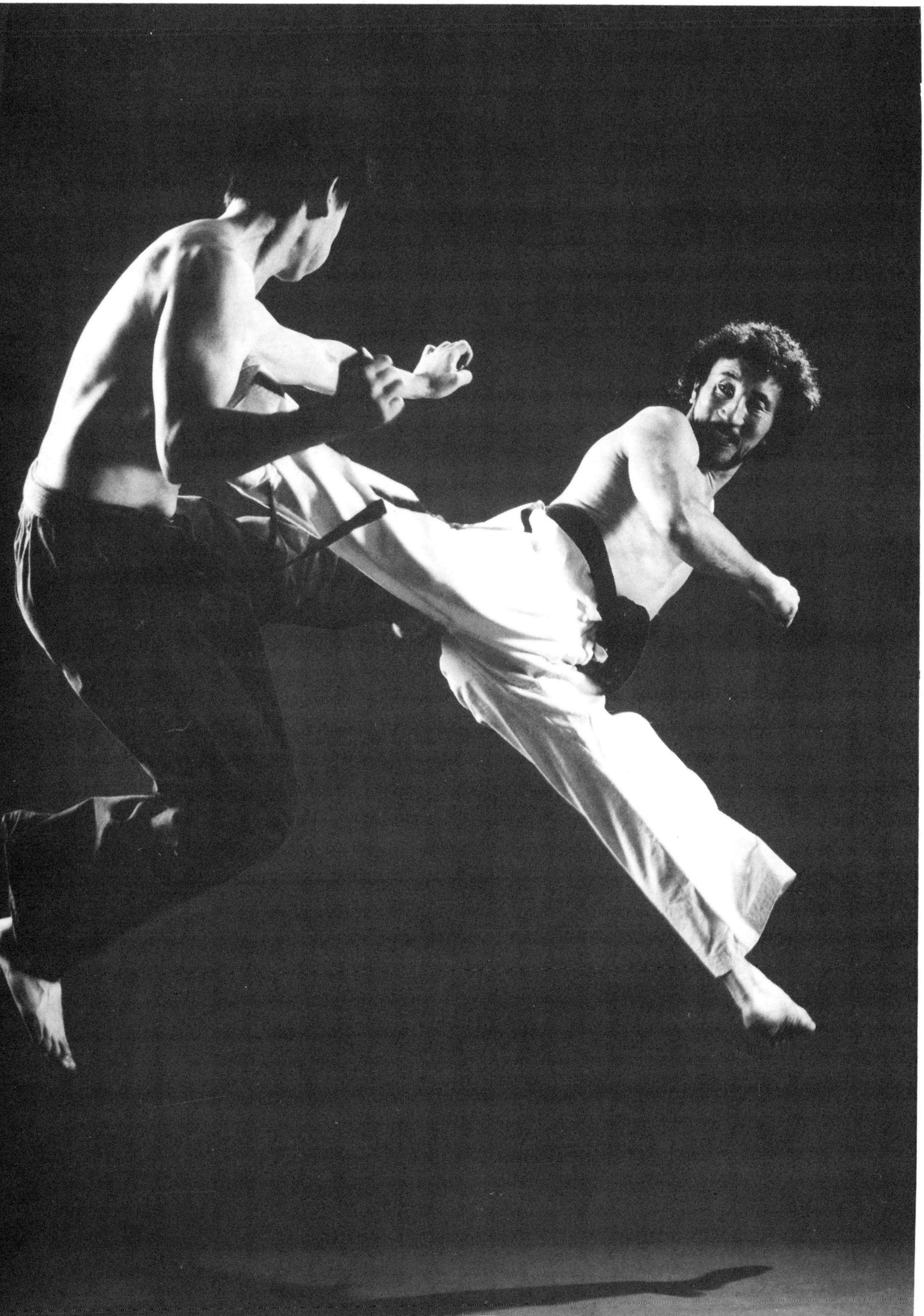

MUSCLES IN GENERAL

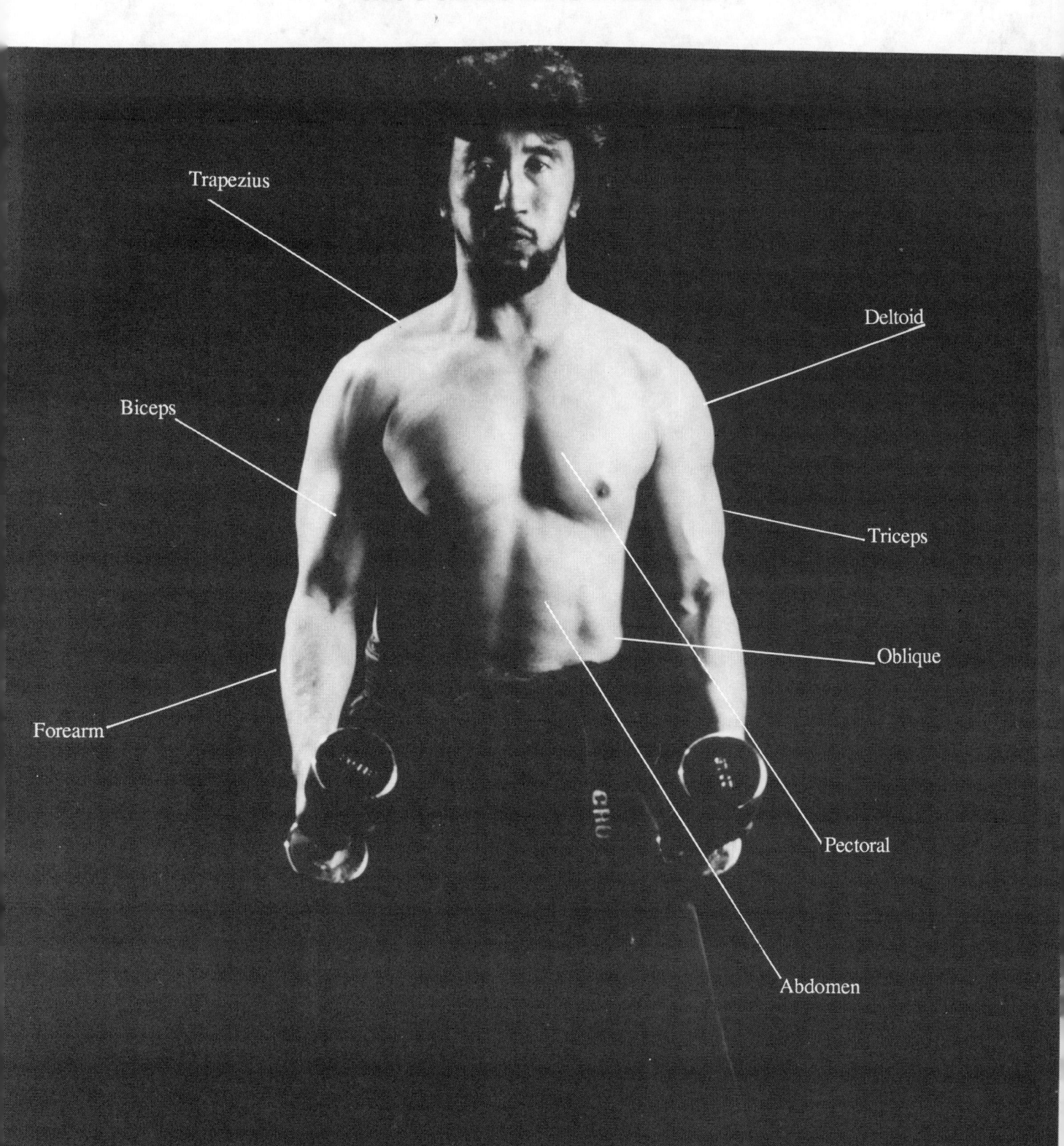

- Trapezius
- Deltoid
- Biceps
- Triceps
- Oblique
- Forearm
- Pectoral
- Abdomen

INTRODUCTION

No volume on kicking technique would be complete without at least a short discussion of the tools which the body uses when kicking - specifically muscles, ligaments, tendons and cartlidge. Without some understanding of how all of these body components interrelate, it is impossible to utilize them to their maximum, much the same as trying to get the most out of a car without reading the owner's manual.

For a person to be considered in "good" shape, he or she must be able as well as physically fit. What good is it to have well developed gastrocnemius muscles in the lower leg (perfect for high jumping) if you have weak ankles? You must learn how the body works as a whole in order to improve individual techniques.

A common myth in training is that if you want to improve a specific kick, figure out which is the most important muscle to that kick and work on developing that muscle. This is only partially true. For example, if you wanted to work on your Spinning Hook Kick, you might think that the muscle to concentrate on would be the biceps femoris (the big muscle in the upper leg) which is responsible for the hooking motion However, as soon as you begin to spin you are using the muscles in your neck, shoulders and waist. As these are the muscles which will generate the torquing power, you'd be doing yourself a great disservice if you failed to condition these muscles as well.

Equally as important as knowing about the muscles, ligaments, tendons and cartlidges involved in kicking is to understand how their flexibilities vary, and what you can do to increase it. Perhaps the single best thing people can do for themselves as they get older is to keep limber by stretching. The connective tissue (ligaments and tendons) tend to bind together and tighten over the years (which contributes to poor posture in older people) unless a conscious effort is made to keep them supple by stretching. To the physically active person, a good stretching program will enable their body to operate more efficiently, leading to improved performance and fewer injuries. It is for this reason that so much attention is spent on various stretching techniques throughout this book that will help the connective tissues as well as the muscles.

MUSCLES IN GENERAL

Muscle tissue is composed of protein, and there are hundreds of different muscles in the body from top to bottom, head to toe. There are actually two different types of fibers within muscles; fast twitching and slow twitching fibers. Muscles create movement in the body, and by using the two different types of muscle fibers, you develop your body to the fullest. The fast twitching muscle fibers are for speed, while the slow twitching muscle fibers are for endurance (which is why sprinters and marathon runners both train very differently.

Every machine needs fuel, and the human machine is no different. Fat stores the energy for the muscles to operate. There is a popular misconception that if you don't work out, your muscles will turn into fat. This is completely incorrect, as fat is a different type of tissue than muscle, and one can never turn into the other. When you stop working out and your caloric intake remains the same, your body starts to store more fat because you are using less for energy, and this fat builds up <u>on top</u> of the muscles, creating the illusion that the muscle had degenerated into fat. Everyone needs a certain amount of body fat, however too much, as you already know, is very bad for your system.

NECK MUSCLES

Whenever you throw a turning or spinning kick, the first part of your body to torque should be your head. Your head is a 16 pound weight which, if used properly, can help to begin the generation of speed in turning. Because of this turning action, the importance of the neck muscles cannot be over-emphasized. In the front of your head these muscles include the sternocleidomastid muscle which runs from just behind the ear to the center of the collarbone and the platysma muscle which fans out from the chin to cover the entire collarbone.

Supporting the head and neck from behind are the trapezius muscles, located on either side of the neck and attached to the base of the skull. In addition to providing support for the head, they also are the key muscles in lifting the shoulders, such as when shrugging. The trapezius muscles are very large, extending halfway down the back on either side.

SHOULDERS

Covering the very top of the shoulders are the deltoid muscles, which provide stability to the shoulder and upper portion of the arms and shoulder sockets. A weak deltoid muscle is the primary reason behind shoulder dislocations (the popping out of the socket) and subluxations (the rapid popping out and back in of the shoulder socket) when executing techniques such as

Knifehand Attacks and Spinning Knifehand Attacks.

UPPER ARMS

There are two main muscles in the upper portion of the arm, the biceps and the triceps. The large muscle in the front of the arm is the biceps. It is this muscle which provides the pulling in action for the arm, such as in a Headlock.

Located on the backs of the upper arms are the triceps, the muscles which provide the arm with the pushing out power needed when punching or extending the lower arm.

FOREARM

The muscles in the forearms are used to contract the hands, forming tight fists and strong grips. There are almost two dozen muscles in the forearm, each one playing an important role in the working of the lower arm, wrist and hand. Well developed forearms are crucial for successful close contact fighting.

UPPER CHEST

The chest muscles are, from a physiological viewpoint, some of the most important to the body's survival. It is these muscles which support and protect all of the internal organs (excluding the brain), providing them with a shield against external forces and traumas.

The pectoral muscle group is the major group of muscles on the front part of the upper body. Working together with the arms, the pectorals generate punching power, as well as provide crucial protection to the upper body organs. The pectorals provide the strength for any pulling motion of the arms towards the center of the body, such as in a Hook Punch or a Bear Hug.

ABDOMEN

Holding your lower internal organs in place are your abdominal muscles. These muscles are some of the most important to the martial artist, and it is for this reason that there are so many exercises in this book which will help to strengthen them.

More than just providing support and protection for your organs, the abdomen is the center of strength for all of the twisting and torquing motions that comprise the main source of power in spinning kicks. These muscles include the rectus abdominis which is the group of muscles which create the "washboard" look on the front of the abdomen, the external obliques on the lower sides by the waist, and the internal obliques in the lower abdomen on either side of the navel. It is really the obliques which provide strength and speed for spinning kicks, with the lower abdomen and obliques (along with the lower back) being the bridge between the upper body and the lower body. A poorly developed mid-section is a serious liability to the martial artist.

BACK MUSCLES

People generally ignore the muscles of the back, maybe because they can't see them on themselves and tend to forget about them. That's too bad, because well developed back muscles are your best defense against back injuries, a problem which plagues almost every martial artist from time to time.

The latissimus dorsi muscles (lats) are located on either side of the back, covering the ribcage like two wings. The lat muscles come into play when the shoulders are moved backwards, such as in a pulling or rowing action, as well as when the upper body is turned side to side. Besides the trapezius muscle (which helps to connect the head to the back) and latissimus dorsi muscles, there are also the lumbar muscles located in the lower back which protect the kidneys, help in supporting the spine, and generate power in torquing the upper body for Spinning Kicks.

THE HIPS AND PELVIS

The major muscles in the upper pelvic region are the gluteus maximus, gluteus medius and the gluteus minimus. Between the three, the gluteus maximus is the key, helping in distance jumping and extending the legs. The gluteus medius helps to extend the legs laterally to the sides such as in the Roundhouse Kick and the Side Kick, while the gluteus minimus helps in moving the leg forward (Front Snap Kick, Axe Kick). These are very strong muscles, and their importance to the physics of the martial arts has been overlooked for some time.

In addition to the gluteus minimus, the picking up (knee to chest) action of the leg is accomplished by the contraction of the illicus, psoas major and psoas minor muscles.

The illicus is attached to the inner wall of the pelvis, beneath the gluteus maximus, and lifts the leg in opposition to the gluteus maximus.

The psoas muscles are support muscles, connecting the very top and front of the leg (right by the joint), through the pelvis and to the spine. If you've ever felt tension in your legs when you do sit ups, you have felt the psoas muscles at work.

THE LEGS

The muscles of the legs are very similar in construction and function to the muscles of the arms, with a large number of muscles devoted to smaller individual functions. Closest to the gluteus muscles is the tensor fascia latae located to the outside of the pelvis. The tensor fascia latae helps to raise the legs laterally as well as provides stability.

The large muscles on the backs of the upper legs are widely thought of as the hamstrings. In reality, the hamstrings are actually a muscle group composed of three different muscles; the biceps femoris, the semitendinosis, and the semimembrenosis. The biceps femoris is the outside muscle, with the semitendinosis located to the inside of the leg on top of the semimembrenosis. They all three are basically working towards the same goal, the flexing in of the lower leg (such as in the Hook Kick), with each one providing a little extra support for whichever side it is located on.

On the opposite side of the thigh from the biceps femoris is the quadriceps muscle group, a grouping of four muscles on the top of the leg - the vastus lateralis (located on the outside), the vastus medialis (located on the inside), the vastus intermedialis (located in the middle, underneath the previous two), and the rectus femoris (located above the vastus intermedialis).

Used when extending the leg outward, the quadriceps come into play whenever you lock out the kicking leg, such as in the Front Snap Kick and the Roundhouse Kick.

The sartorius muscle, the longest muscle in the body, stretches all the way from top of the hip, over the quadriceps, down to the inside of the knee. The sartorius muscle provides increased control of the leg's lateral movement, coming largely into play during kicks such as the Inside Crescent Kick and Outside Crescent Kick.

In the lower leg, the gastrocnemius muscle is a little muscle with a big job. The gastrocnemius is the principle muscle involved in the springing off of the balls of your feet. It is usually the first leg muscle to go into action whenever kicking, and because of this it is the first link to generating speed in your kicks.

Many people neglect to pay any attention to the development of the gastrocnemius muscle, and as a result have much slower kicks.

Located in the ankle, the arch tendon, while not a muscle, is the primary force which helps to both get your foot into the proper position for kicking (flexing for Side Kicks, pointing for

Roundhouse Kicks) as well as providing the initial strength in pushing off of the feet for jumping.

LIGAMENTS, TENDONS AND CARTLIDGE

Ligaments are the connective tissues which bridge the gap from bone to bone. While muscles can be stretched to quite a distance, ligaments will only stretch about 15% past their resting size before becoming damaged.

Tendons on the other hand, are the connective tissue which attaches muscles to bones. Tendons are very tough and inflexible, only stretching 10% past their resting size. Usually it is a person's tendons, not their muscles which will determine how flexible they are.

Cartlidge is a soft material which is located in the joints to serve, on one hand, as a shock absorber, and on the other hand as an area for lubrication for the joint. While it is possible to heal a tendon or a ligament injury, a cartlidge injury is much more serious, usually requiring surgery. This is especially true for the knee, which is a complicated hinge-type joint that is very vulnerable to injury.

55

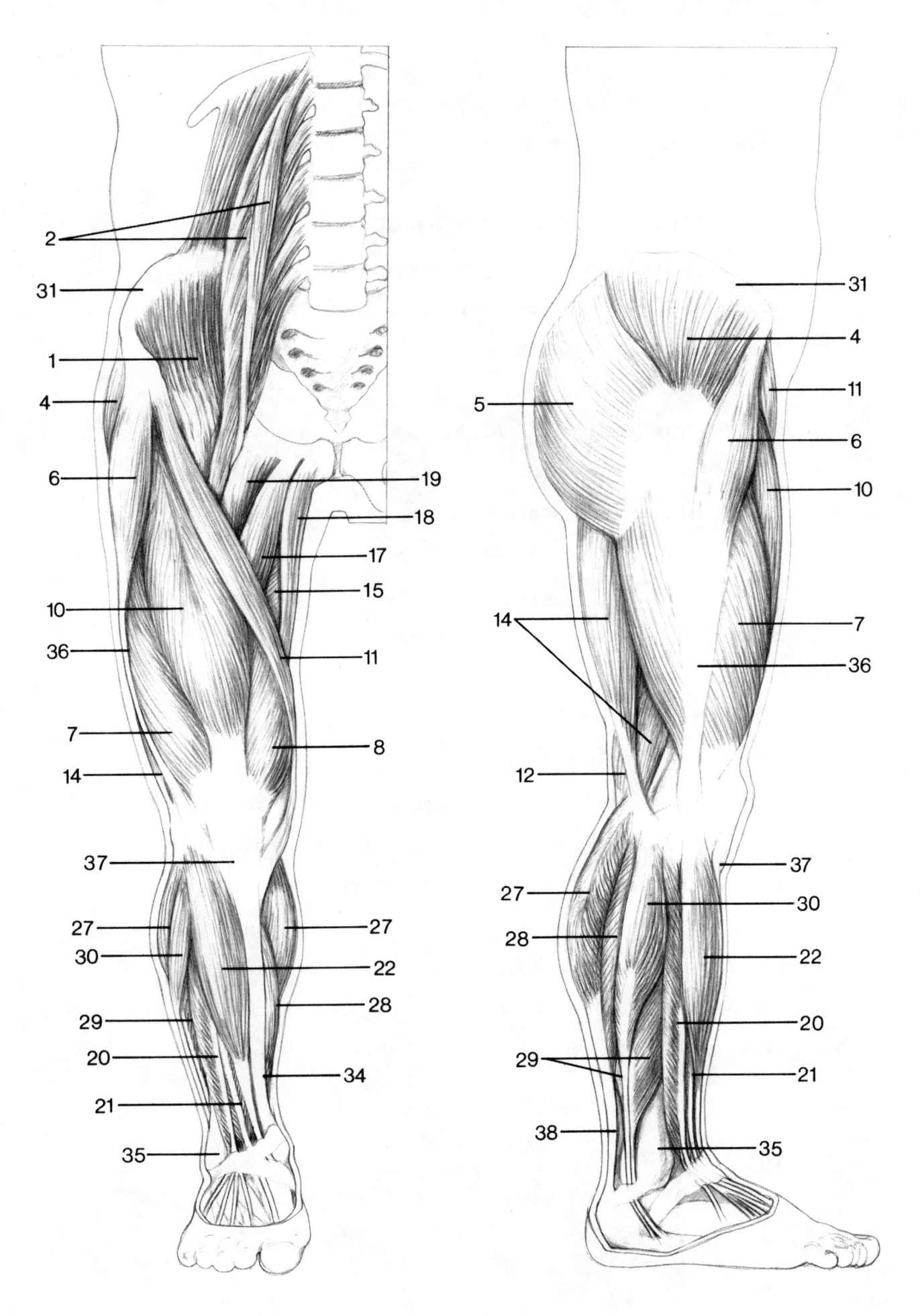

ILIOPSOAS (Internal Pelvic Muscles)

1. Iliacus
2. Psoas Major and Minor

EXTERNAL PELVIC MUSCLES

3. Gluteus Minimus (not shown; deep muscle under Gluteus Medius)
4. Gluteus Medius
5. Gluteus Maximus
6. Tensor Fasciae Latae

THIGH MUSCLES

(Quadricepts)
7. Vastus Lateralis
8. Vastus Medialis
9. Vastus Intermedialis (not shown; deep muscle under Vastus Medialis)
10. Rectus Femoris
11. Sartorius

(Hamstrings)
12. Semimembranosus
13. Semitendinosis
14. Biceps Femoris

(Abductors)
15. Abductor Magnus
16. Abductor Brevis
17. Abductor Longis
18. Gracilius
19. Pectineus

57

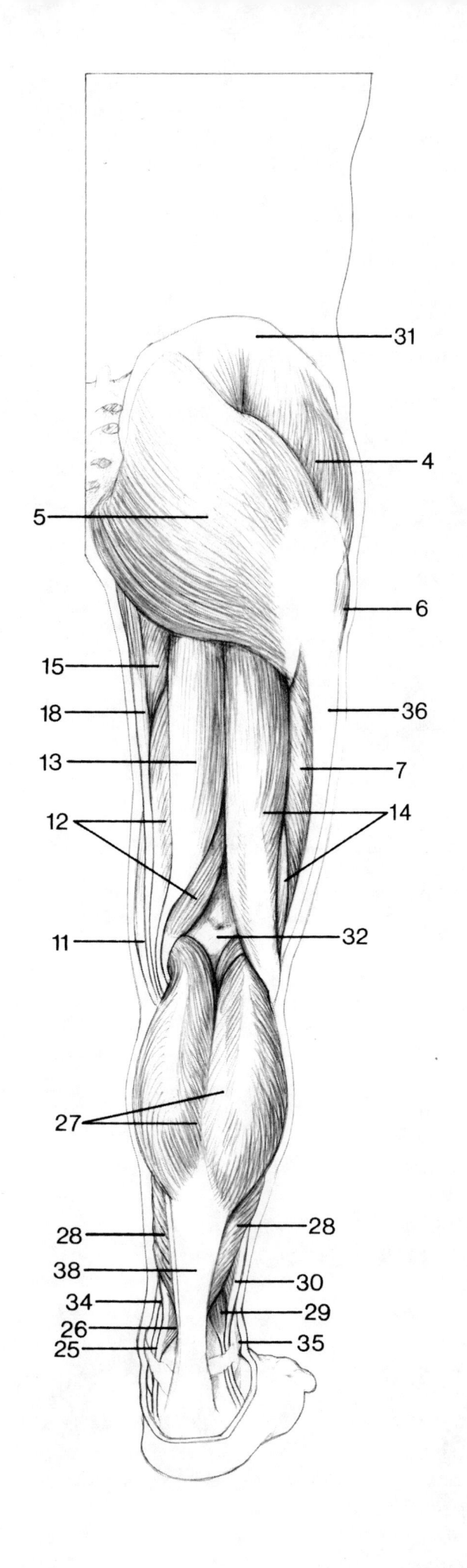

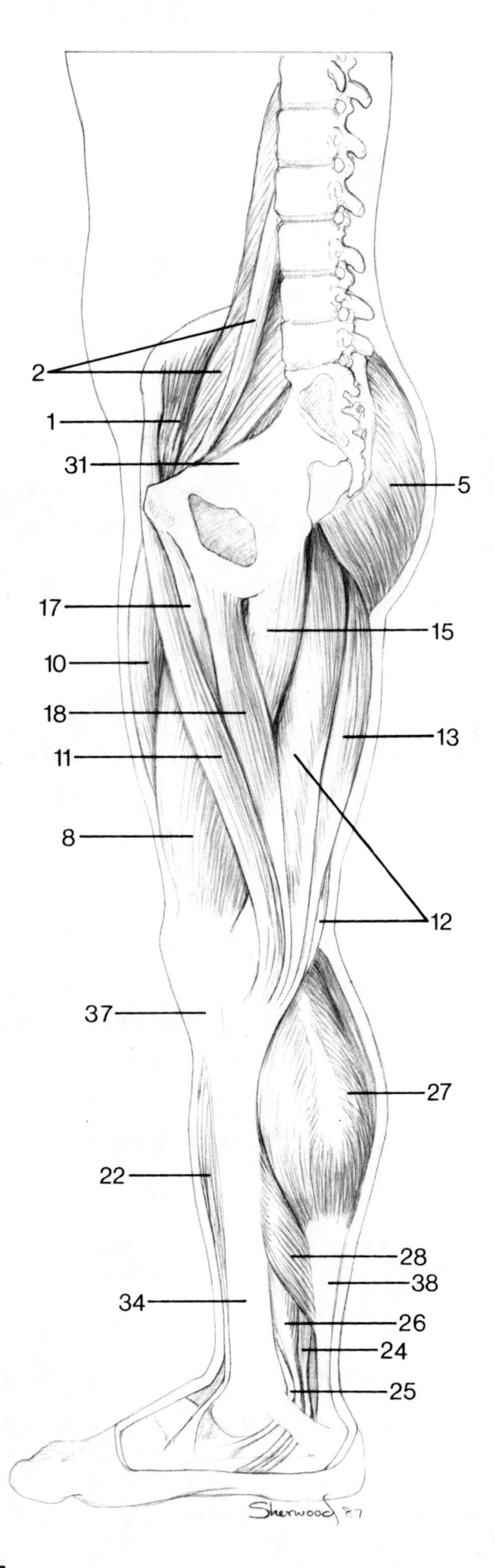

LOWER LEG MUSCLES

    (Extensors)

20   Extensor Digitorum Longus
21   Extensor Hallucis Longus
22   Tibialis Anterior

    (Flexors)

23   Popliteus
24   Flexor Hallicus Longus
25   Tibialis Posterior
26   Flexor Digitorum Longus
27   Gastrocnemius
28   Soleus
29   Peroneus Brevis
30   Peroneus Longus

BONES

31   Pelvic
32   Femur
33   Patella (kneecap, not shown; under Patellar Ligament)
34   Tibia
35   Fibula

CONNECTIVE STRUCTURES

36   Iliotibial Band of Fasciae Latae
37   Patellar Ligament
38   Achilles Tendon

Injuries

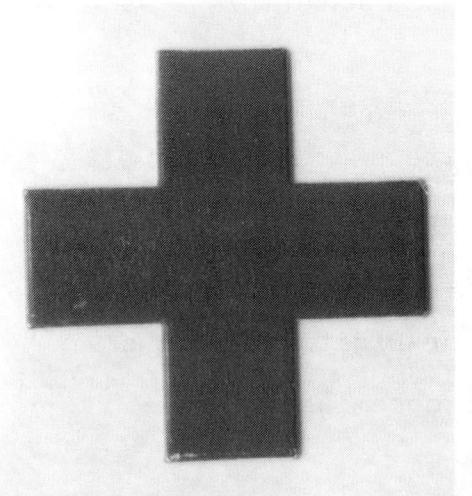

COMMON INJURIES: THEIR PREVENTION AND TREATMENT

Every martial artist faces a whole catalog of injuries which can affect their performance. Some injuries are merely inconvenient, while others can be more serious. In dealing with injuries, common sense is the rule. Never substitute good advice for a professional opinion. If there is any question, see a doctor immediately.

Some injuries are unavoidable as well as unforeseeable, and anyone who indulges in any contact sport is going to live through a lot of minor cuts and scrapes. Occasionally, unfortunately, more serious injuries occur, such as broken bones, dislocations, and serious cuts. If this should happen, obviously the best thing you can do is to get a doctor's help. Minor injuries, however, can easily be treated by yourself.

PULLED MUSCLES

The most common injury, not just in the martial arts but in most sports, is what is known as a "pulled" muscle, which is in reality a tearing of the muscle tissue beneath the skin. A tear in a muscle is not unlike a cut on the skin; you feel pain, the muscle bleeds (beneath the skin) and you must allow it to heal. If you are careful not to reinjure the muscle, it will heal completely.

If on the other hand, you constantly break

the wound open again and again, just like skin the muscle will scar. Muscle scar tissue can build up, becoming very rigid and inflexible. Constant reinjury can limit a muscle's usefulness for life. It is for this reason that if you do pull a muscle you must heal it completely before attempting to use it to its fullest.

The best way to avoid pulling muscles is to make sure that your body is warmed up before attempting any strenuous techniques. Stretch for at least ten minutes, and then begin your workout slowly, building up gradually to the more challenging techniques. By paying attention to your body and knowing its limitations, you will be able to avoid most injuries.

Unfortunately, no matter how conscientious you are, chances are that at some point in your training you will pull a muscle. As soon as you realize that this has happened, stop your workout and apply an ice pack to the entire affected area for at least thirty minutes. This will limit the amount of bleeding around the tear. Use the ice pack for thirty minutes, take it off for ten, and then put it back on, keeping up this rotation for at least an hour and an half. If possible, keep the part of your body with the torn muscle elevated, also to inhibit bleeding.

A torn muscle is a real nagging injury, sometimes lingering for four or five months. This doesn't mean that you should stop training for that time, but you should take it very slowly, building up again gradually. Don't fall victim to the urge to try and regain your abilities in one workout after having knocked off for a while. All you will do is reinjure the same muscle, thus starting the healing process all over again.

STRAINED LIGAMENTS, TENDONS AND CARTLIDGE

Because of the strain that the martial arts places on the joints, other very common injuries are strained ligaments, tendons and cartlidges. The severity of these injuries vary; usually with an injured cartlidge being more serious than an injured ligament or tendon.

These types of injuries tend to happen as a result of hyperextending (over extending) a joint when throwing various techniques by snapping out your arm or leg rather than controlling it with the appropriate muscles. The two most common areas for these injuries are the knees and the elbows.

Because of the proximity of the ligaments, tendons and cartlidge to each other, it might sometimes be difficult for you to determine the exact nature of your injury. Don't hesitate to see a trained professional in the event that you feel you have injured yourself. Typically, if you feel the pain deep within the joint, it will be a combination of ligaments, tendons and cartlidge damage. As with a muscle injury, ice packs are the treatment of choice, helping to relieve the pain and reduce the accumulation of fluid. In the event that the joint begins to swell up dramatically, the chances are that you have a much more serious cartlidge injury and you should see a doctor immediately.

HEAT ILLNESS AND STITCHES

While not dealing specifically with the muscles, tendons, ligaments or cartlidge, two very common problems, heat illness and stitches, deserve a brief mention here, largely because they are so easily avoided.

Heat illness is a very common problem, especially if you haven't trained in a while. While not an actual injury, heat illness refers to the problems of exhaustion, dehydration, dizziness and/or shortness of breath that usually accompanies someone who trains hard after not having trained in a while. Heat illness can even affect someone who has been training, but who is just more sensitive to the conditions on a given day.

The best prevention for heat illness is to drink a lot of fluids, either water or juice, around two hours before a workout, as well as starting your workout slowly, building up to a faster pace as your tolerance for that type of workout increases.

Also, be aware of the conditions where you are working out. You will be more apt to feel heat illness on a hot and humid day than you would in the middle of the winter, though in the middle of the winter you are more likely to pull a muscle. Be alert as to the type of conditions you are training in, and take the appropriate precautions to avoid a variety of injuries.

A case of the stitches is real uncomfortable and quite easy to avoid. Most people feel the stitches - a spasm in the diaphragm which causes a sharp pain below the ribcage - when they workout shortly after having eaten a big meal. You should eat no less than three hours before working out, allowing your body a chance to devote its energy to the task of digestion. People can also get the stitches from breathing improperly when working out, usually holding their breath while executing techniques, and from not stretching the stomach muscles properly.

In the event that you get the stitches, stop

your workout and rest. Place your hands over your head and breathe in and out deeply, contracting the diaphragm.

Look at the idea, don't run away from reality. If you perfect your idea you will become a winner.

THE ORIENTAL METHOD OF FIRST AID USING TRADITIONAL ACUPUNCTURE POINTS

In addition to the martial arts, the orient's other great export to the west has been acupuncture. Studied and used in this country for several decades now, acupuncture has gotten increased respect as a legitimate healing art.

It is not surprising to discover that acupuncture points have been used widely by martial artists in the the orient for many years, both for the purpose of first aid and for general relaxation and health. While a number of different methods and techniques will be described over the next few pages, they are in no way meant to take the place of competent medical attention in the case of an emergency or accident.

There are literally dozens of acupuncture points located over the body, each one serving a different and distinct function. The points are actually channels; located on the skin and tying directly into the nervous system. Acupuncture is usually seen being performed using small needles (which are used to stimulate the points), but wonderful results can be obtained by simply applying direct, firm pressure to the point with the tip of the thumb or index finger. This pressure can either be applied by yourself (if possible in the situation) or by others.

There are two suggested methods of applying this pressure. The first one - apply pressure directly to the point for three to five seconds, then remove pressure for three to five seconds. This pressure on/pressure off method should be continued until you achieve the desired result. The second method is to apply and maintain direct pressure until you achieve the desired result.

Following are some revival points that can be used in the event a person becomes unconscious (knocked-out) or light-headed. They can be used individually, or in any combination.

1. GV-26:
Governing channel point #26 located in the philtrum, ⅓ the distance from bottom of nose to top of the upper lip.

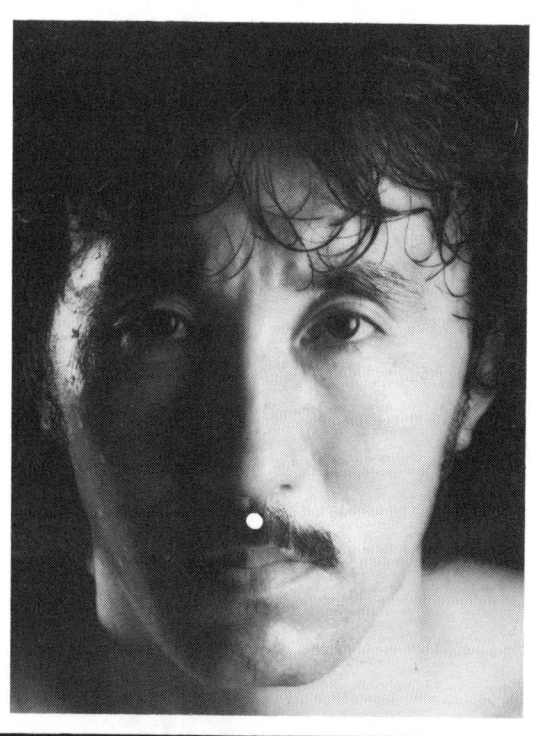

2. LI-4:
Large Intestine channel point #4 located in the web between thumb and index finger. With thumb and index finger opened as wide as possible, locate the point slightly on the side of index finger between 1st & 2nd metacarpal bones.

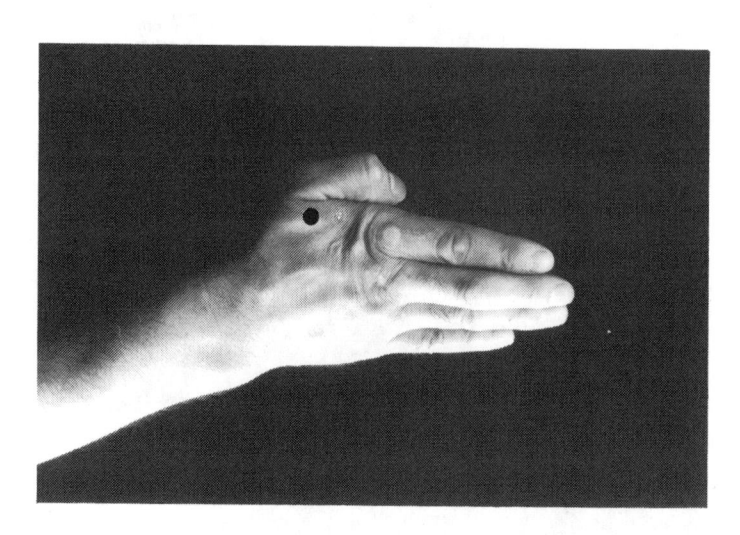

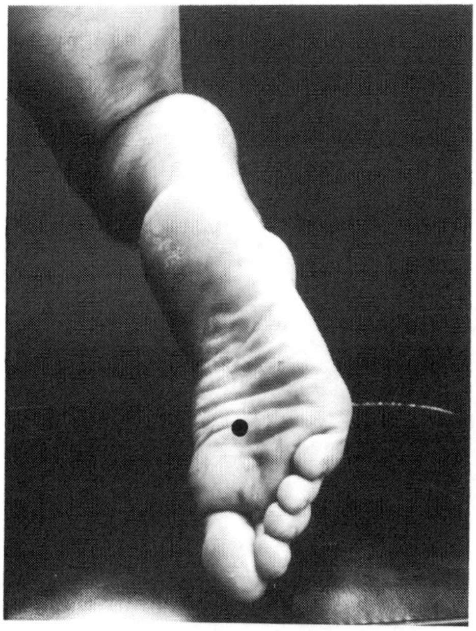

4. ST-36:
Stomach channel point #36 located on lower leg, approximately 4 finger width below the hollow next to patellar tendon below the knee.

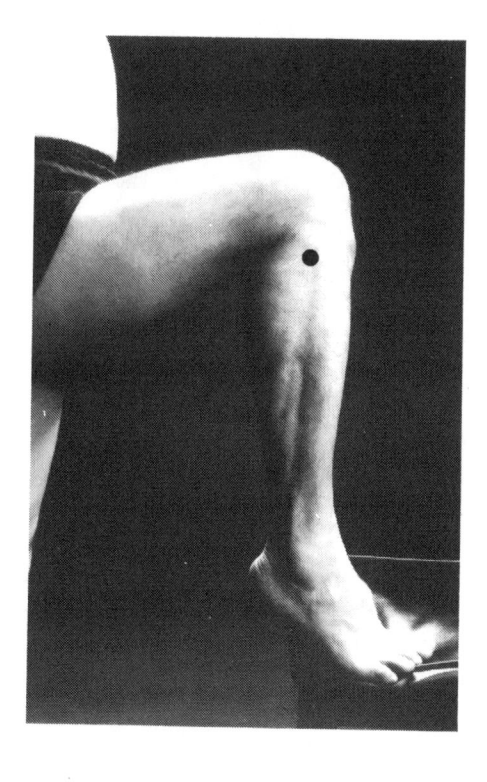

3. K-1:
Kidney channel point #1 located on the bottom of the foot, ⅓ the distance from base of 2nd toe to the edge of heel.

5. P-9:
Pericardium channel point #9 located in the center tip of middle finger.

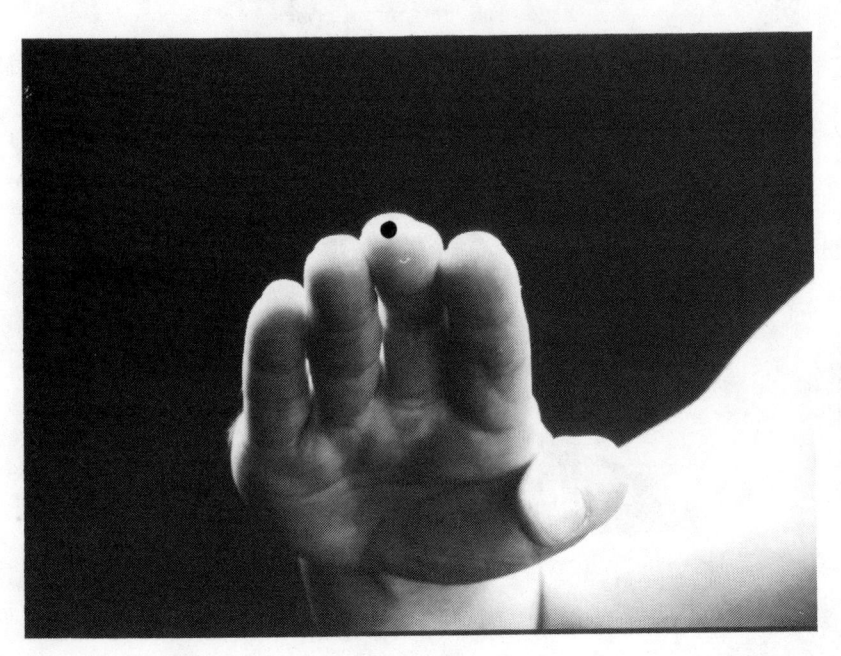

6. Special point on the thumbnail: press on the white half moon shaped area on the thumbnail.

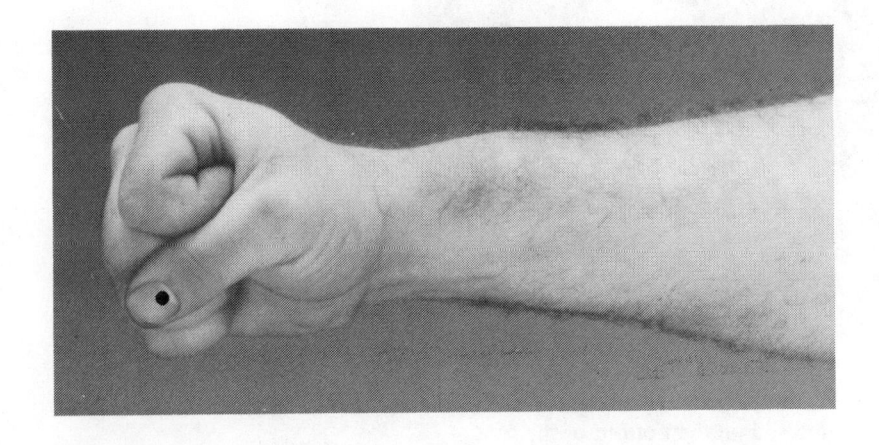

II. THE TRADITIONAL ACUPUNCTURE POINTS USED IN IN RELAXATION

The following points are commonly used to relax, rejuvenate, and strengthen one's body and mind in Traditional Oriental Medicine. These points can be used before and after training or competition to relieve tension and stress placed on one's body and mind. Some of these points are the same as in the first aid treatments.

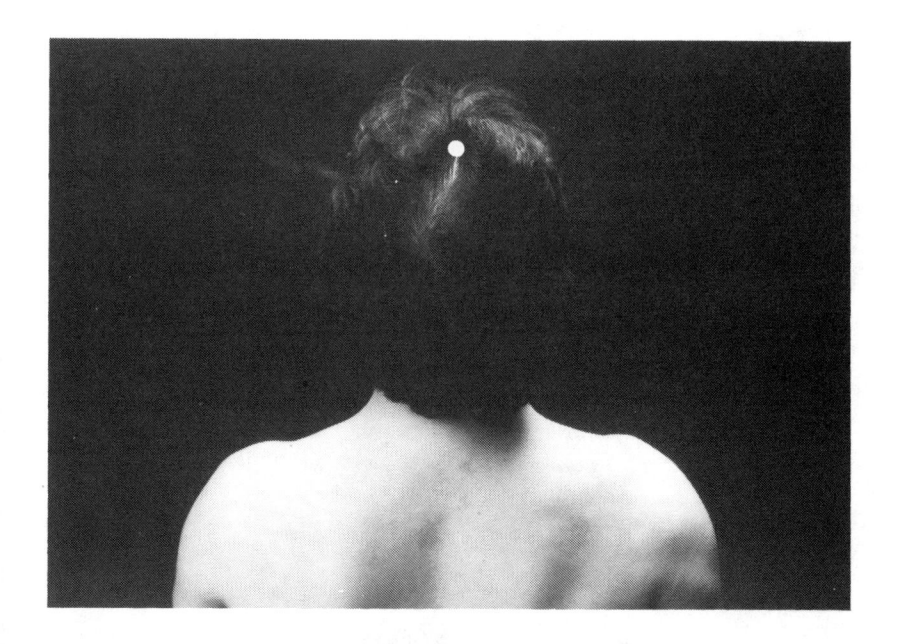

HEAD REGION:

1. GV-20:
Governing channel point #20 located on the top of head on the midpoint of a line connecting tips of both ears. This point will calm the mind and relieve headache and dizziness.

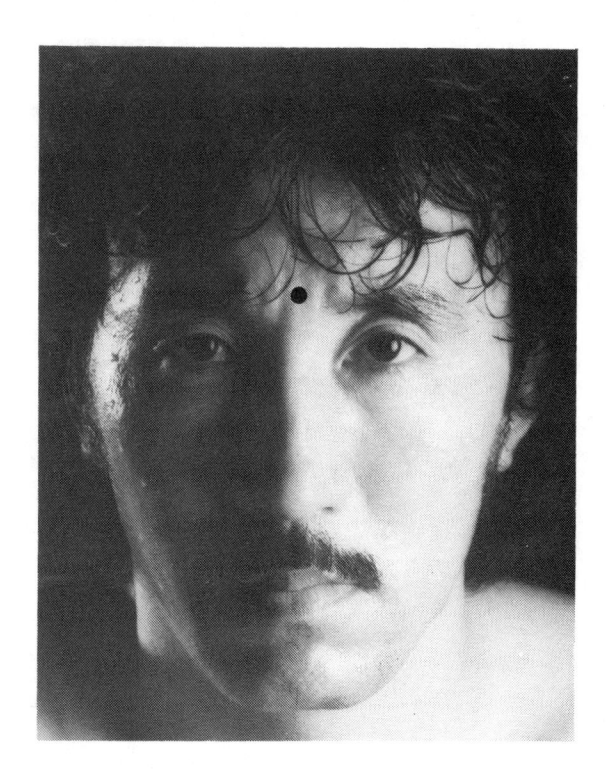

2. Yintang:
located on midpoint between two eyebrows. This point will calm the mind and relieve headache and dizziness (same as GV-20).

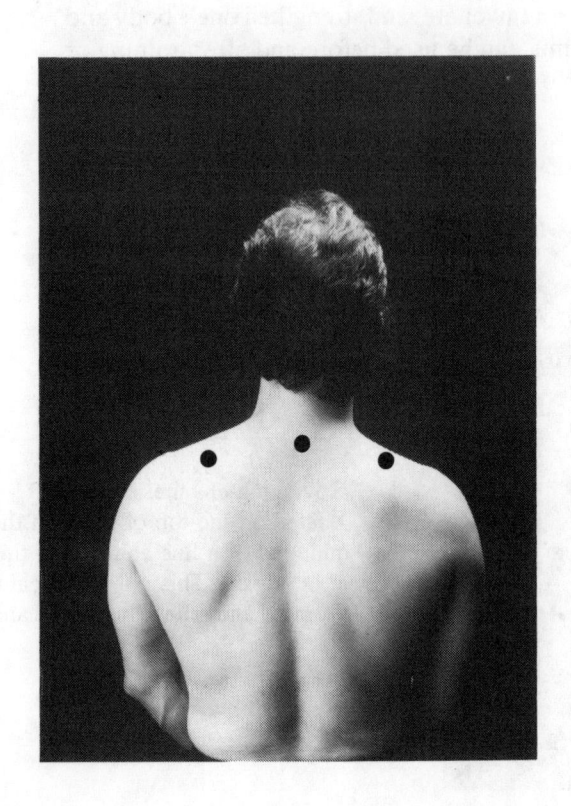

NECK REGION:

1. GV-14:
Governing channel point #14 located between the spinous process of the 7th cervical vertebrae and 1st thoracic vertebrae. This point will calm the mind.

2. GB-21:
Gall Bladder channel point #21 located on shoulder ½ way between lower border of 7th cervical vertebrae and acromion. This point will relieve tension built around the shoulder area.

HAND REGION:

1. LI-4:
this is the same point as used on first aid. Pressing this point will relieve fatigue and relax all the muscles in the body. In addition, it will relieve headache in front part of the head.

3. P-6:
Pericardium channel point #6 located on the medical side of the forearm, 3 finger width above the center of wrist crease between two tendons (palmaris longus & flexor carpi radialis). This point will calm the mind and help stop pain. It will also relieve migraine headache.

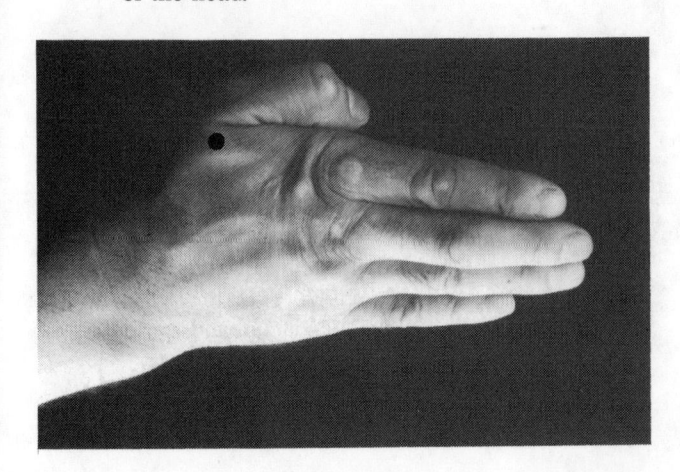

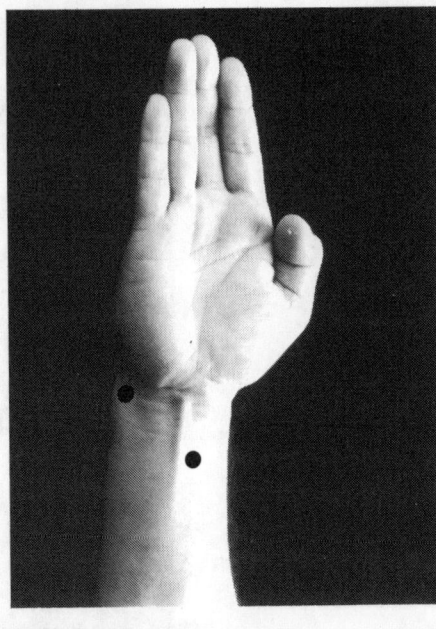

2. H-7:
Heart channel point #7 located on the wrist. With palm up, locate the point at transverse crease of the wrist medial to the tendon of flexor carpi ulnaris. This point has calming action on the heart and mind.

4. SI-3:
Small Intestine channel point #3 located lateral and posterior to head of 5th metacarpal bone at the end of the transverse crease with hand clenched into fist. This point will calm the mind and relax all the muscles in the body.

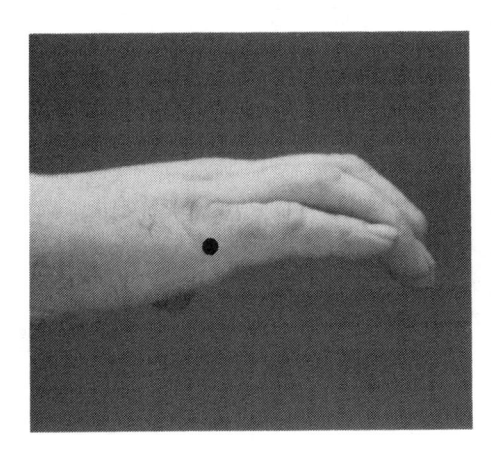

LEG REGION:

1. ST-36:
This is the same point as used for first aid. Traditionally, this point has been used for longevity, and pressing this point will relieve fatigue and relax all the muscles in the body. In addition, this point will strengthen all the muscles and help the digestion and elimination.

2. GB-34:
Gall Bladder channel point #34 located on the lower leg in the hollow anterior and inferior to the head of the fibula. This is an influential point, and it can relax and/or strengthen all the tendons in the body.

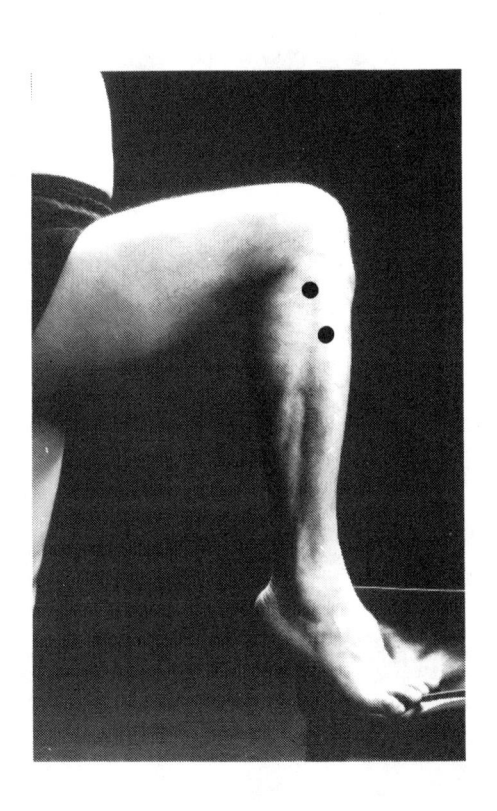

FOOT REGION:

1. LIV-3:
Liver channel point #3 located on the foot about 1.5 inch above web between 1st and 2nd toes. This point has a calming action on the whole body and will relieve "top of the head". Headaches.

2. UB-60:
Urinary Bladder channel point #60 located in the depression ½ way between lateral malleolus and the Achilles' tendon. This is one of the most commonly used points for relieving pain, especially due to injury. It will relax the muscles and tendons in the body. It can also strengthen the lower back and remove headaches at the back of the head.

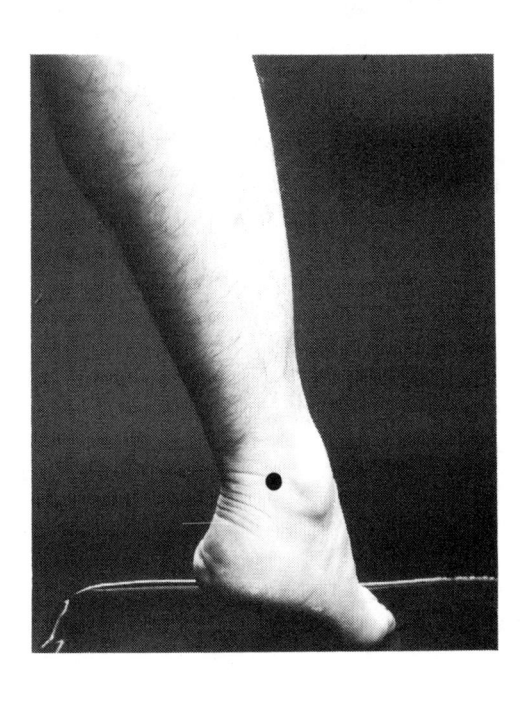

"ailure" does not exist.
The experience is merely a chance
To learn and prepare
For success.

Philosophy of Master Hee Il Cho

In the days following World War II, Korea was a country looking for an identity, searching aimlessly for its soul.

More than 30 years of Japanese occupation had destroyed the country's culture and all but buried one of its most important resources -- martial arts. Oh, there were scores of young martial artists looking for fights, thinking they were the toughest kid on the block. And I was one of them. But the foundation of the Korean arts, its philosophy, had disappeared with the country's independence. Three decades of imposed rule had robbed Korea of most of its true masters. Gone were most of the old-world instructors who considered martial arts to be an equal combination of spirit and techniques. Mastering one without learning the other was like having a body, but no mind, they believed.

Still, in those early days we didn't know any better. No one talked about philosophy; only fighting. It wasn't how disciplined you were, but who you could beat. We had struggled to survive for so long, we forgot when the war was over that so was our conflict. Instead, the emphasis was still on surviving, taking care of yourself before anyone else. Back then martial arts catered to the street people, those not so well-educated. There were a few exceptions, such as some students living and training in the mountain monasteries, but I didn't believe studying with old masters would teach me how to fight. As with most of us, I believed the only way you could learn how to fight was to experience the thrill of combat.

I guess you could say we had a philosophy, but I know now it was not the right philosophy. When I started practicing, the master was the God image. I believed he could blink an eye and kill anybody. Or if he worked out, he would be so fast no one could see him. His speed was that mysterious. I seldom saw him, just a lot of his black belt students teaching us. He gave a little speech before testing and then he was gone.

As far as the martial artists, they hated each other. They would say "We are the best, we are the strongest" and we would fight at different street corners, different dojo, almost like a Bruce Lee movie. I believed my master was the best. I showed him true loyalty. It was almost as if I was brainwashed. I couldn't see what was good or evil. And I believed my style was the best. I was willing to die to prove it. But as I found out later, if the frog stays in a little pond, he thinks he knows the world. But when he gets to the ocean, he is lost.

That's exactly how I felt when I came to the United States in 1969. I was lacking a philosophy, a true meaning for studying my discipline, but I didn't know it. I came here thinking I was the toughest, meanest fighter that ever lived. And that my style, Taekwon Do, was second to none. I wanted to prove that, to challenge every one and anything that crossed my path. I did, and I got the shock of my life. As time went by I competed and lost a couple of matches in point tournaments. I couldn't believe it. I was using my jumping spinning kicks and the Japanese stylists would not even move. They would just stand there, throw a reverse punch to my ribs and score.

I realized that at the age of 27, I would have to develop my own philosophy. Hundreds of years ago, philosophy was the foundation upon which all form and technique were built. Martial artists searched for the meaning in their lives and tried to instill order. From this order came form and from form came technique. Philosophy is not just religion, as in Buddhism or Taoism, but is using its practical applications in our daily lives. Masters in ancient Korea had the right idea, but somehow the principles of martial arts philosophy got lost in wanting to be the best, the strongest or the fastest. I remember someone once suggesting to me that sooner or later I would have to give up being a performing martial artist and start being a teacher. At the time I maintained I would still be doing demonstrations when I was 70 years of age. I'd still do jumping spinning kicks off the ceiling, I promised. Well now I'm approaching 50 and would you believe it, I can't do it! When I was 30 I thought masters weren't actively teaching and demonstrating because they were phonies, frauds. They didn't do it because they couldn't do it. I never had respect for my seniors because they never did anything. I never saw one do a demonstration, so how could they be in shape? I realized there was more to being a black belt, more to being a good teacher than wiping up the floor with another fighter or tickling the chandelier with a kick. I learned you must first develop a philosophy, a guiding light for both you and your students to follow through the rigors of training in one of life's most demanding disciplines.

Being a good martial arts student involves time, dedication and motivation, as well as a rock solid philosophy that will help you through the rough times. The components of that philosophy are: flexibility, timing, discipline, humility, ego, concentration and focus, fighting, and training. These are the values I continually impart to my students and these are the values I will share with you.

Flexibility

You have to develop a philosophy of being flexible, of being adaptable to change, to progress in the martial arts. This means you have to be open to new ideas as well as training principles. I realized when I came to this country that my style was not the only good style around. I noticed after losing on several occasions that Taekwon Do was not the lone superior style, although that has not prevented it from becoming the most popular martial arts style in the world.

In Korea, since most people studied Taekwon Do, kicks were prevalent and hand techniques were seldom used. But we never faced fighters from other styles. At a tournament soon after I came here, I saw most of the martial artists win by using the reverse punch or the ridge hand. So I adopted that. I opened my mind. After all, what good are high or flashy kicks if they don't work in a practical fighting situation?

Every athlete is getting better in the United States because they are opening their minds to new theories. What coaches and trainers do not understand, they study. They discover that the body may produce more if trained a certain way, or an athlete may execute a technique better if positioned at a different angle. I kept entering tournaments here because I wanted to learn more about something I didn't know. If you have a narrow mind, very still, then you won't grasp other styles or grasp the philosophy behind the techniques. For example, when Taekwon Do fighters face Shotokan stylists, they must use more hand skills. Subsequently, Taekwon Doists become better fighters with their hands. The more knowledge you have, the better off you are.

Also, when your attitude is flexible, you can adapt more things more quickly into your style. You can understand why certain techniques work a certain way, and why you might have to discard a favorite move in favor of one that might be more effective.

To increase your effectiveness, you must be physically flexible. Your kicks look better and your techniques are easier to execute. If your attitude is flexible, you can push yourself towards physical flexibility. As time and age come, you must understand your physical flexibility will decrease. But if your attitude is strong, yet open to change, your mind will grow as it absorbs more. You get better and better. You become more flexible, and better off in a martial arts sense.

Timing

A fighter whose timing is off just one half second can end up on the wrong side of a punch or kick. Timing is very important in martial arts training or any field of endeavor. The philosophy of timing deals with organizing your life in such a manner that it is always working in your favor. Being there at the right time and at the right place with the right execution will make you a winner most of the time.

Life is full of examples of good and bad timing. Sometimes, through no fault of your own, your may be at the wrong place at the wrong time. Say for instance you're involved in an accident. But there are times when better timing could produce a happy ending. If you have a big business meeting and you're a half hour late or you miss your flight, it could cost you your livelihood. You have to train your mind to use good timing and you can use that in your martial arts endeavors.

Adjusting your timing is not nearly as difficult as it appears. You just have to constantly be thinking about what you're doing. If you go to church and merely listen, you're not understanding what is being said. If you concentrate on the preacher's words, and try to live your life accordingly, then you're letting timing work for your. You should also think about developing that skill.

And that brings us back to martial arts. Timing is one of the martial artist's greatest allies. I know I sometimes have trouble with my timing. But I know that, and I continually work towards improving that deficiency. The first time you try, you may fail. If you continue to work, you'll find you get better. That's like punching 10 times. If it doesn't work, try 20 times. And if that doesn't work, try 2,000 times. It's the same thing in life. Some people actually reach their goals and others fall by the wayside. The people who have actually made it have worked on improving their timing. When you have a problem with timing, you must work to eliminate it.

Discipline

I am much more publicized than most of the masters around the country or the world. But many think the 11 books I've written and the 30 video tapes I've done somehow came after one day's work. However, I worked weekends, 12-hour days. Whenever I had a free moment. I knew what I wanted and I was determined to get it. I was willing to spend the time. This is called discipline.

Training is difficult for many people who join my school. It's after work, you're tired, you might like to sit in front of the tv and drink a beer. It's very inviting. But if you decide to push yourself a little more now, you'll be happier later in life. As a more disciplined person, you will have brought order into your work and personal life.

What makes a disciplined martial artist? That's hard to say, but in many cases it starts with the instructor. If he teaches you the right way with the right philosophy, he will create in you a drive to become better. Hopefully, you'll take care of the rest. Unfortunately, there are many unqualified instructors out there who think total training begins and ends with sparring. The undisciplined martial artist will be taught that philosophy means nothing, that being competitive is the path to take. Martial arts is not just for competition; it is for realizing your limitations and then using your discipline to wipe away those limitations. If you look at a brown belt and say , "He's better than me," well, he may be younger stronger and faster. Instead of looking at someone else, look at what you've accomplished. Now you have discipline. You've been training for a long time and you have courage.

Ego

I have many students and their biggest problem is to bow when they enter the dojo. They have trouble saying "Yes sir," and "No sir," to people they don't know or respect. People having the most problems are degreed personnel such as doctors and lawyers. They have worked hard to achieve a position and are not very willing to bow to someone else. The problem is one of ego.

But if they don't give up and keep training, they will reconstruct their whole attitude and discover they lacked confidence when they came in. When your whole attitude changes, you have true self-confidence and have lost your ego. Then you can respect yourself and easily say, "Yes sir," "No sir." If you don't respect yourself, you cannot respect anybody else. If a person can bow and realize he doesn't know something, or that he knows less that the instructor, he can be a great asset to the martial arts. And the martial arts can be a great asset to him.

Mind and Body

When your mind and body are harmonized, you will be much calmer. You won't be nervous and you won't suffer physically. If your mind and body can be fused as one, you'll be much happier because you'll be understanding, accepting.

As with any phase of life, you'll suffer if your mind is one place and your body somewhere else. An instructor cannot just teach the physical, or just teach the spiritual. There's no way you can accentuate body over mind. If you take away the brain, you are paralyzed; you no longer function. That means if you take out the brain and place it on the table, the brain itself will be useless.

The brain and the body are one, and you try to harmonize the body and mind. Sometimes it can be very difficult, especially during martial arts training. There's so much concentration during forms practice, your mind and body must function together. When sparring, if these two entities are a single unit, you will be difficult to hit. If not, you can get nailed by a slow moving truck.

Don't get me wrong. As with most martial arts training, learning to harmonize the body and the mind takes time. It is especially difficult to teach children. Their minds and bodies are not working together. They're young and their attention span is limited.

Most people who join a karate class are in their early 20's. Unfortunately, their minds have been set. It's very difficult to change their characters. The problems they had while growing up are still with them. They won't change in two months or two years. Maybe 10 years. But if they're children, we can bring mind and body together in two years or less.

Mind and body harmonization is most important in the execution of forms. If the master is trying to teach you a 68-step form, and your mind and body are not together, you'll never memorize the steps. But if you're focusing, flowing, allowing your mind and body to become one, then sooner or later you're no longer thinking, just doing. You will do it automatically.

Fighting

Gaining self-confidence is the most important aspect in our lives. However, many people go through life lacking confidence. You can achieve an academic-type confidence by graduating from college or a skill-type confidence from learning a trade. But in the martial arts, physical confidence can only be gained by learning how to fight and knowing how to take care of yourself in a real situation.

Many martial arts schools won't emphasize sparring. Some business people don't want to be hit hard in the face, while other instructors fear the possibility of lawsuits brought about by injury. But if you're not going to emphasize sparring, you must teach them self-confidence and self-control, but how can you expect true confidence without an emphasis on sparring ? You won't know what a true martial art is and what it can offer you.

Fighting is imperative in the martial arts. Without fighting, you're not understanding total and complete martial arts, because until you get physically hit by someone, you won't know if something works. The instructor must bring his student along slowly, so he can allow his confidence level to grow. And his confidence can grow only by getting as close as possible to real physical training. If all you do is forms, touch hands, shadowboxing and working out alone, then you go into the ring and get hit, you'll' be in trouble because you won't know how to react.

Training

You can eat breakfast, lunch and dinner in one sitting and then not eat for the rest of the day. Or you could try to eat a month's worth of meals in just one week. Your stomach couldn't take the pace and you would get sick. The same holds true for your training regimen. If I haven't worked out for a week, my workouts are different than if I had been working out for that week. When I take a vacation, I've found I've lost everything when I return to the dojo. My muscles hurt, my reactions are slower.

Your philosophy of training should be the same as breathing. You need to do it every day to survive. To stay in shape, to hone your skills, you need to train on a regular basis.

Many people get disillusioned with training. At first the gains are considerable., But after a while, as your skills become sharper, the improvements are barely noticeable. And it's easier to get frustrated. What you have to consider is what you'll look and feel like if you stop.

This goes back to the philosophy on discipline. Even when you feel like quitting, you must reach back and gather the strength to continue. You must have faith in your routine and your instructor. You have to say to yourself that this is a necessary part of my life.

If you can get through these low periods, you'll soon find you can't go without training. You know if you stop your body will become flabby and you'll lose pride in yourself. You won't want to throw your body in a junkheap.

Conclusion

In this day and age, it is rare to find an instructor who emphasizes philosophy as much as physical technique or training. For most instructors today, the most important thing is to find a good location and develop a business. Martial arts teachers have become businessmen. As such, the spiritual aspect may become lost in their drive for success.

In the same vein, students are not as apt to request teaching in the philosophical side of martial arts. For the two or three hours they spend at the dojo, they may just want to exercise the body. It is virtually impossible in that small time period to explain the roots of the discipline. Most practitioners cannot be expected to desire the things their ancestors did in ancient Korea.

But for those few who want more from their martial art than self-defense techniques and a well-built frame, there should be instructors who are willing to provide the total foundation.

The philosophies outlined in the preceding pages are merely a map to follow during your martial arts training. No one said it would always be easy. As with anything worthwhile in life, martial arts takes time, dedication discipline, a will to excel and a willingness to accept and respect those more talented than you.

Most of all, the martial arts are a microcosm of life. They have philosophies that work as well outside as when you're training. If you concentrate on the virtues of flexibility, fighting and training, and allow them to spill over into your daily life, you will be happier and more successful in anything you do.

Does Kihap help?

Yes, it does. Morehouse and Miller, in their text, Physiology of Exercise, report that studies show that "maximum pulls against a tensometer were enhanced by 12.2% when the subject shouted loudly during a random final pull" (p. 56). Yelling makes you stronger, Morehouse and Miller suggest, by reducing inhibitions.

What Research Says About Rest Pauses.

In Master Cho's classes, rest pauses are about 30 seconds long. It turns out that 30 seconds may be optimal - longer rests would not be much better in restoring strength:

"Short, frequent rest pauses result in greater efficiency in muscular work than do prolonged, infrequent rests and are equally important in preventing loss of efficiency in skilled performance. Even after an elbow flexor muscle had been allowed to work to exhaustion, 69% of its strength was regained after 30 seconds. After a rest of 2.5 minutes only 13% more was regained, and after 7.5 minutes an additional 18% was regained. After a long pause of 42.5 minutes a total of 95% of its original strength was regained - only 26% more than after a 30 second rest." (From Morehouse and Miller, Physiology of Exercise, p. 54).

Does Rotating the Fist Help?

While some varieties of martial arts recommend rotating the fist while delivering a punch, very little seems to be gained. Physicist J. Walker calculated that the fist rotation adds about 0.4 joules of energy to a punch (one joule is the energy needed to lift one kilogram 10 centimeters). Since the energy contained in a good punch, according to Walker's calculations, is about 150 joules, Walker concludes that fist rotation makes a negligible contribution.

Walker, J. 1975. "Karate Strikes" American Journal of Physics 43:845-849

Three Workouts Per Week?

Master Cho requires three workouts a week. According to research, three workouts per week may be just about right. Studies show that three workouts per week produces a significantly better conditioning effect than two or one workouts. More than three workouts means little or no additional gain, however. Studies cited by Morehouse and Miller (1976) show that five workouts per week result in only a 3.5% increase in aerobic power when compared with three workouts, and that "cardiovascular fitness is retained nearly as effectively by three sessions per week as by four sessions per week." (p. 235) Other studies (Crews and Roberts, 1976) show no difference between three and five days per week. Morehouse and Miller also point out, however, that one or two sessions per week will give some improvement if training is intensive: "The notion that one workout per week is worse than none at all is invalid." (p. 235)

References:

Crews, T. and Roberts J. 1976. "Effect of Interaction of Frequency and Intensity of Training", <u>Research Quarterly</u>

Morehouse, L. and Miller, A. 1976. <u>Physiology of Exercise</u>, Saint Louis: Mosby. Seventh Edition.

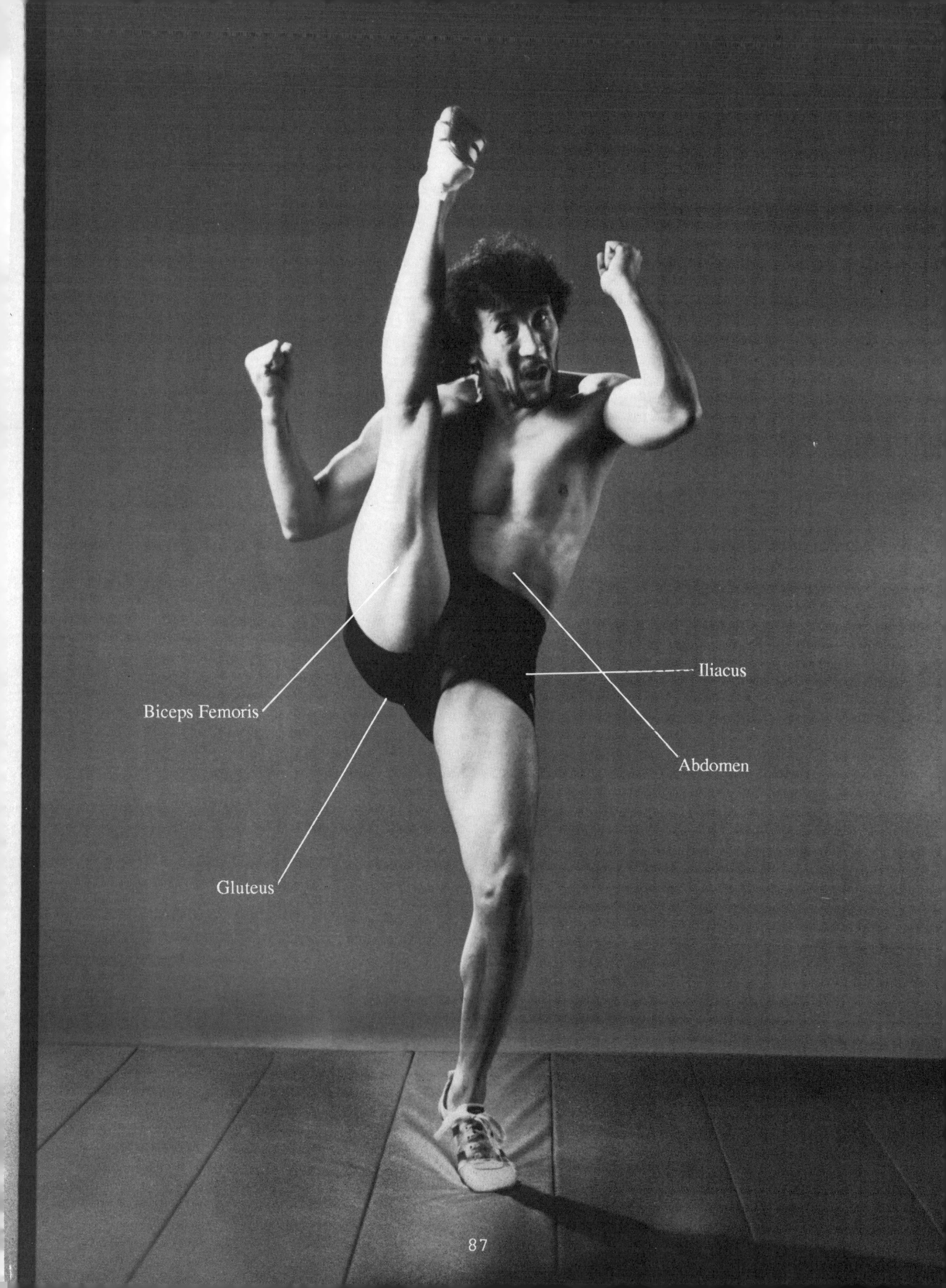

Biceps Femoris

Gluteus

Iliacus

Abdomen

FRONT RISING KICK

The Front Rising Kick is a powerful technique which, done right, will help sharpen your other basic kicks. As a stretching technique, it develops and strengthens the biceps femoris area as well as the illicus and gluteus muscles, arch tendon, hamstring and lower abdominal areas. It will also help you develop balance and speed.

The practical applications of this kick are varied. Rising up with the ball of the foot, the Front Rising Kick is a powerful attack to either the groin or under the chin, and using the back of the heel on the way back down, the kick can be a devastating blow to either the face or collarbone.

HOW TO

1. Assume a right fighting stance.

2. Shift balance onto the right leg. Generating speed with your hip as well as your leg, bring the right leg upward sharply. The kicking leg should be straight, ankle pulled forward, hips leaning forward in the direction of the kick, drawing an arc rising in front of you.

1

2

5

4. After rising up, flex the biceps femoris bringing the kicking leg straight down, exerting force and focusing energy to the back of the heel. This will help you develop your front quadriceps, as well as give you a kick that is as effective coming down as it is rising up.

3. The balancing foot should remain flat on the surface, or you can rise up on the ball of the foot. The knee of the balancing leg should be slightly bent, and the upper torso leaning slightly back. Make sure you keep your guard up; both fists protecting your jaw and your arms covering your ribs.

3

4

APPLICATION

MOST COMMON MISTAKES

A common error of The Front Rising Kick is to just swing the leg without leaning the hip into it. This will reduce both the speed of the kick as well as its power. Other errors are leaning forward, which will keep your leg from rising as high as it can, and over-bending the balancing leg, which robs the hamstring and hips of the full benefit of the stretch.

REPETITIONS

Beginners - 5 to 10 times, each leg.
Advanced - 15 to 20 times, each leg.

BREATHING

INHALE before the kick, as you rise up with the kick, EXHALE SHARPLY. When you return to the ready stance, INHALE again.

WEIGHT LIFTING

If you want to maintain size, but increase your strength, you should work with lighter weights, between 30 and 80 pounds, and do 15 to 20 repetitions for 10 sets. Rest time between sets should only be 10 to 15 seconds.

If you want to increase your size, start with a lighter weight as a warmup for 2 sets of 10 repetitions, a medium weight for 5 sets of 5 to 6 repetitions, and then go for the maximum weight you can handle, 2 to 3 repetitions for 2 or 3 sets. Between each set, you should rest for 20 to 30 seconds.

If you are just maintaining size, this workout can be done every day. If you are trying to increase your size, this workout should be done every other day, concentrating on different muscle groups.

1. QUADRICEPS & HAMSTRINGS
Carefully place the weight on your shoulders and trapezius muscles, not on your neck (a very common mistake). With your feet one shoulder width apart, bend your knees without leaning forward, keeping your back as straight as possible. Squat down until your legs are at 90 degree angles, like a narrow Horse Riding Stance. An angle of 90 degrees isolates the quadriceps area, but if you can squat deeper than 90 degrees you will also get your biceps femoris muscles involved and your entire leg will benefit.

1   2

1   2

5. ILLICUS & LOWER ABDOMEN - An especially good exercise for someone with a bad back is to sit upright in a chair, supporting yourself with your hands and keeping your legs together, bring your knees close to your chest. Keeping your knees bent will make things easier on your lower back, while straightening your legs will put a little more strain on the lumbar muscles. Repeat this for 5 sets of 10 repetitions.

4. OBLIQUES - To work your oblique muscles, assume a position as if you were going to do a bent leg sit-up, but instead of lying flat on the floor, sit up and turn your upper body so that you are facing either your right or your left side. Leaning back at about a 45 degree angle, quickly torque your waist side to side. Work both sides for 5 sets of 15 repetitions. If you are more advanced, do 7 sets of 30 repetitions. If you have trouble keeping your feet flat on the floor while doing this, place your feet underneath a sofa or some other heavy object.

1

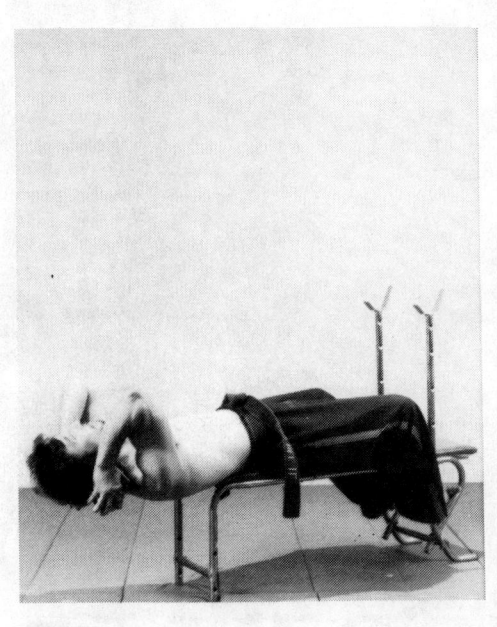

1 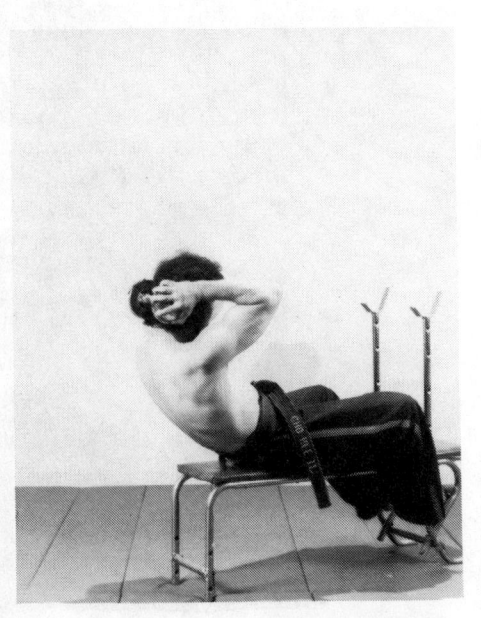   2 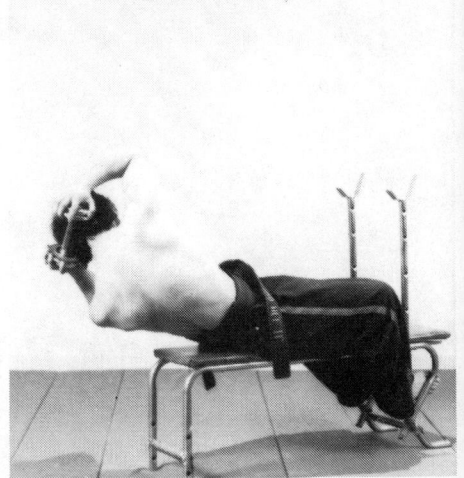   3

2   3

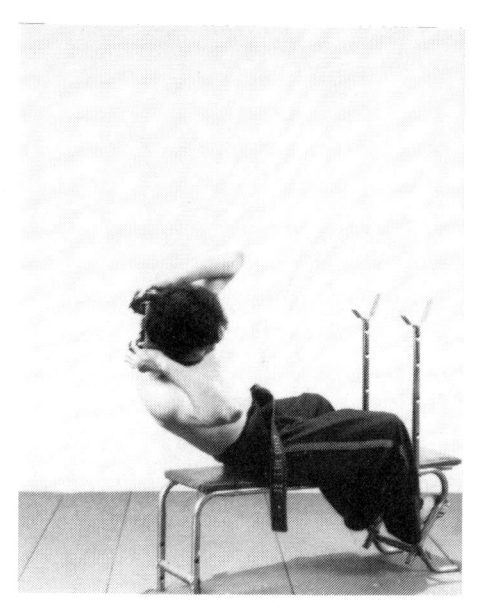

2. ABDOMINALS - Because the stomach muscles play such an important role in keeping the leg raised, they must be strengthened. Using a bench, lie flat on your back with the small of your spine at the edge of the bench. Rise up to an angle of 45 degrees, and then lower yourself back down. Repeat this for 5 sets of 10 repetitions. Advanced students can hold a light weight or dumbell behind their heads.

3. OBLIQUES - Do the same exercise as above, except only rise up about 15 degrees, and then rotate your upper body from side to side for 5 sets of 10 repetitions.

4

STRETCHING

1. HAMSTRINGS I - Sitting flat on the floor with both legs straight out in front of you, bend your upper body forward. Try not to arch your back, but rather bend at the hips. This will increase the stretch you achieve. You can also work one leg and then the other by extending your leg onto a chair or a ladder, heel flat and toes pointing upward. Bend your body downward towards the middle, bringing your upper body below your leg. As you stretch, it is important that you continue breathing properly as well as isolate whichever muscle group are working, giving it full attention.

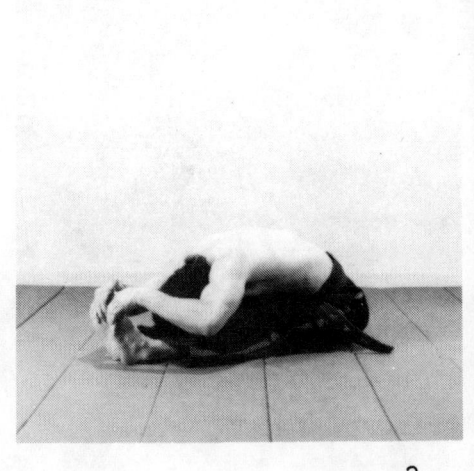

1

2

6. HAMSTRINGS - An excellent stretch for the biceps femoris muscle group is to place your leg on an high object (in this case a ladder). Keeping your toes point upward and your rear leg as straight as you can, bend your upper body down lower than your raised leg. Repeat this three or four times for each leg, holding yourself there for 20 seconds.

1

2

95

1   2

2. HAMSTRINGS II & QUADRICEPS - Get into a front split position with the heel of your front foot flat on the floor, toes pointing upward. The instep of the rear leg should be flat on the floor. In this position, your front leg will be stretching the biceps femoris while your back leg will be stretching the quadriceps. Leaning backwards will emphasize the quadricep stretch, while leaning forward will add to the biceps femoris stretch. Hold yourself in both positions for 20 seconds, and then switch direction. Repeat this three or four times.

Biceps Femoris — Abdomen — Iliacus — Quadriceps

PUSHING KICK

In between the Axe Kick and the Front Snap Kick is the Pushing Kick. The Pushing Kick, whose action is just as it sounds - a solid pushing motion with the bottom of the foot, has been developed and used to great advantage lately by Olympic Tae Kwon Do stylists who see it as an effective technique which rises above the restrictions of fighting while wearing chest protectors.

Used both offensively as well as defensively, the Pushing Kick serves a lot of needs while sparring. If an opponent is rushing in, a Pushing Kick can help to keep them off of you. If you are trying to set up your opponent for a hand or foot technique, the Pushing Kick can move them to a proper distance. Also, since the chamber for the Pushing Kick is halfway between those of the Front Snap and Axe Kicks, the Pushing Kick can be thrown as an afterthought when the Front Snap or Axe Kick that you were getting ready to throw turns out to be the wrong move at the wrong time.

Because your body remains upright while throwing this technique, it is fairly easy to keep your balance. The Pushing Kick gets its power from the quadriceps which thrust out the kicking leg and the abdominal, illiacus and biceps femoris muscles which help to keep the leg in chamber position.

HOW TO

1. Assume a left fighting stance.

2. Shifting your balance onto your left leg, quickly raise your right leg, knee as high and as close to your chest as possible. You must keep you lower leg almost parallel to the floor.

1   2   3

MOST COMMON ERRORS

The single most common mistake made while executing the Pushing Kick is the failure to bring the kicking leg up into a high chamber position with the flat of the foot facing the opponent. The pushing action is straight out from your chest to the opponent's. The other most common error is to not follow the Pushing Kick with an effective follow up technique or techniques. The Pushing Kick is a good technique, but it cannot stand on it's own.

REPETITIONS

Beginners - 5 to 10 times, each leg.
Advanced - 15 to 20 times, each leg.

BREATHING

INHALE before the kick and as you perform the kick, EXHALE SHARPLY. When you return to the ready stance, INHALE again.

3. Flexing your quadriceps muscles, push out your right leg, driving your body weight into the target and pushing with the flat of your foot. You can even lean your upper body back in the opposite direction of the kick to increase the reach of the kicking leg.

4. Because this is a distancing technique, you should immediately follow the Pushing Kick with either another, more aggresive kicking technique (such as a Roundhouse or Back Turning Kick), or with hand techniques.

4

5

6

APPLICATION

WEIGHT LIFTING

If you want to maintain size, but increase your strength, you should work with lighter weights, between 30 and 80 pounds, and do 15 to 20 repetitions for 10 sets. Rest time between sets should only be 10 to 15 seconds.

If you want to increase your size, start with a lighter weight as a warmup for 2 sets of 10 repetitions, a medium weight for 5 sets of 5 to 6 repetitions, and then go for the maximum weight you can handle, 2 to 3 repetitions for 2 or 3 sets. Between each set, you should rest for 20 to 30 seconds.

If you are just maintaining size, this workout can be done every day. If you are trying to increase your size, this workout should be done every other day, concentrating on different muscle groups.

1 **2** **3**

1. QUADRICEPS & HAMSTRINGS - Placing a slight lift beneath your heels (in this case a piece of wood) hold a light weight across your shoulders and trapezius muscles. With your legs about one and a half shoulder widths apart bend your knees, squatting down as far as you can go. The wood places a little more emphasis on your quadriceps and your balance, rather than if you were to do this flat-footed. Repeat this for 5 sets of ten repetitions.

ILIACUS MUSCLE -
Sitting on any sturdy chair, support yourself with your arms and rapidly raise and lower each leg as high as you can. There are a few variations on this exercise; you can work one leg at a time, you can scissor your legs, or you can raise both legs simultaneously which will also help to strengthen your abdominal muscles.

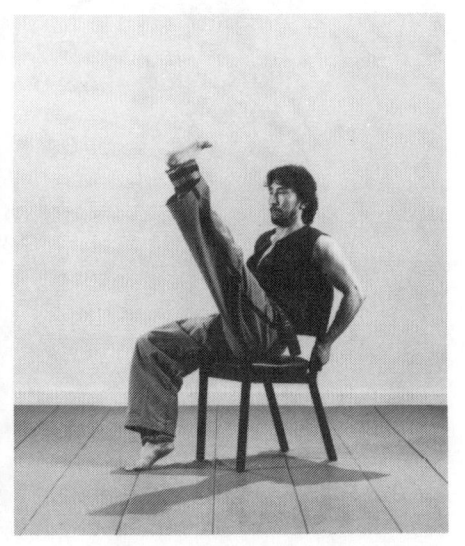

1
2
3

1
2
3

4. LUMBAR & OBLIQUES -

Placing a barbell behind your neck on your trapezius muscles and keeping your legs slightly greater than one shoulder width apart, first bend your waist 90 degrees forward and return to standing 5 to 10 times. Be careful not to jerk your body when you do this and also not to use too much weight. After this exercise, stand upright with the barbell still behind your neck and torque your waist 90 degrees both left and right. This will exercise your oblique muscles. Do this 10 to 15 times in each direction. This exercise is widely called the "Good Morning" exercise.

1

2

1

2

3

GLUTEUS MUSCLES & LUMBAR REGION II - This exercise is most easily performed on a "roman bench". If you do not own or have access to one, you can use any sturdy table or bench as long as you have someone hold down your feet and are able to lower yourself almost totally to the ground. Keeping your hands behind your head, raise your upper body up slightly greater than 90 degrees to the ground. At the top of the extension, flex your buttocks muscles. Repeat this exercise for 10 sets of 10 repetitions.

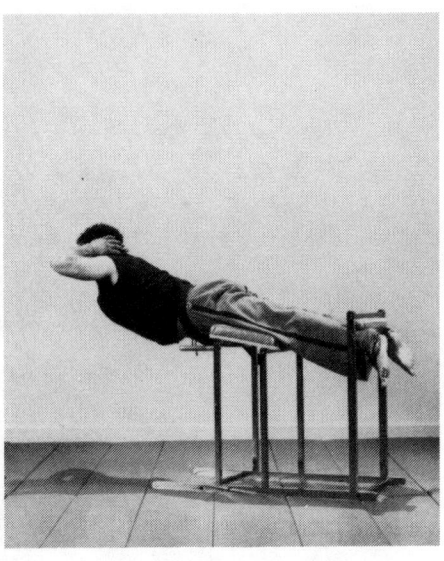

1

2

3

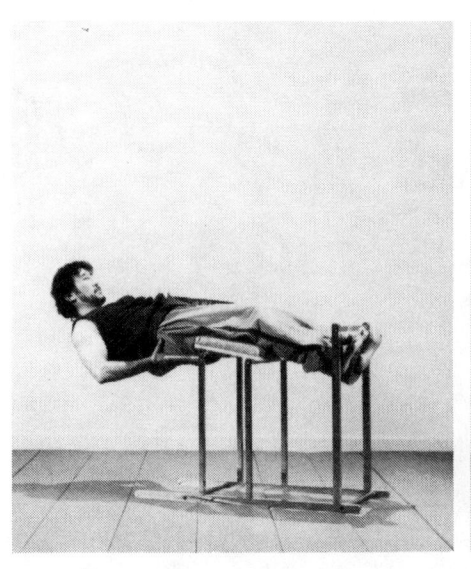

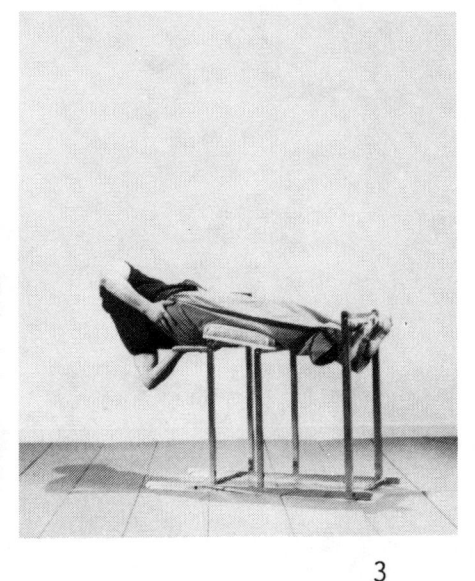

1

2

3

ABDOMINAL & OBLIQUE MUSCLES - This exercise is best performed on a "roman" bench, though if you don't have access to one the exercise can be done by laying on any bench with someone holding down your ankles. Keeping your hands on your lower back, lean backwards and keep your upper body to an angle no greater than 180 degrees from your legs. In this position, rotate your upper body left and right as far as you can. Keep going until you feel a burning sensation in the muscles, and then rest. Repeat for 10 sets.

QUADRICEPS & ILLIACUS MUSCLES - Sitting on the floor, lean backwards, supporting yourself with your hands behind you. Keeping your feet together and off the ground, flex your entire leg upward, both raising your legs high as well as extending them outward as far as you can. The upward motion of the legs will benefit the illiacus muscles, while the extension of the legs will help the quadriceps muscles. Wearing ankle weights will help to make this a more effective exercise. Repeat this exercise for 10 repetitions of 10 sets.

1

2

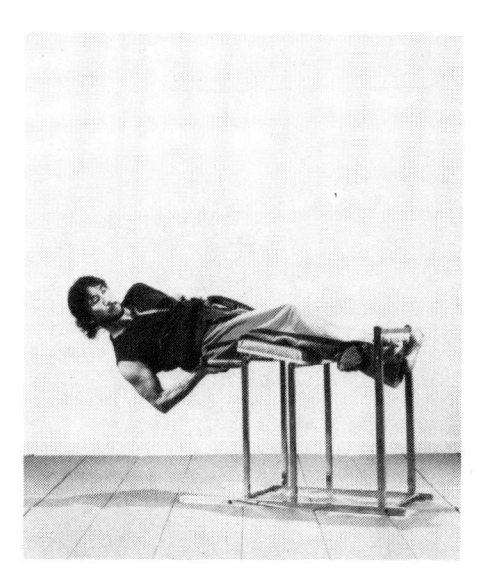

4

STRETCHING

HAMSTRINGS III & QUADRICEPS -
Get into a front split position with the heel of your front foot flat on the floor, toes pointing upward. The instep of the rear leg should be flat on the floor. In this position, your front leg will be stretching the biceps femoris while your back leg will be stretching the quadriceps. Leaning backwards will emphasize the quadricep stretch, while leaning forward will add to the biceps femoris stretch. Hold yourself in both positions for 20 seconds, and then switch legs. Repeat this three or four times.

1 2 3

QUADRICEPS -
Kneeling on the floor, reach behind and grab your left ankle with your right hand. Take a deep breath and as you exhale lean forward, pulling your left leg as far forward as possible. You should think that you are trying to touch your foot to your head. Hold yourself in this position for 20 seconds, rest for a few moments, and then repeat 5 times for both legs.

HAMSTRINGS & SARTORIUS II -
Standing with your legs as close together as possible, bend over and grab the back of your ankles with your hands, and then pull yourself down trying to touch your head to your knees. Hold yourself there for 3 sets of 20 seconds each.

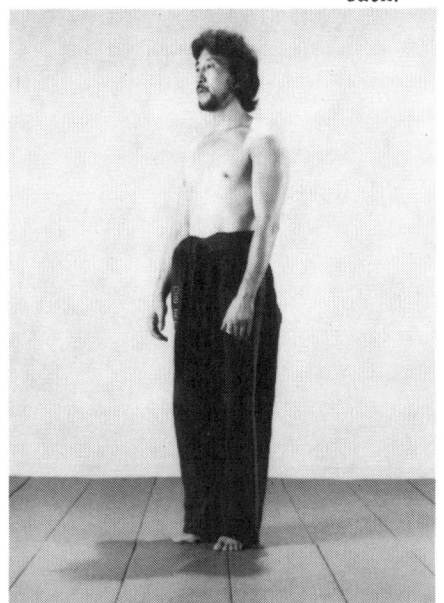

1   2   3

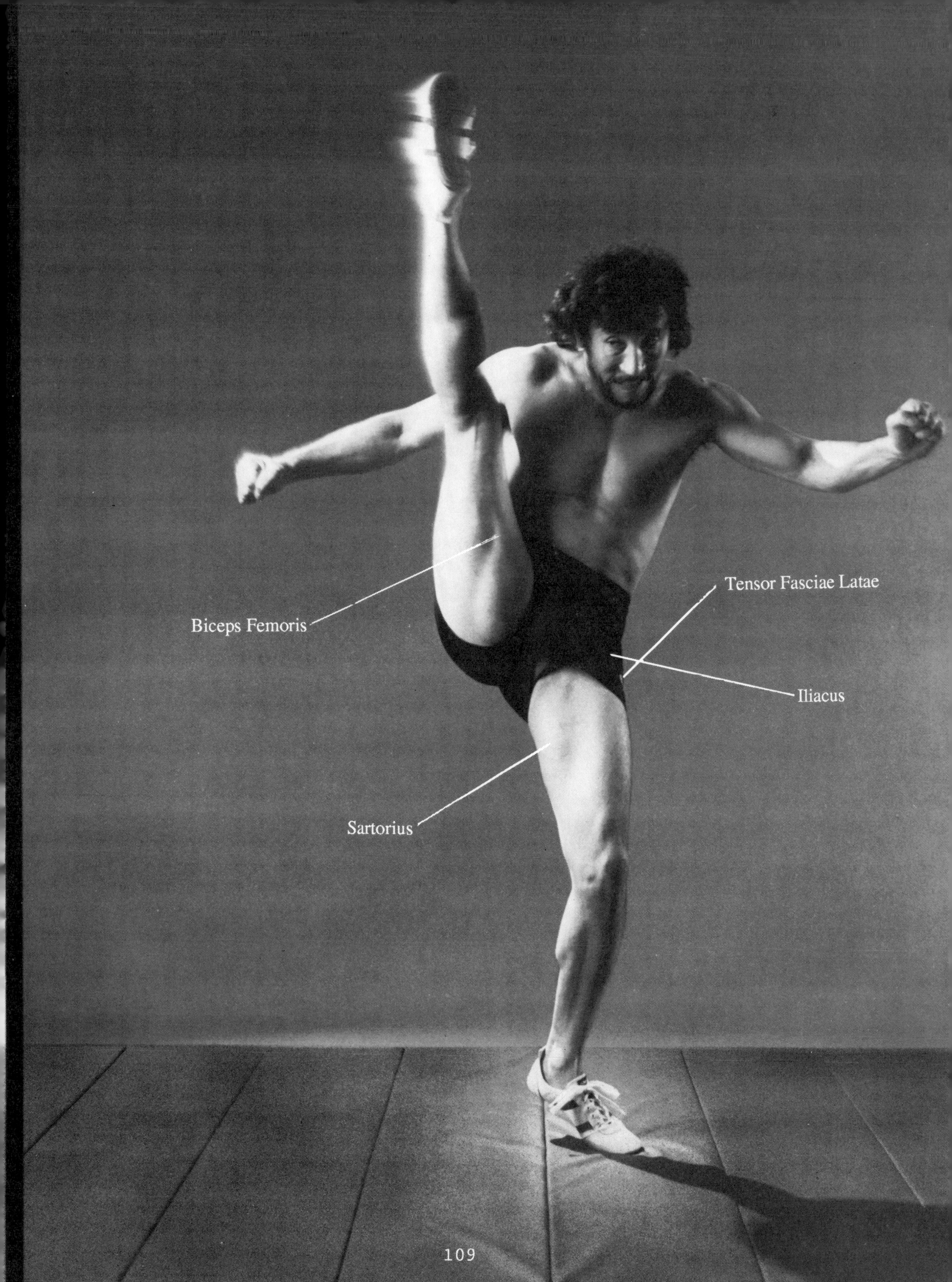
Tensor Fasciae Latae
Biceps Femoris
Iliacus
Sartorius

CRESCENT KICK
(Inside to Outside)

A very powerful attacking tool, the crescent kick gets its power from the sartorius, illicus and tensor fascia latae muscles as well as the hamstrings and groin area. As effective a stretch as it is a kick, the crescent kick is a tremendous aid to increasing balance.

The practical application of the Crescent Kick is when in close quarters with an opponent, delivering a strong blow with the side of the foot to the face. Without flexibility and a good stretch, this kick is hard to throw, but if you have these qualities, then the Crescent Kick is a terrific addition to your arsenal of techniques.

HOW TO

1. Assume a left fighting stance.

2. Shifting balance onto your left leg, torque your waist to your left (counter-clockwise), simultaneously raising your right leg, knee slightly bent. Your balance leg should also be slightly bent.

3. Shooting it straight out, whip your leg from left to right (inside to outside) using your hips to generate speed and the sartorius muscle to generate the power that pushes your leg out. The Crescent Kick should start to the left of your target, with the full execution of the kick bringing it through your target on the way to the right side. At the point of contact (midway through its swing) straighten your knee and tense your muscles. The arc of the kick should be as close to 360 degrees as you can make it. The balancing foot can be either flat on the ground or you can rise up on the ball of the foot for extra reach, and the upper body should be leaning slightly back. Keep your hands in a good, protective fighting position.

4. After executing the technique, flex your biceps femoris, pulling your leg sharply down, rather than letting momentum and gravity do all the work. You will keep better control that way, enabling you to be ready to follow the Crescent Kick with another technique if necessary.

4 5 6

APPLICATION

MOST COMMON MISTAKES

The most common mistakes made while executing the Crescent Kick include using just the leg to generate speed without torquing the hips and waist, as well as leaning the torso too far forward (usually done to compensate for a lack of stretch). Either mistake will rob the kick of both speed and force, making it less effective than it could be.

REPETITIONS

Beginners - 3 sets of 5 to 10 times, each leg.
Advanced - 4 sets of 15 to 20 times, each leg.

BREATHING

INHALE before throwing the kick, and as you execute the technique, EXHALE SHARPLY. As you return to the ready stance, INHALE again.

WEIGHT LIFTING

Working every day with 20 to 40 pounds will enable you to maintain size but improve strength. Do 8 sets of 10 to 15 repetitions. Rest for 10 to 15 seconds between sets.

To increase your size, start with 2 sets of 5 repetitions using light weights, 5 sets of 5 to 6 repetitions using medium weights, and then go for the maximum weight you can handle for 2 or 3 sets of 2 or 3 repetitions. Rest between sets for 15 to 20 seconds. This type of workout should only be done every other day.

1

2

1. QUADRICEPS & HAMSTRINGS - The best exercise for both the quadriceps and biceps femoris muscles is bicycling - either on a regular bicycle or on a stationary "Life Cycle". If you don't own a bicycle, light ankle weights can be worn an you can "bicycle" by sitting in a chair and moving your legs in a pedaling motion.

1

2

2. SARTORIUS & QUADRICEPS - Placing a weight on your shoulders and trapezius and keeping your legs two shoulder widths apart, slowly lower yourself into a horse riding stance, knees bent, back straight. With your legs that far apart, it is strongly urged that you DO NOT try to bend your knees any further than 90 degrees; that is how back injuries occur. Repeat this for 5 sets of ten repetitions.

3

. SARTORIUS - Another good exercise for the sartorius muscles requires no weights at all, just isometric resistance. Keeping your knees together while in a sitting position, place your hands on the outsides of your knees and while applying pressure, attempt to separate your legs. Once you have them spread as wide as they can go, reverse the pressure as you now try to bring your legs back together again. Repeat this for five sets of ten repetitions. (Don't be surprised to discover that your arms get as good a workout from this as your legs!)

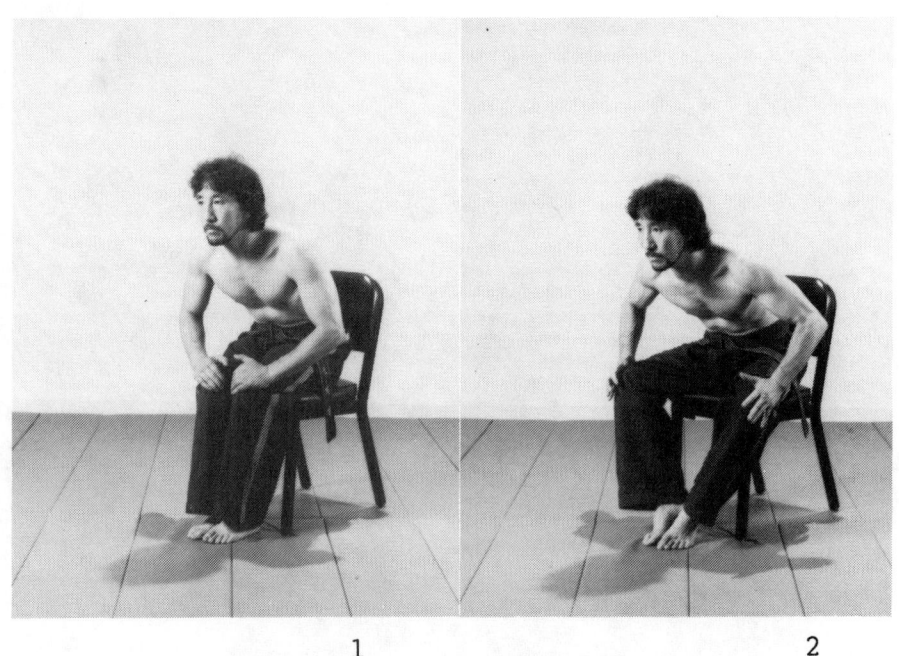

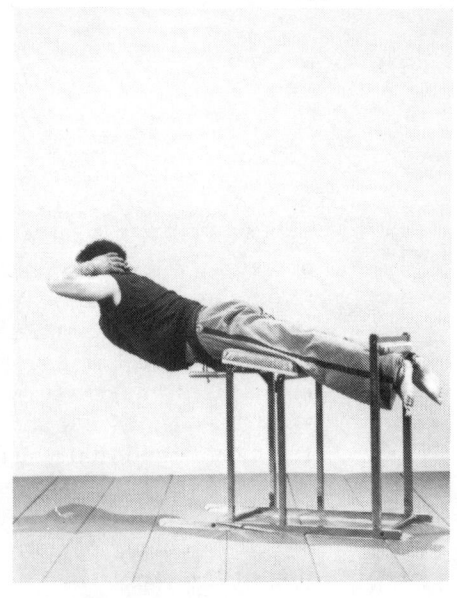

1 2

1 2 3

LUMBAR MUSCLES - Using a either a "roman" bench or a straight bench with someone holding down your ankles, lie on your stomach and from a deep bent position raise yourself up at least 90 degrees from your starting position. Raising yourself higher than 90 degrees will benefit your gluteus muscles as well as your back muscles. Repeat this for 5 sets of 10 repetitions.

GLUTEUS & TENSOR FASCIA LATAE - Supporting yourself by leaning against a chair or some other stationary object, balance yourself on your left leg and raise your right leg away from your body 90 degrees, ankle pulled back, foot parallel to the floor. Using short movements, raise and lower your leg slightly for 10 repetitions of 10 sets, working both legs. NOTE - the movement of the leg is very slight...do not swing the leg. Also, the leg is not being lifted behind you as in a side kick, but 90 degrees away to the side.

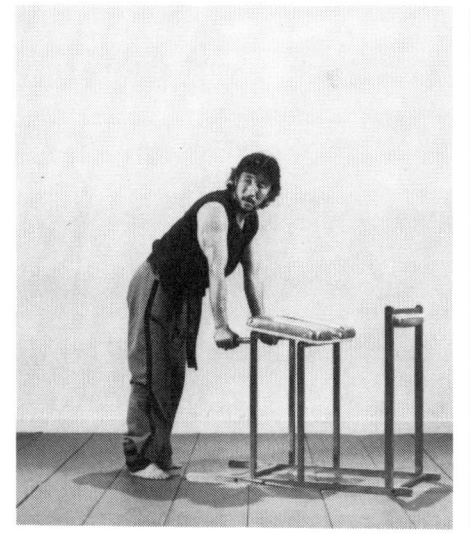

1 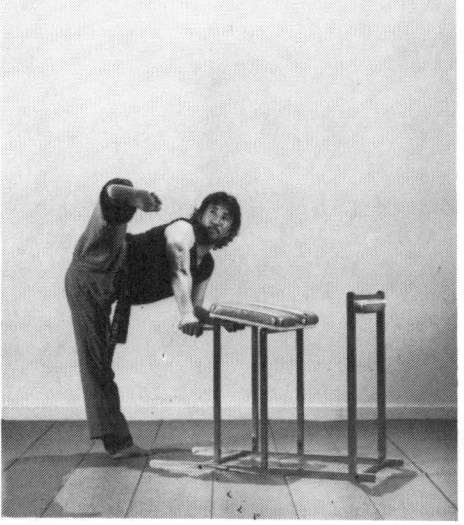   2    3

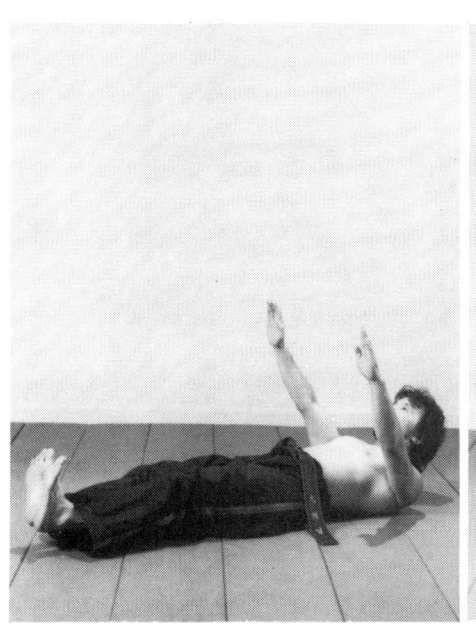

---

1    2

ABDOMINALS - Lying flat on your back with your arms raised in front of you, simultaneously lift your legs straight kneed and raise your upper body, trying to tough your toes with your finger tips. Do as many repetitions as you can, 10 sets worth.

1　　　　　　　　　　　　2　　　　　　　　　　　　3

ABDOMINALS - Exercising your abdomen can done by doing leg raises on a bench, lowering your legs below the level of your body. Make sure you keep your legs as straight as you can. If you have a back problem you can do this same exercise except bring your legs up bent kneed. In order to really see an improvement, you must do as many repetitions as you can for five sets.

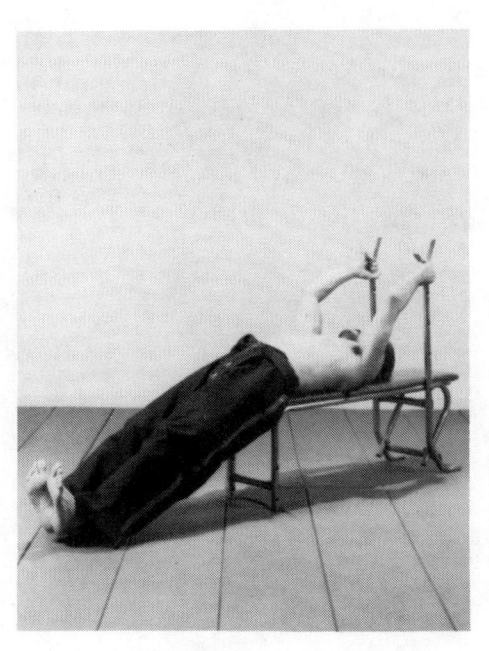

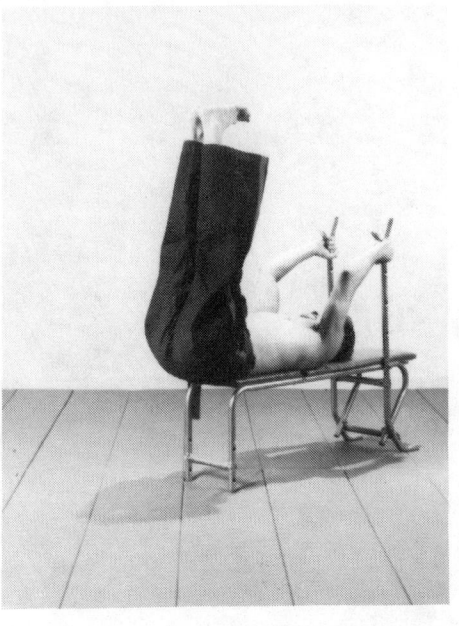

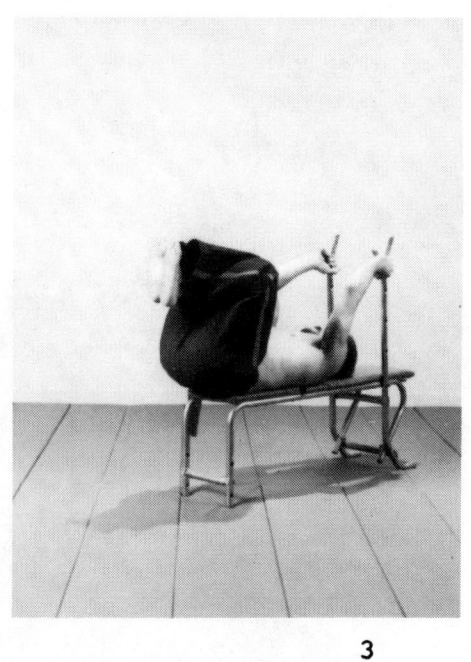

OBLIQUES - A good exercise for the obliques is to place a light weight on your shoulders and trapezius muscles, and keeping your legs one to one and a half shoulder widths apart torque your waist slowly side to side. Do 5 sets of ten repetitions in each direction.

1

2

3

STRETCHING

1. SARTORIUS - With your feet on the floor, separate your legs as wide as you can, locking your knees and keeping your legs straight. Slowly bend over, and with your hands and arms first pull yourself forward, holding for 20 seconds, and then push yourself back, also holding for 20 seconds. Rest for a few moments, and then repeat two more times.

1 2 3

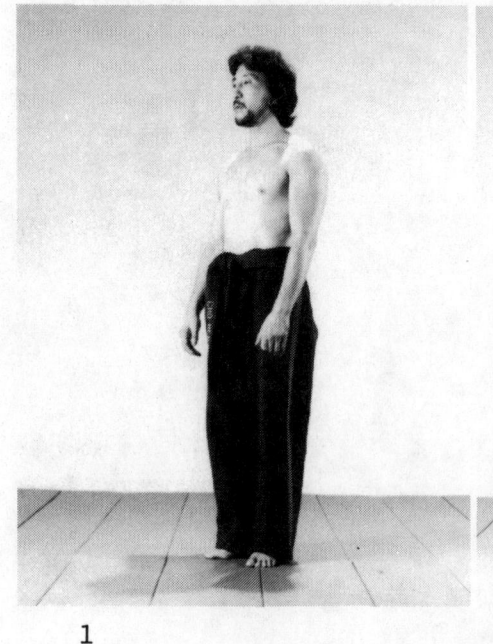

1 3

HAMSTRINGS & SARTORIUS II - Standing with your legs as close together as possible, bend over and grab the back of your ankles with your hands, and then pull yourself down trying to touch your head to your knees. Hold yourself there for 3 sets of 20 seconds each.

1	2

HAMSTRINGS & SARTORIUS I - An excellent stretch for the biceps femoris is to place your leg on an high object (in this case a ladder). Keeping your toes pointed upward and your rear leg as straight as you can, bend your upper body down lower than your raised leg. Repeat this three or four times for each leg, holding yourself there for 20 seconds.

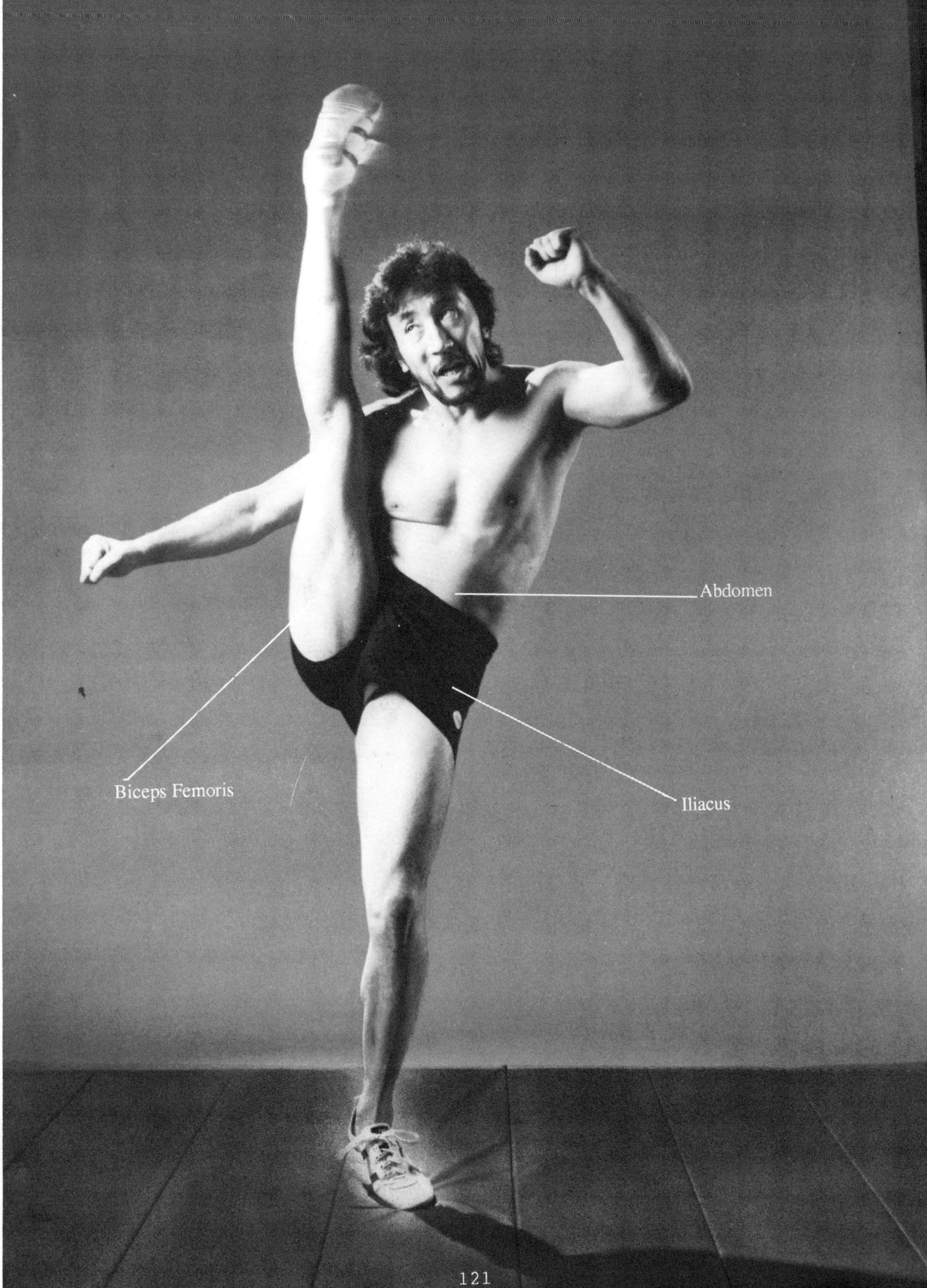
Abdomen
Biceps Femoris
Iliacus

THE AXE KICK

In a modern Tae Kwon Do championship fight, the contestants wear cumbersome chest gear which restricts movement. It was because of this lack of mobility that the Axe Kick was developed in Korea over the last 15 years. The Axe Kick is now the most uniquely comprehensive fighting kick in use in Korea, being thrown about 80 percent of the time. For self defense purposes, the Axe Kick is a powerful addition to anyone's arsenal, requiring not a lot of distance in order to throw it effectively.

The Axe Kick places a great strain on the hamstrings, and because of this it cannot be thrown safely unless these muscles are well stretched and conditioned. Additionally, this kick is aided by the illicus muscle which holds the leg high and the lumbar muscles in the back which provide support as the kick is brought crashing down on the target.

HOW TO

1. Assume a left fighting stance.

2. Rapidly exchange your legs, bringing you right leg forward and your left leg back. Shifting balance onto the right leg and generating speed with your hip as well as your leg, bring the left leg upward sharply. The kicking leg should be straight, ankle pulled forward, hips leaning forward in the direction of the kick, drawing an arc rising in front of you.

1

2

3

4. Hold the leg in a raised position for a moment, sighting in on your target. As you start to bring the kicking leg down, lunge in towards your opponent, covering the distance and exerting force while focusing energy to the back of the heel. Depending on where your opponent is, flex the sartorius muscle of the kicking leg inward or outward, giving the kick a little extra energy. At the moment of impact, lean your upper body backwards. After executing the technique, drop the kicking leg into a fighting stance, or follow with a hand technique.

3. The balancing foot should remain flat on the surface, or you can rise up on the ball of the foot. The knee of the balancing leg should be slightly bent, and the upper torso leaning slightly back. Make sure you keep your guard up; both fists protecting your jaw and your arms covering your ribs.

4

5

APPLICATION

MOST COMMON MISTAKES

A common error of this kick is to just swing the leg without leaning the hip into it. This will reduce both the speed of the kick as well as its power. Other errors are leaning forward, which will keep your leg from rising as high as it can, and over-bending the balancing leg, which robs the hamstring and hips of the full benefit of the stretch. Also, don't just drop the kicking leg - you must flex the biceps femoris muscle and pull your leg down sharply across your target.

REPETITIONS

Beginners - 5 to 10 times, each leg.
Advanced - 15 to 20 times, each leg.

BREATHING

INHALE before the kick, as you rise up with the kick, EXHALE SHARPLY. When you return to the ready stance, INHALE again.

WEIGHT LIFTING

If you want to maintain size, but increase your strength, you should work with lighter weights, between 30 and 80 pounds, and do 15 to 20 repetitions for 10 sets. Rest time between sets should only be 10 to 15 seconds.

If you want to increase your size, start with a lighter weight as a warmup for 2 sets of 10 repetitions, a medium weight for 5 sets of 5 to 6 repetitions, and then go for the maximum weight you can handle, 2 to 3 repetitions for 2 or 3 sets. Between each set, you should rest for 20 to 30 seconds.

If you are just maintaining size, this workout can be done every day. If you are trying to increase your size, this workout should be done every other day.

1. QUADRICEPS & HAMSTRINGS - Exercising your quadriceps and biceps femoris can be done by holding as heavy a dumbell as you can manage in each hand and squatting all the way down. Keep your back as straight as you possibly can to prevent straining it as you squat and stand. Do ten repetitions for five sets.

2. BACK & LUMBAR - This exercise is called the "Good Morning" exercise. Placing a light weight on your shoulders and trapezius muscles behind your head and keeping your legs one and a half shoulder widths apart, bend forward at the waist to an angle of 90 degrees. Make sure that you keep your legs straight.

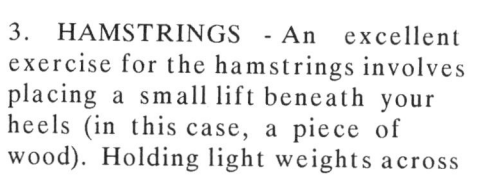

1

2

3. HAMSTRINGS - An excellent exercise for the hamstrings involves placing a small lift beneath your heels (in this case, a piece of wood). Holding light weights across the top of your chest, squat down until your legs are at a slightly greater angle than 90 degrees. Repeat this ten times for five sets.

5. QUADRICEPS & HAMSTRINGS - The best exercise for both the quadriceps and biceps femoris muscles is bicycling - either on a regular bicycle or on a stationary "Life Cycle". If you don't own a bicycle, light ankle weights can be worn an you can "bicycle" by sitting in a chair and moving your legs in a pedaling motion.

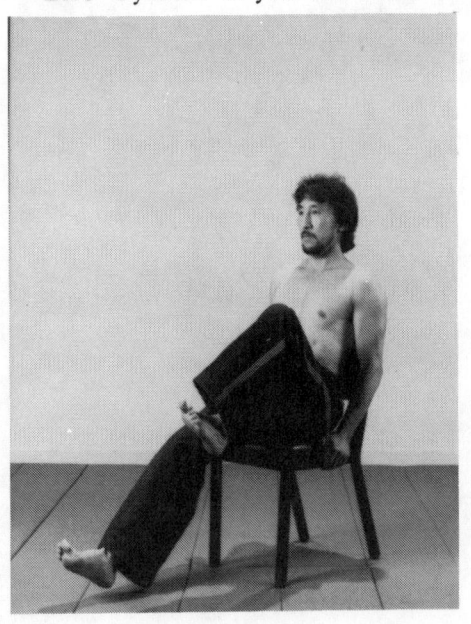

1

2

1 GLUTEUS MUSCLES - Either holding onto a chair or assuming a squat position on the floor, support yourself on your hands by leaning forward. Keeping your right leg straight, raise it as high off the floor as you can, foot perpendicular

2

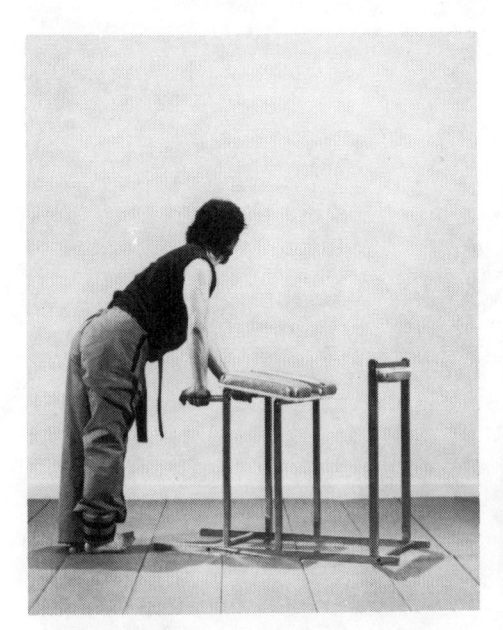

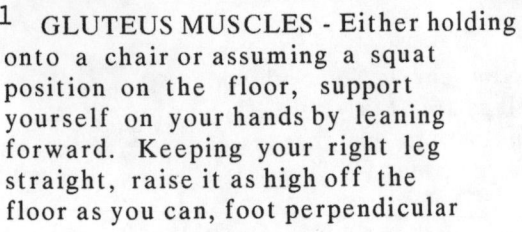

to the floor. Switching legs raise and lower each leg for 10 repetitions of 5 sets. You can add to the effectiveness of this exercise by wearing light ankle weights.

4. SARTORIUS - Another good exercise for the sartorius muscles requires no weights at all, just isometric resistance. Keeping your knees together while in a sitting position, place your hands on the outsides of your knees and while applying pressure, attempt to separate your legs. Once you have them spread as wide as they can go, reverse the pressure as you now try to bring your legs back together again. Repeat this for five sets of ten repetitions. (Don't be surprised to discover that your arms get as good a workout from this as your legs!)

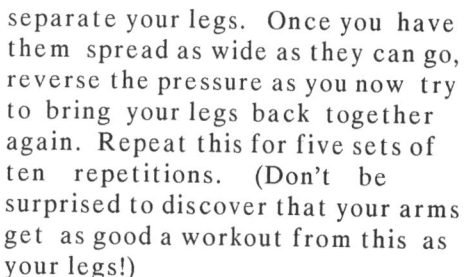

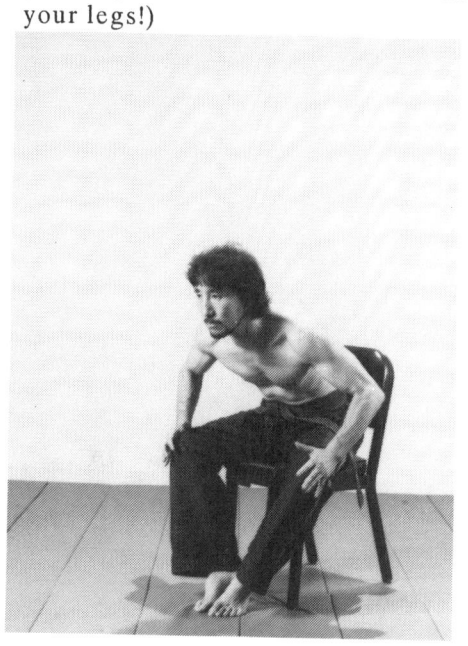

1

2

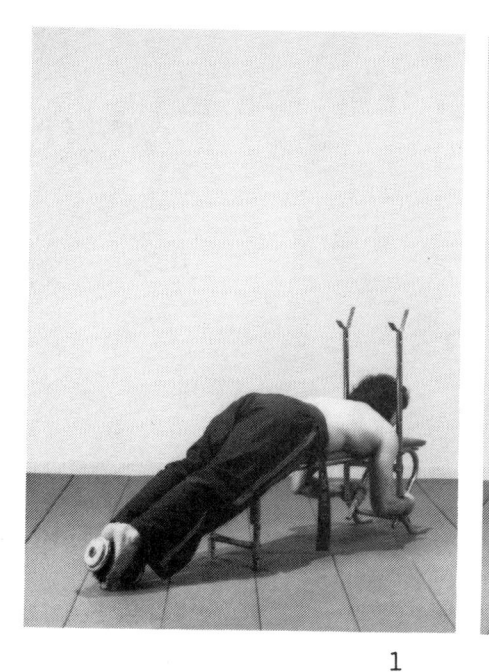

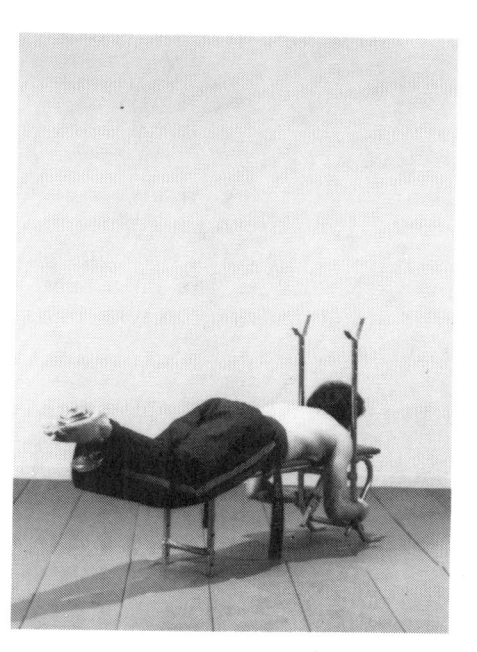

1

2

3

3. HAMSTRINGS - Exercising your hamstring muscles can be done by lying down on your stomach on a long bench and doing reverse curls, also with leg weights on your ankles. Do the same number of sets and repetitions as the leg raises. Following these three fairly simple exercises will increase your strength dramatically.

128

STRETCHING

1. **QUADRICEPS & SARTORIUS** - Kneel on the floor Japanese style, except keeping your knees spread out as wide as you can. Supporting your weight with your hands, lean backwards, dropping your neck and raising your hips as high off the floor as you can. Remember to breath deeply and isolate the quadricep and sartorius muscles. Hold yourself there for 20 seconds. Repeat this exercise three or four times.

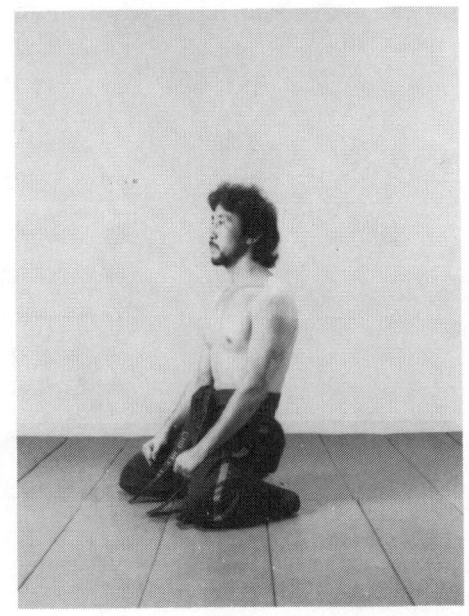

1  2

3. **HAMSTRINGS** - Sitting flat on the floor with both legs straight out in front of you, bend your upper body forward. Try not to arch your back, but rather bend at the hips. This will increase the stretch you achieve. You can also work one leg and then the other by extending your leg onto a chair or a ladder, heel flat and toes pointing upward. Bend your body downward towards the middle, bringing your upper body below your leg. As you stretch, it is important that you continue breathing properly as well as isolate whichever muscle group are working, giving it full attention.

1  2

1 2 3

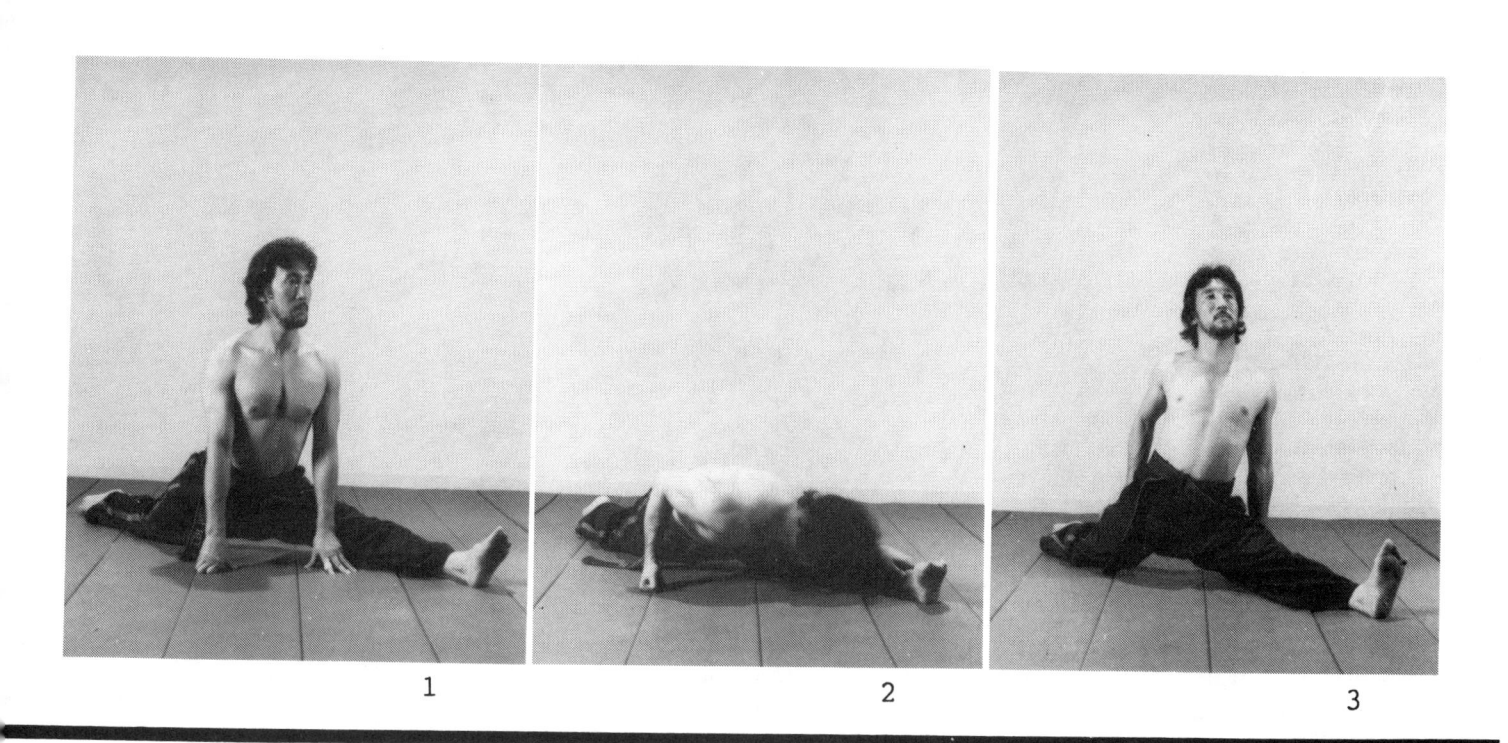

2. HAMSTRINGS & QUADRICEPS - Get into a front split position with the heel of your front foot flat on the floor, toes pointing upward. The instep of the rear leg should be flat on the floor. In this position, your front leg will be stretching the biceps femoris while your back leg will be stretching the quadriceps. Leaning backwards will emphasize the quadricep stretch, while leaning forward will add to the hamstrings stretch. Hold yourself in both positions for 20 seconds, and then switch direction. Repeat this three or four times.

Gastrocnemius

Sartorius

Gluteus

Quadriceps

TWISTING KICK

The Twisting Kick is a difficult kick for the beginner to throw, however it is a good technique to use as a sudden and unexpected attack. Because of the attacking angle, this technique isn't as powerful as some other kicks, yet still utilizes the full strength of the quadriceps and gluteus medius muscles, as well as the gastrocnemius muscles.

As a stretch, this technique works out the sartorius area to its maximum because the kick can be thrown in a number of different ways; high section, mid section and groin areas can all be attacked with the Twisting Kick. With a balance similar to that of the Front Snap Kick, the Twisting Kick can be followed by a variety of hand techniques.

HOW TO

1. Assume a left fighting stance.

2. Shifting balance onto your left leg, torque your waist to the left, turning your hips almost 90 degrees. Cock your right leg at a 90 degree angle, with your lower leg as parallel to the floor as is possible extended over your balance leg.

1

2

3

APPLICATION

3. Keeping the right leg bent, quickly torque your hips to the right (clockwise), and using the quadriceps muscles as well as the gastrocnemius muscles in your lower leg, snap your right leg out at the last moment. The striking area for this kick is the ball of the foot (especially if you are barefoot), though for sparring you can also use the instep. Your hips should be bent into the kick, not leaning back.

4. After executing the Twisting Kick, you can either draw your leg back and place it behind you for a good fighting stance, or you can bring the kicking leg down in front of you in preparation for other kicking techniques. When just practicing the Twisting Kick, try to throw the kick a few times before bringing your kicking leg back down.

4

5

MOST COMMON MISTAKES

The most common mistake made while attempting the Twisting Kick is failing to have your kicking leg bent as parallel to the floor as it can be. This results in throwing a kick that is more of a Crescent Kick than a Twisting Kick. Hand in hand with this is the mistake of not using your knee and lower leg to generate power; relying soley on your hips and thighs.

REPETITIONS

Beginners - 7 to 12 times, each leg.
Advanced - 17 to 25 times, each leg.

BREATHING

INHALE before throwing the technique, and as you execute the kick EXHALE SHARPLY. When you return to the ready stance, INHALE again.

WEIGHT LIFTING

Weight lifting is, to me, the real "Fountain of Youth". No matter what your sport is, if you train with weights your body will keep its tone well into your later years.

Different people set different goals for themselves when weight lifting. If you want to maintain size but increase your strength, you should work with lighter weights rather than heavier ones. By experimenting, find a weight which you can comfortably work with for 10 sets of 15 to 20 repetitions. Rest between sets for 10 to 15 seconds.

If you want to increase your size, start with a lighter weight as a warmup for 2 sets of 10 repetitions, a medium weight for 5 sets of 5 to 6 repetitions, and then go for the maximum weight you can handle, 2 to 3 repetitions for 2 or 3 sets. Between each set, you should rest for 20 to 30 seconds.

If you are just maintaining size, this workout can be done every day. If you are trying to increase your size, this workout should be done every other day, concentrating on different muscle groups.

1

2

3

1. QUADRICEPS & SARTORIUS- Placing a weight on your shoulders and trapezius, keep your legs two shoulder widths apart. Slowly lower yourself into a horse riding stance, knees bent, back as straight as possible. To increase size, start with a lighter weight for 2 sets of 10 repetitions, then move on to a medium weight for 5 sets of 5 to 6 repetitions. Finish by using the maximum weight you can handle for 2 or 3 sets of 2 to 3 repetitions. Rest between sets for 20 to 30 seconds. This exercise will also help to strengthen your sartorius muscles.

6. ILLICUS & LOWER ABDOMEN - Sitting either on a chair or on the floor, support yourself with your hands and raise first one leg and then the other straight up in front of you as high as you can. Wearing ankle weights will speed up your progress as you do 5 sets of 10 repetitions for each leg.

1 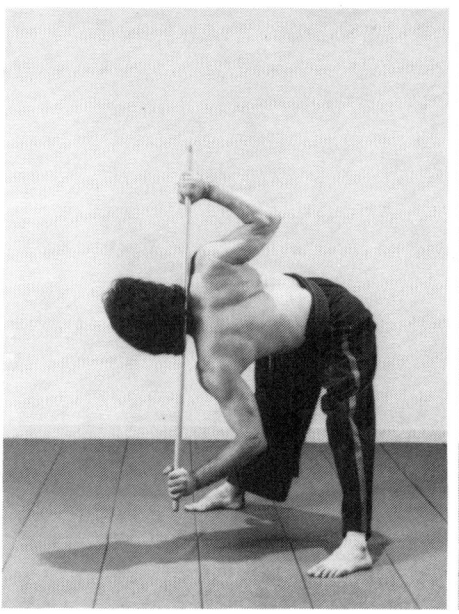 2  3

4. OBLIQUES II - Exercising your obliques can also be done by standing with your legs two shoulder widths apart. Holding a stick behind your head, bend forward 90 degrees at the waist. From this position, rapidly torque your waist side to side. Work both sides for 5 sets of 15 repetitions. If you are more advanced, do 7 sets of 30 repetitions.

2. **GASTROCNEMIUS** - Exercising your gastrocnemius muscles can be done quite simply by quickly and repeatedly rising up on your toes. Holding a weight across your shoulders and trapezius while doing this will increase the efficiency of this exercise. You can also use a chair for support if your balance is a little weak. Do this for 3 sets of 20 repetitions.

1

2

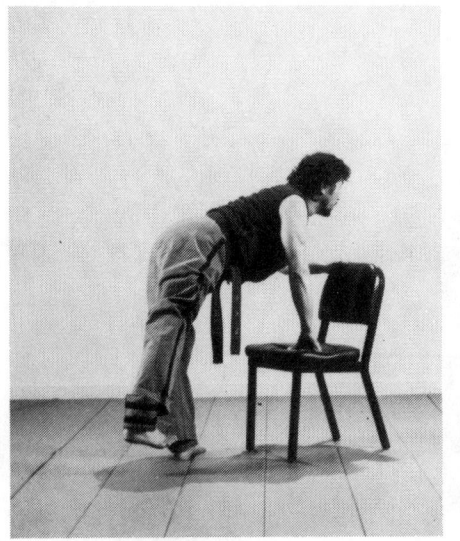

GLUTEUS MUSCLES II - Supporting yourself by leaning against a chair and support yourself on your hands. Working first one leg and then the other, place your leg directly behind you as far as you can, knee straight. Raise the leg as high as you can behind you for 10 repetitions of 10 sets for both legs. Wearing ankle weights will help make this a better exercise.

1

2

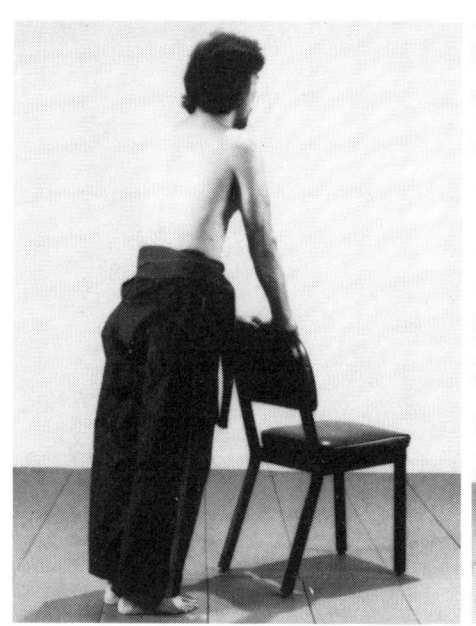

1　　　　　　　　　　　　2

1　　GLUTEUS & TENSOR FASCIA LATAE - Kneeling on your left knee, support your upper body with your hands and arms. Using long motions, swing your right leg up and down, keeping the knee locked and the foot in a side kick position with the edge of the foot parallel to the floor and your heel higher than your toes. Repeat this 5 times for 5 sets, and then switch sides. If you are more 　2　advanced, do this exercise 10 repetitions for 10 sets. Lifting to the side works out the tensor fascia latae, while lifting your leg behind concentrates the exercise more in the gluteus muscles. You can also work up to adding ankle weights to increase the effectiveness of the exercise.　3

138

3. OBLIQUES I - Lying on a flat bench with your lower back at the very edge and holding a light weight behind your neck, rise up to a 45 degree angle. From this position, quickly torque your waist to both sides. You should try to do this as many times as possible, until you feel a burning sensation in the obliques muscles.

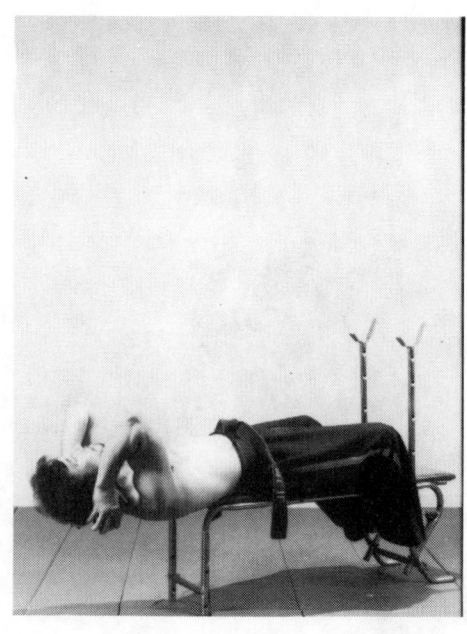

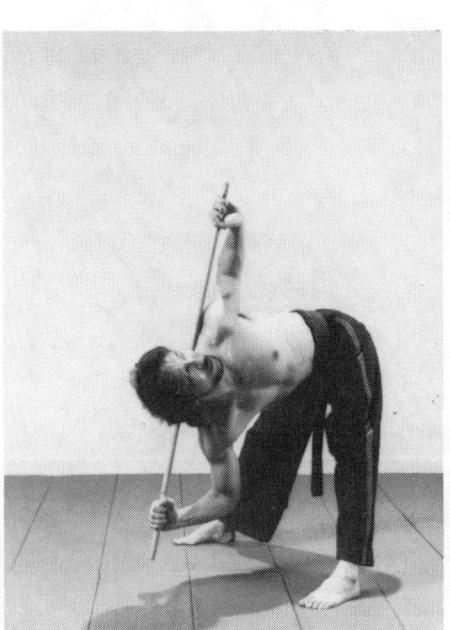

OBLIQUES - With your legs two shoulder widths apart and holding a stick behind your head, bend forward 90 degrees at the waist. Rapidly torque your waist to both sides for 20 repetitions each side. Repeat this for 5 sets.

2   3   4

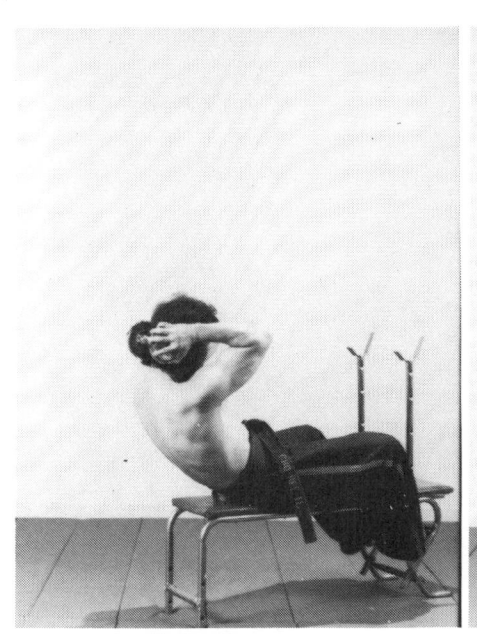

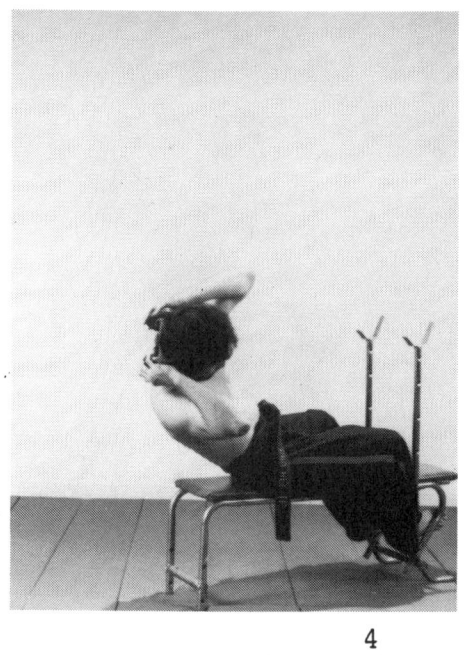

STRETCHING

1. SARTORIUS - From a standing position, spread your legs as wide as you can, keeping your feet flat on the floor. Locking your knees, lean your body as far forward as you can, hold yourself there for 20 seconds, and then push yourself back as far as you can, also holding yourself there for 20 seconds. Repeat this three or four times, resting slightly between sets.

1

2

3

1

2

3

3. HAMSTRINGS - Separate your legs 2 shoulder widths apart. Grabbing your ankles with both hands, bend your body forward, pulling yourself down to the center. After 20 seconds, slowly bring yourself over to your right side, trying to touch your head to your knee. After 20 seconds slowly pull yourself over to your left side, again trying to touch your head to your knee. Hold yourself there for 20 seconds.

4

1   2

2. KNEE TENDON - Because of the strain placed on the knee by the Twisting Kick, it is a good idea to do deep knee bends (without weights) in order to tone up your knee's tendons and ligaments.

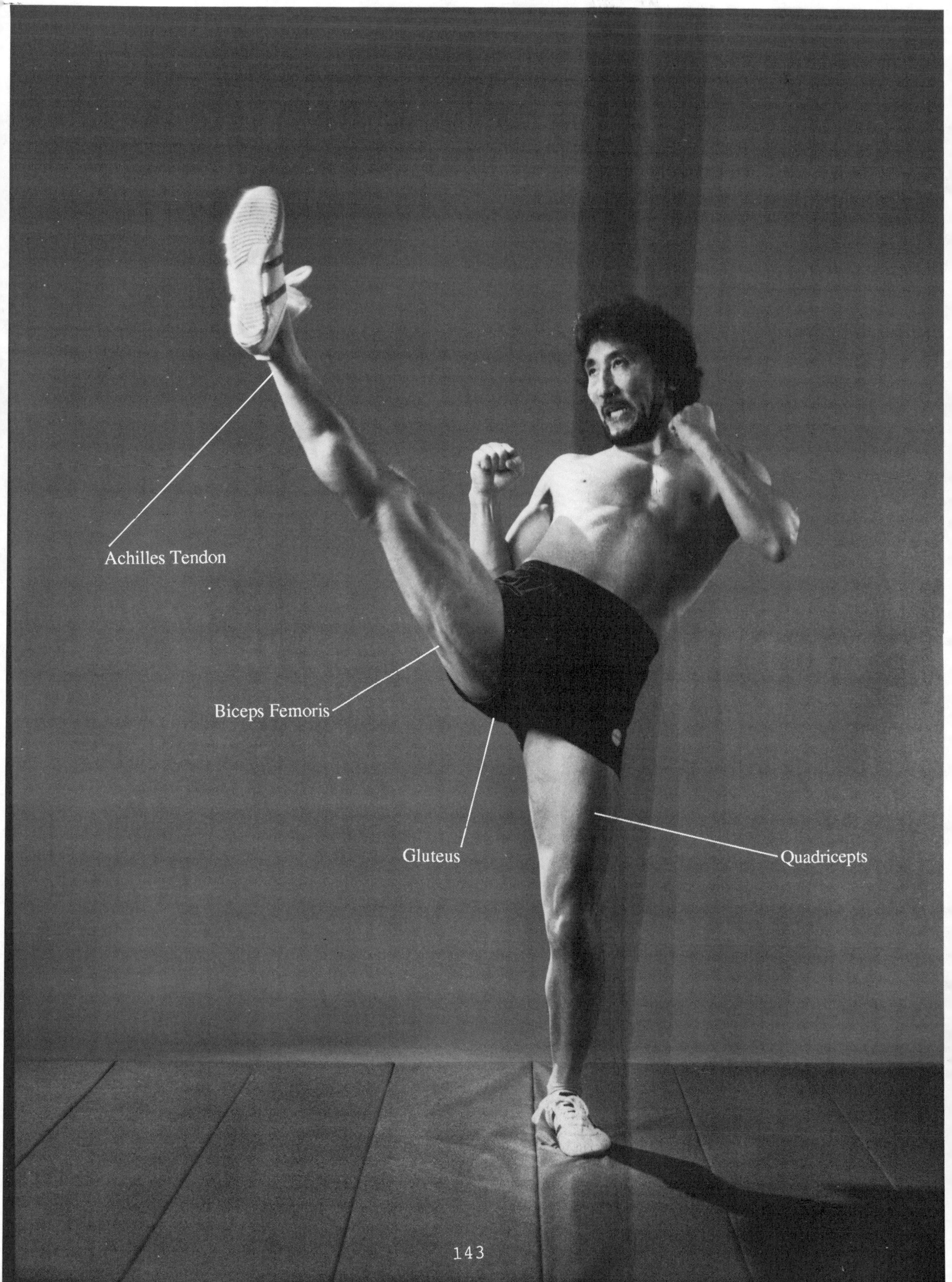
Achilles Tendon
Biceps Femoris
Gluteus
Quadricepts

FRONT SNAP KICK

The Front Snap Kick is a reasonably easy technique to throw, which makes it both fast and versatile. Getting its force mostly from the quadriceps and gluteus muscles as well as the knee tendon and arch tendon areas, the Front Snap Kick is an attacking technique, as compared to the Front Rising Kick which is a stretching technique.

The kick can be thrown a number of ways for a variety of purposes. Thrown high, the kick is an attack to the face. Thrown straight out in front or lower, the kick is a powerful attack to the solar plexus or groin. Because balance is so easily placed on the rear leg while executing this technique, the Front Snap Kick can be easily followed with hand attacking techniques. In Korea, the Front Snap Kick is enjoying a renewed following with tournament fighters using it as a pushing type of technique for defense, as well as backing it up as a double technique for offense.

HOW TO

1. Assume a left fighting stance.

2. Shifting balance onto left leg, torque your waist slightly forward using your hips. Cock your right leg in such a way so that your heel is closer to your buttocks, rather than parallel to the floor.

1

2

3

APPLICATION

3. Draw your right leg up with your quadricep, and simultaneously throw the kick out using your knee. Your upper body can either lean back (which gives the kick reach) or lean slightly forward (which throws the kick in a closer distance). Lock your ankle forward and pull your toes back so that the contact area for the kick is the ball of your foot. Once again, you must be careful not to drop your guard; keep your face protected at all times.

20

4. After executing the kick you can either drop the leg in front of you which gives you forward momentum to follow the kick with a lunging punch, or re-cock the leg which sets you up for another kick or a shorter distance punch.

4   5   6

MOST COMMON MISTAKES

The most common mistake made when executing the Front Snap Kick is to bring the kicking leg too far in front of you before throwing the technique. This prevents you from gaining the speed and power from your hips and quadricep muscle. This is also a common cause of knee injuries, because the knee must bear the full brunt of the kick's forward force. Other mistakes include not pulling the toes back, striking the target with the toes rather than with the ball of the foot, separating the cocking of the leg and the throwing of the kick (these should happen together), and leaning too far forward.

REPETITIONS

Beginners - 7 to 12 times, each leg.
Advanced - 17 to 25 times, each leg.

BREATHING

INHALE before throwing the kick, and as you execute the technique, EXHALE SHARPLY. As you return to the ready stance, INHALE again.

WEIGHT LIFTING

Weight training is the most effective way of increasing and maintaining muscle tone. The idea that it will slow a martial artist down is a myth as far as I am concerned. I've been lifting weights steadily for over 30 years, and it hasn't slowed me down in the least.

Increasing muscle mass and maintaining muscle tone require two different types of workouts. To increase size you must first warm up with light weights for 2 sets of five repetitions. Rest for no more than 30 seconds between sets. After you have done your 2 sets, move on to a medium weight for 5 sets of 5 to 6 repetitions. Finish your workout by training with the heaviest weight you can handle for 2 or 3 sets of 2 or 3 repetitions each. This type of workout should be done only every other day.

To maintain a desired muscle tone without increasing mass, work with 30 to 80 pounds and do 10 sets of 15 to 20 repetitions, resting for no more than 15 seconds between sets.

---

3. GLUTEUS MUSCLES - Either holding onto a chair or assuming a squat position on the floor, support yourself on your hands by leaning forward. Keeping your right leg straight, raise it as high off the floor as you can, foot perpendicular to the floor. Switching legs raise and lower each leg for 10 repetitions of 5 sets. You can add to the effectiveness of this exercise by wearing light ankle weights.

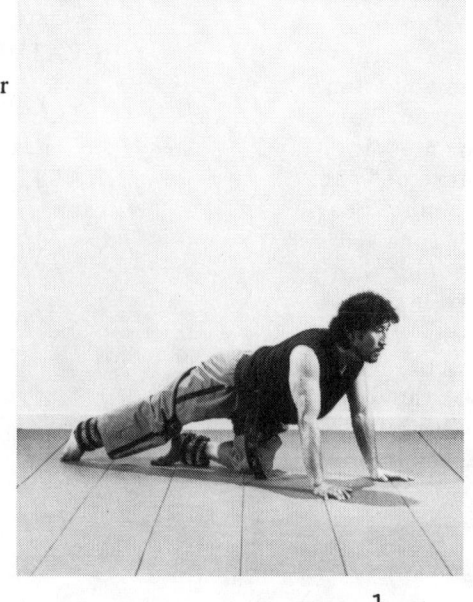

1. QUADRICEPS & HAMSTRINGS - Placing a light weight across your shoulders and trapezius muscles, lunge forward from a standing position into a deep forward stance. Make sure that you keep your back straight and that you press into the forward stance deeply. Come back up to a standing position. Repeat this 5 sets of ten repetitions with each leg.

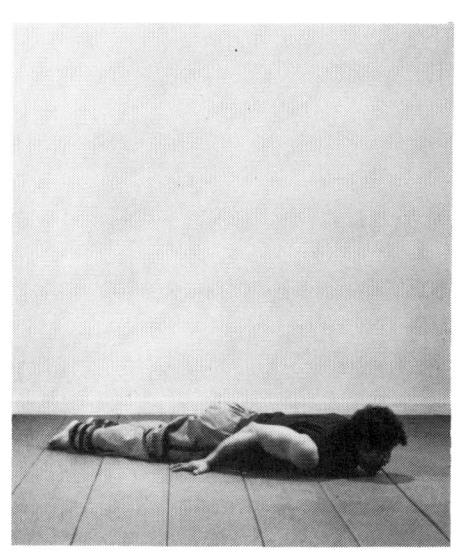

1   2   3

4. GLUTEUS MAXIMUS - An excellent tool to use to develop the gluteus muscles is a Roman bench. Lying face down and bending at the waist, arch your back upwards as far as you can go for 10 repetitions of 10 sets. If you don't have a Roman bench to use, this exercise can be done by lying down on the floor, face down, arms out in front of you. Raise your upper body and legs simultaneously, tensing your gluteus muscles and holding yourself like this for 10 seconds. Repeat this 10 times.

1   2   3

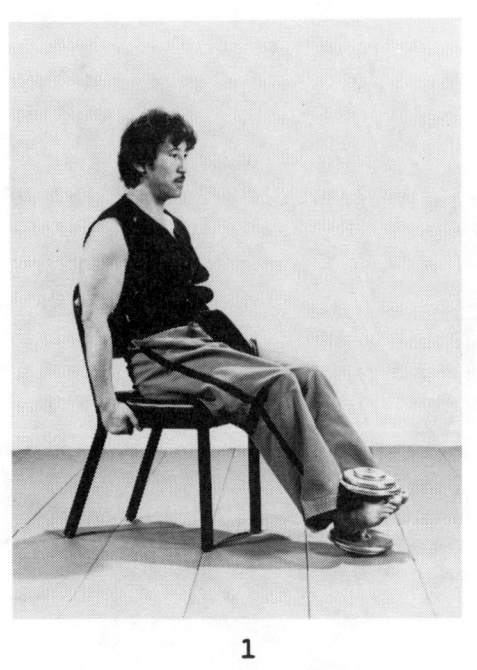

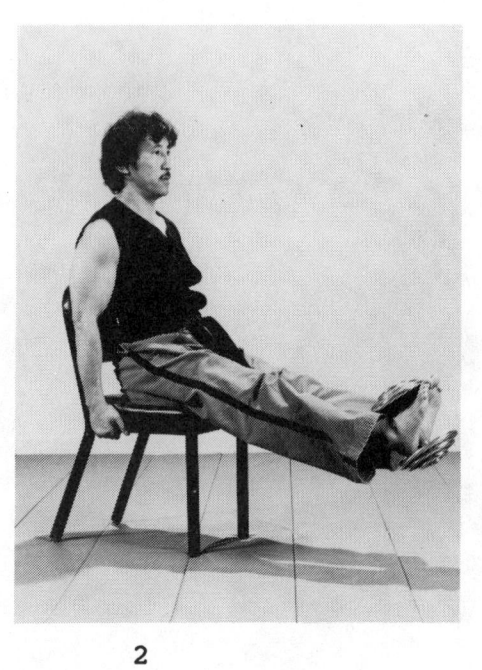

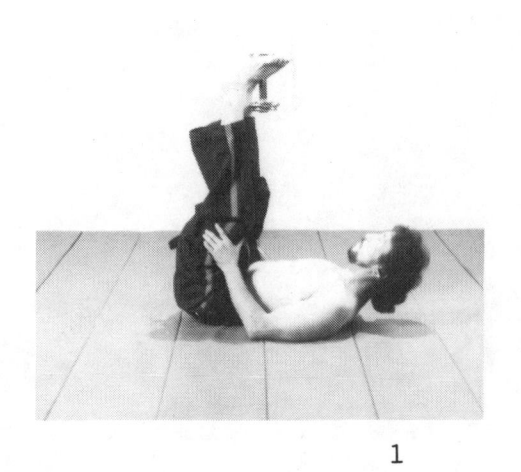

1

2

1

2

149

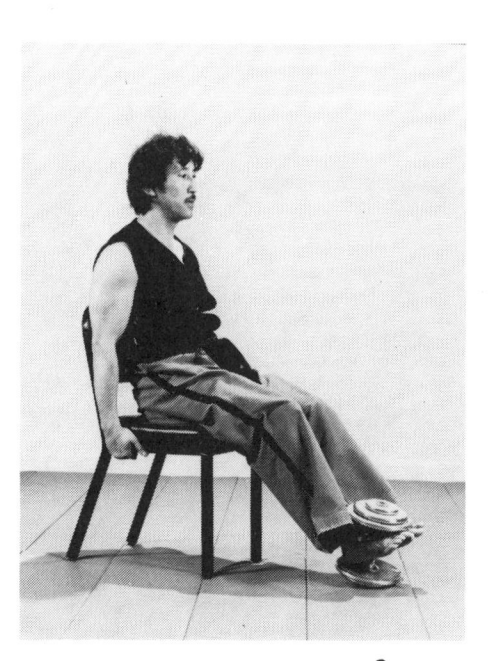

2. QUADRICEPS - If you don't have a leg rising machine to use, you can do this exercise with a chair. Placing weights on your ankles (tying them down if necessary) sit with your back straight and hold onto the bottom or back of the chair with your hands. Straighten and lower your legs directly in front of you. Another method of doing this exercise is to lay down flat on the floor, and with weighted ankles, bring your knees to your chest and then push upward, flexing with your quadriceps muscles and extending your legs as close to a 90 degree angle into the air as you can.

3

3

STRETCHING
1. QUADRICEPS - Kneeling on the floor with your legs bent beneath you (Japanese style), lean backwards supporting yourself with your hands and raise your hips off the floor. This will concentrate the stretch in your quadriceps. A forward split is also a very good stretch for the Front Snap Kick, and by leaning slightly backwards you focus the stretch heavily in the quadricep of the rear leg.

1

2

1

2

151

3. HAMSTRINGS II - One of the best stretches for the hamstrings is also one of the most commonly done. Sitting on the floor with both legs straight out in front of you, reach forward and grab your toes, pulling yourself forward and down. Remember, the goal of this stretch is not to touch your forehead to your knee, but your chin to you shinbones - you want to bend from the waist, not from the back.

1

2

1

2

3

2. HAMSTRINGS I - Separate your legs 2 shoulder widths apart. Grabbing your ankles with both hands, bend your body forward, pulling yourself down to the center. After 20 seconds, slowly bring yourself over to your right side, trying to touch your head to your knee. After 20 seconds slowly pull yourself over to your left side, again trying to touch your head to your knee. Hold yourself there for 20 seconds.

Tensor Fasciae Latae
Quadriceps
Gluteus
Biceps Femoris
ABDOMINALS

SIDE KICK

SIDE KICK

Perhaps the most widely used as well as the most powerful kick is the Side Kick. Every martial arts discipline has some form of the Side Kick as part of its basic system. This kick is as versatile as it is common, being used as both an offensive and defensive technique. Strength is generated in a straight line from the mid-section, and because of this the recommended attacking area is the opponent's torso area, or in the case of street self defense, the knee area. The side kick is often demonstrated as being thrown face level, but that is not where is is the most effective.

The Side Kick uses more muscle groups than any other kick, relying on the tensor fascia latae and gluteus muscles to raise the leg; the abdomen, oblique and biceps femoris muscles to draw the leg into the chamber position; and the quadriceps muscles to push the leg out. Each group of muscles must work properly with the next in order for this kick to be thrown effectively. The Side Kick can be thrown from both a stationary position, or while moving in towards the target for extra power as well as covering a greater distance.

Many full-contact fighters use a modified form of the Side Kick during their bouts, throwing the kick at a 45 degree angle rather than leaning their bodies back as in good martial arts technique. Either way, the Side Kick is as effective as it is powerful.

HOW TO

1. Assume a right fighting stance.

2. Shifting balance onto your right leg, simultaneously bring your left leg past and behind your right leg, turning your upper body counter-clockwise 45 degrees. Once your left foot is past your right and firmly planted on the floor, shift your weight onto your left leg and raise your right leg up, knee as close to your chest as you can with your leg high and lower leg parallel to the floor.

3. Simultaneously now turn your body 45 degrees clockwise and push your leg out with the quadriceps muscles in your upper leg. Your balance foot (the left) should pivot sharply on the ball of the foot, so that as you kick your left heel turns in a direct line towards the target. Keeping your ankle back, strike the target with the blade of the foot or the heel. At the height of the kick you should be looking over your shoulder and your heel, hip, and shoulders should all be a perfect vertical line.

4. After executing the technique, you can either draw back and throw the kick again, drop the kicking leg in front of you and throw another kick, or drop the kicking leg and follow up with hand techniques.

4 5 6

MOST COMMON MISTAKES

The most common error made during this technique is not drawing the kicking leg up far enough to the chest, keeping the lower leg perpendicular to the floor rather than parallel. Other mistakes include kicking like a roundhouse kick (which when done as a side kick is the cause of the majority of knee related injuries), leaning your body forward rather than back in a vertical line, and separating the movements of the kick rather than keeping them all one continuous motion.

REPETITIONS

Beginners - 10 to 12 times, each leg.
Advanced - 20 to 27 times, each leg.

BREATHING

INHALE before throwing the technique, HOLD YOUR BREATH as you move forward, and then EXHALE SHARPLY as you execute the kick.

APPLICATION

WEIGHT LIFTING

I have found weight training to be a great asset to the martial artist. If done properly, it can tremendously increase both kicking and punching power.

There are two goals that the martial artist can set for himself with weight training. One is to increase muscle mass, while the other is to maintain muscle mass and increase tone and endurance. These involve two different types of workouts.

To increase size begin with light weights for 2 sets of five repetitions taking no more than 30 second rests between sets. Next move on to a medium weight for 5 sets of 5 to 6 repetitions, and end the sessions with the maximum weight you can handle for 2 or 3 sets of 2 or 3 repetitions. This type of workout should be done only every other day.

To maintain a desired muscle tone without increasing mass, work with 30 to 80 pounds and do 10 sets of 15 to 20 repetitions, resting for no more than 15 seconds between sets.

1

2

3

1. QUADRICEPS & HAMSTRINGS - Placing a slight lift beneath your heels (in this case a piece of wood) hold a light weight across your shoulders and trapezius muscles. With your legs about one and a half shoulder widths apart bend your knees, squatting down as far as you can go. The wood places a little more emphasis on your quadriceps and your balance, rather than if you were to do this flat-footed. Repeat this for 5 sets of ten repetitions.

2. QUADRICEPS - If you don't have a leg rising machine to use, you can do this exercise with a chair. Placing weights on your ankles (tying them down if necessary) sit with your back straight and hold onto the bottom or back of the chair with your hands. Straighten and lower your legs directly in front of you.

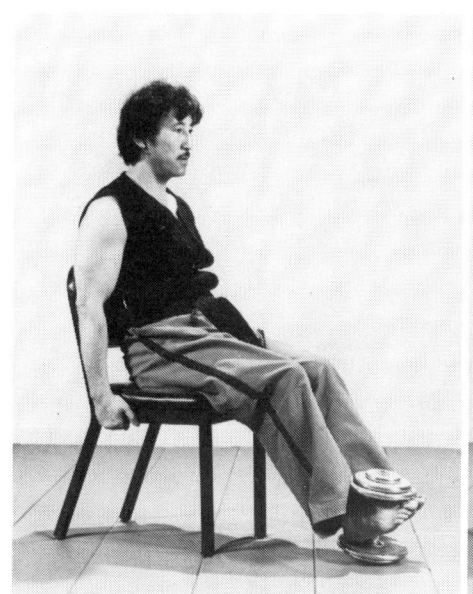

1

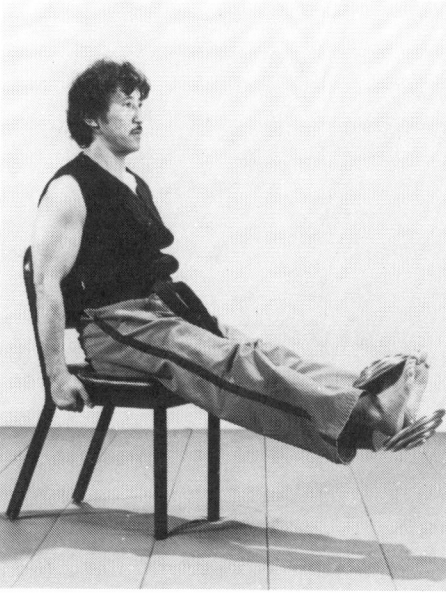

2

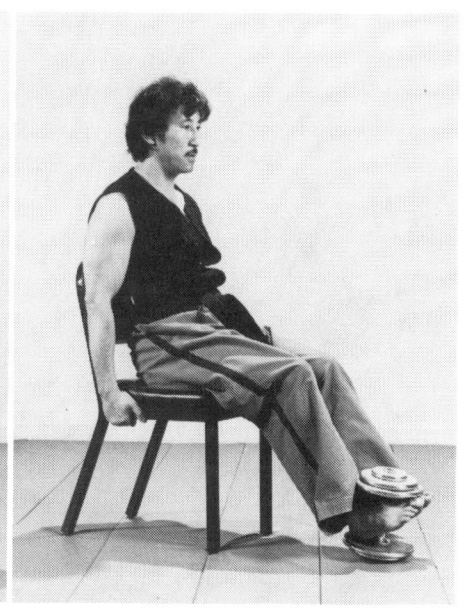

3

1

2

TENSOR FASCIA LATAE & OBLIQUES - Supporting yourself by holding onto some stationary object (in this instance a "roman" bench), raise and lower your leg behind you in a side kick position with your toes parallel to the ground using a long, swinging motion. The higher you bring the leg, the better will be the workout that your oblique muscles get. Repeat this for 10 sets of 10 repetitions.

1 2 3

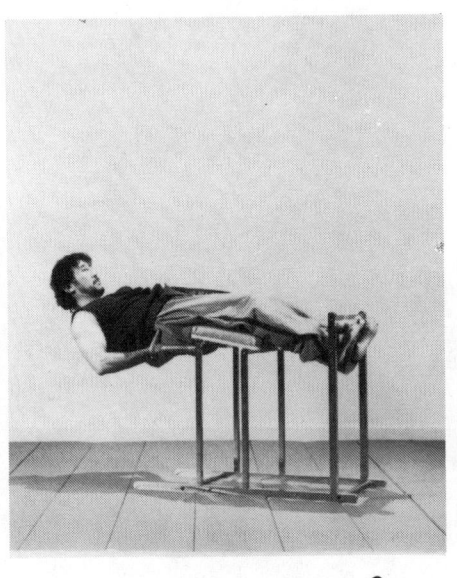

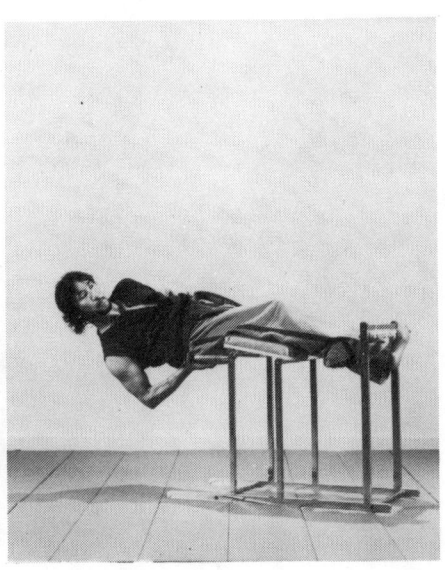

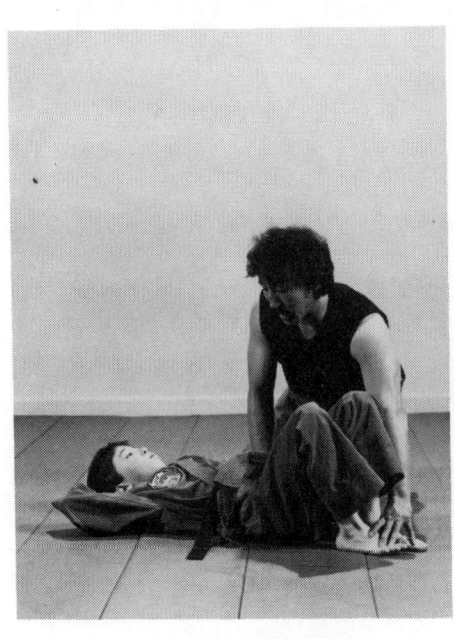

1 5. UPPER ABDOMEN -
Getting into a bent leg sit up position, raise
your upper body to your knees repeatedly. Try
not to return to a full lying position until
the set is over. Do as many as you can for 5
sets. This type of sit up is called
"Crunchers". You'll find out why.

2 3

159

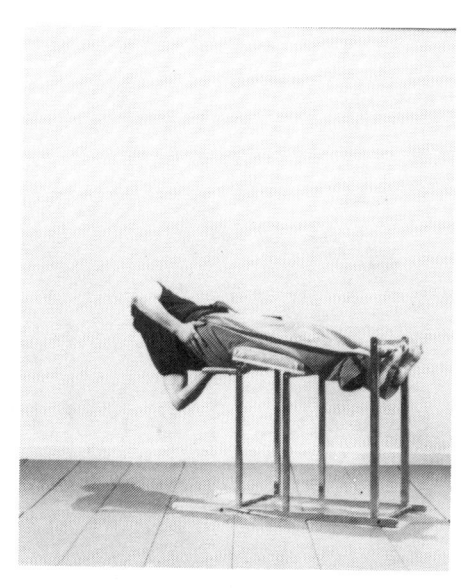

ABDOMINAL & OBLIQUE MUSCLES -
This exercise is best performed on a "roman" bench, though if you don't have access to one the exercise can be done by laying on any bench with someone holding down your ankles. Keeping your hands on your lower back, lean backwards and keep your upper body to an angle no greater than 180 degrees from your legs. In this position, rotate your upper body left and right as far as you can. Keep going until you feel a burning sensation in the muscles, and then rest. Repeat for 10 sets.

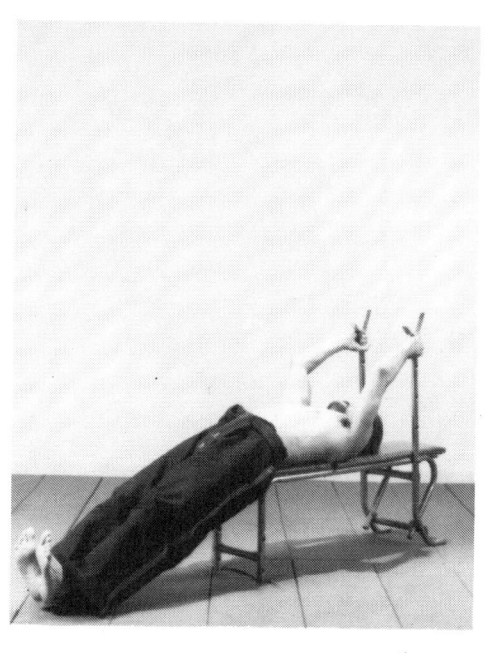

4

---

4. LOW ABDOMEN -
Exercising your lower abdomen can be done by doing leg raises on a bench, lowering your legs below the level of your body. Make sure you keep your legs as straight as you can. If you have a back problem you can do this same exercise except bring your legs up bent kneed.

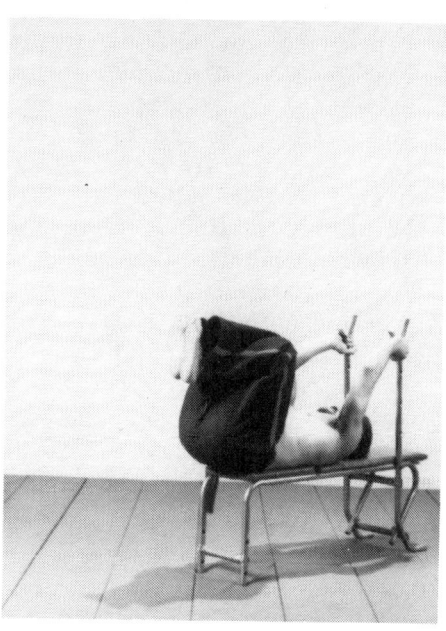

In order to really see an improvement, you must do as many repetitions as you can for five sets. This same type of exercise can be done on the floor, using a partner to apply a little pressure to your abdomen as you raise your legs.

1 2

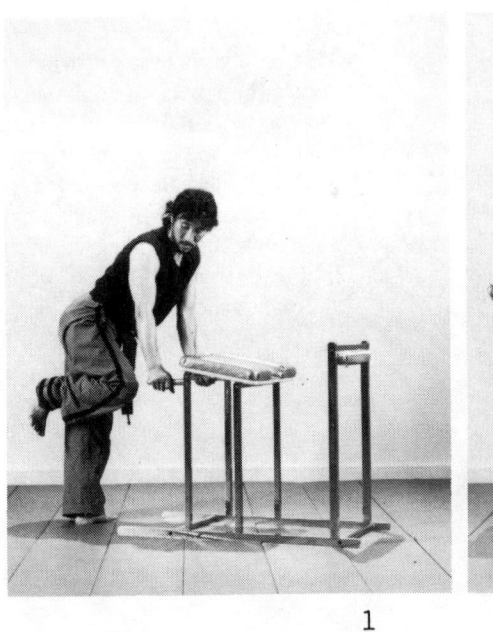

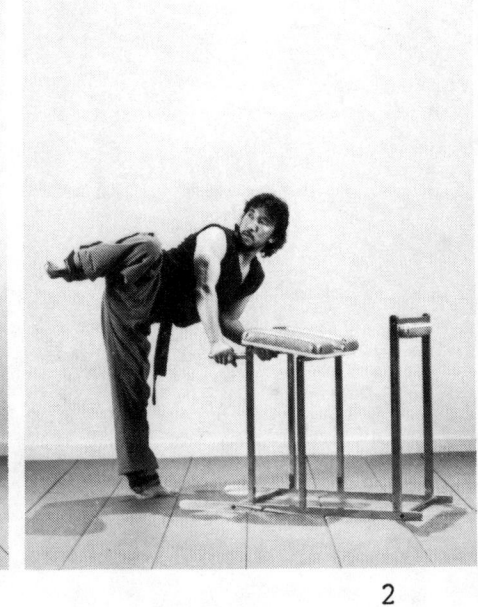

3. GLUTEUS & TENSOR FASCIA LATAE - Supporting yourself by leaning against a chair or some other stationary object, balance yourself on your left leg and raise your right leg away from your body 90 degrees, ankle pulled back, foot parallel to the floor. Using long, slow movements, raise and lower your leg for 10 repetitions of 10 sets, working both legs. NOTE - at the height of the swing, hold your leg in the raised position for a few moments.

4. GLUTEUS & LUMBAR MUSCLES - Lying on the floor, support yourself with your hands by the edge of your body and lift your legs as high off the floor as possible. Keep yourself in this position for at least 10 to 20 seconds. Rest for 10 seconds and then repeat for 10 repetitions. Wearing ankle weights will greatly improve your strength.

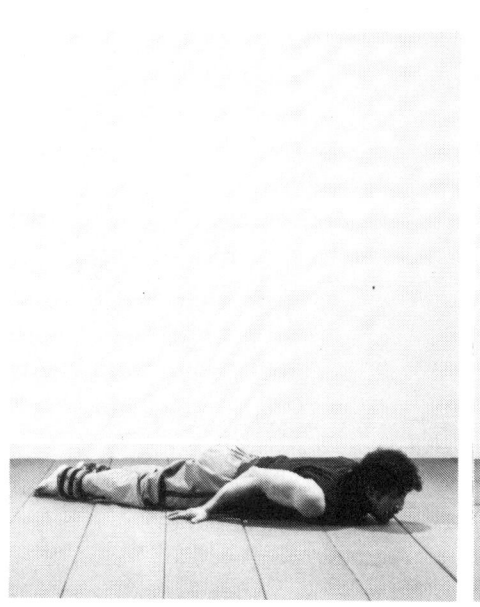

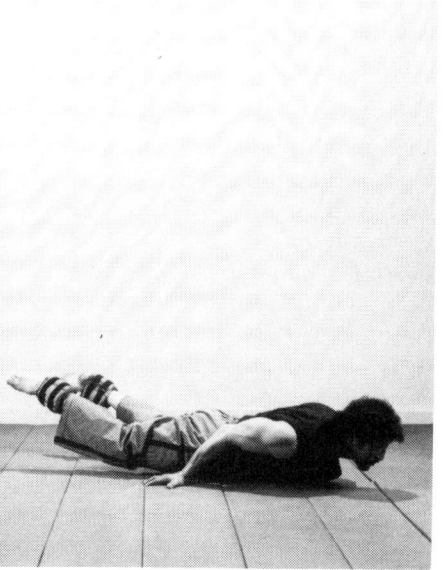

1
2
3

STRETCHING

1. QUADRICEPS & SARTORIUS - Kneel on the floor Japanese style, except keeping your knees spread out as wide as you can. Supporting your weight with your hands, lean backwards, dropping your neck and raising your hips as high off the floor as you can. Remember to breath deeply and isolate the quadricep and sartorius muscles. Hold yourself there for 20 seconds. Repeat this exercise three or four times. Your back and lumbar muscles will also benefit from this stretch.

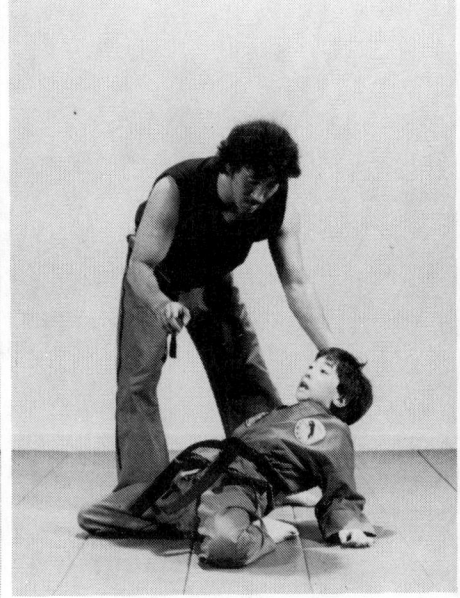

1   2   3

---

2. SARTORIUS - From a standing position, spread your legs as wide as you can, keeping your feet flat on the floor. Locking your knees, lean your body as far forward as you can, hold yourself there for 20 seconds, and then push yourself back as far as you can, also holding yourself there for 20 seconds. Make sure you keep your hips as low as possible as you repeat this three or four times, resting slightly between sets.

1

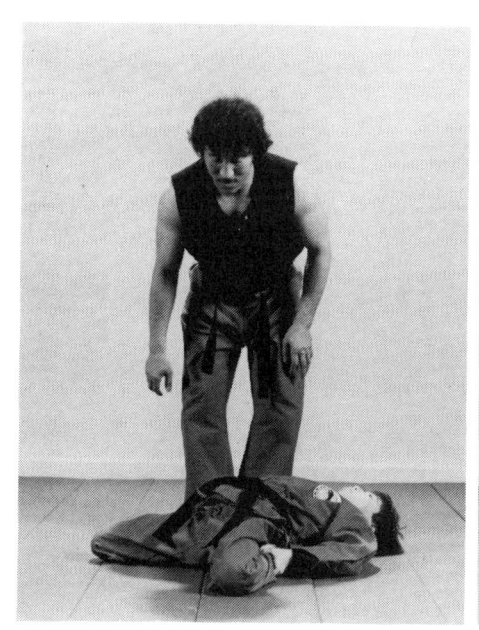

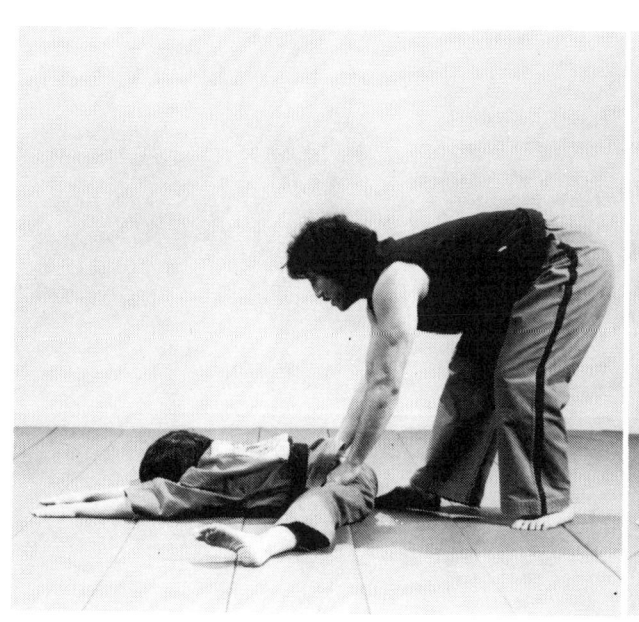

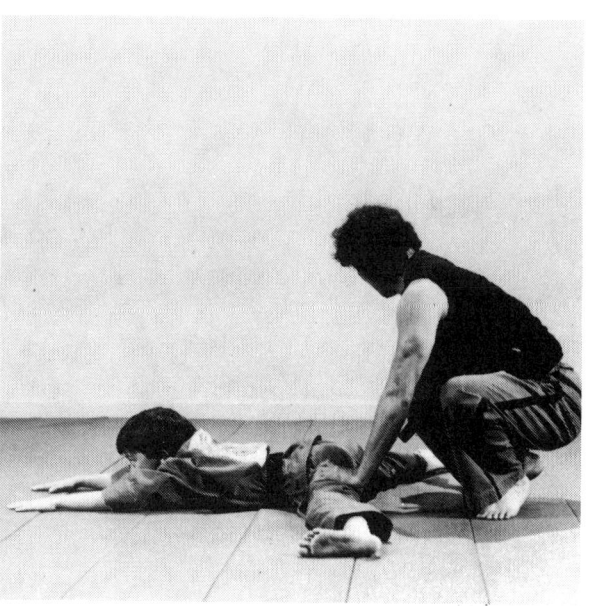

4

5

6

2

3

HAMSTRINGS & QUADRICEPS - Get into a front split position with the heel of your front foot flat on the floor, toes pointing upward. The instep of the rear leg should be flat on the floor. In this position, your front leg will be stretching the biceps femoris while your back leg will be stretching the quadriceps. Leaning backwards will emphasize the quadricep stretch, while leaning forward will add to the biceps femoris stretch. Hold yourself in both positions for 20 seconds, and then switch direction. Repeat this three or four times.

1

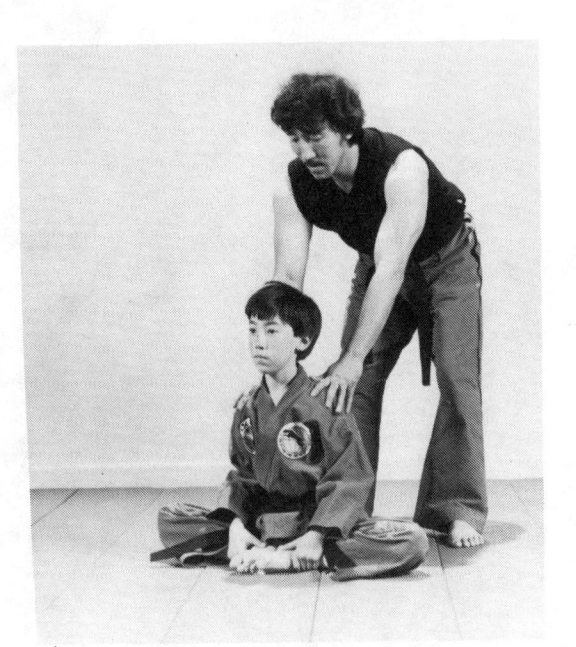

1 **SARTORIUS & LUMBAR** - Sitting on the floor with your back straight, bend your legs inward, bottoms of the feet touching. As you try to keep your knees down to the floor, bend yourself forward at the waist, arms straight out in front of you.

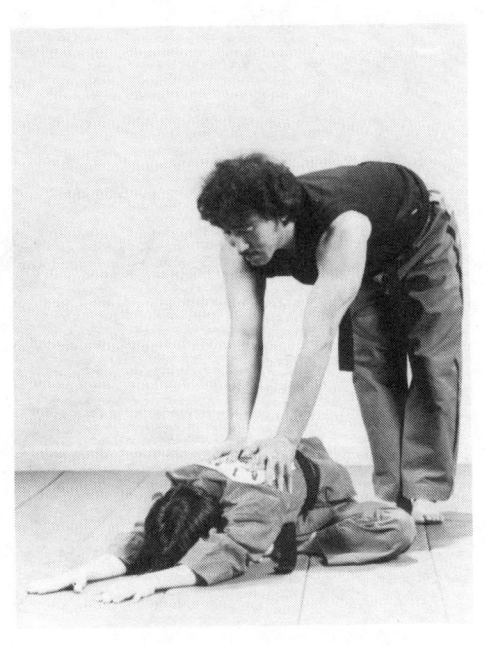

The object of this stretch is not to touch your head to your feet, but the tops of your feet to your chest. If you have a partner, a little extra push on your lower back will help to increase the efficiency of this stretch.

2

165

2

3

HAMSTRINGS - Sitting on the floor with one leg bent inward, foot as close to your groin as possible and your other leg straight out in front of you, reach forward, grabbing your foot (this is a little easier than trying to do the same stretch with both legs straight out in front).

1

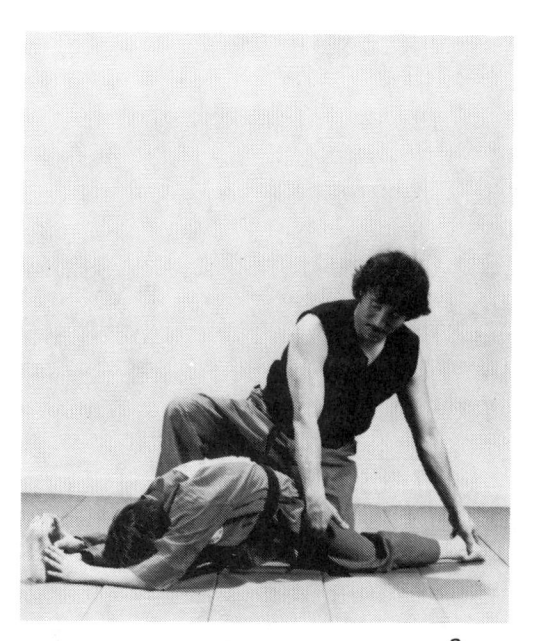

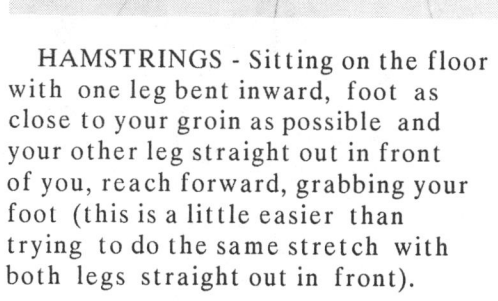

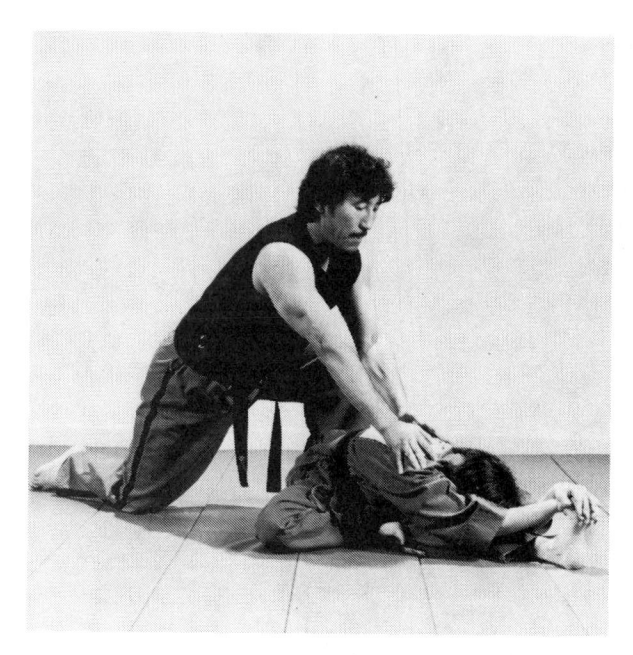

Bending at the waist, bring your chin to your shin, keeping your back as straight as possible. Hold yourself in this position for 20 seconds, and then rest for a few moments. Repeat this three or four times with each leg.

2

Quadriceps

Biceps Femoris

Gluteus

Tensor Fasciae Latae

HOOK KICK
(Front Leg, Moving In)

Developed primarily by Americans for point-style fighting, the Front Leg Hook Kick is a powerful kicking technique as well as an effective sparring/counter attack technique. The Hook Kick can be used as a fake (usually followed by a Roundhouse Kick) as well as a block, making it a very versatile move. Because the main target area for the Hook Kick is the face, this is a very difficult kick for someone who is lacking in flexibility to throw. The Hook Kick also makes a very good foot sweep, which can be thrown by anyone regardless of their stretch.

Like the Side Kick, the Hook Kick uses the tensor fascia latae to raise the leg, the hamstring and gluteus muscles to bring the leg to the chamber position, and the quadriceps to push the leg out. The hooking motion is created by the hamstrings, however care must be taken not to over-tax the knee tendons and ligaments so as to avoid any injury. The striking surface is the heel or bottom of the foot.

HOW TO

1. Assume a right fighting stance.

2. Shifting balance onto your right leg, simultaneously bring your left leg past and behind your right leg, turning your upper body counter-clockwise 45 degrees. Once your left foot is past your right and firmly planted on the floor, shift your weight onto your left leg and raise your right leg up, knee as close to your chest as you can with your lower leg parallel to the floor.

APPLICATION

4. After executing the technique, you can either draw back and throw another Hook Kick, throw a Roundhouse Kick (an excellent combination), or you can drop the kicking leg and follow up with hand techniques.

3. Simultaneously turn your body 45 degrees clockwise and push your leg out with the quadriceps muscles in your upper leg. Your balance foot (the left) should pivot sharply on the ball of the foot, so that as you kick your left heel turns in a direct line towards the target. Keeping your ankle back, shoot your right leg barely 15 degrees to the left of the target, and at the last moment hook your leg back towards and through the target, striking with the bottom of the foot or the heel. The most effective way of throwing this technique is to not only hook the leg across but also down through the target, using gravity to help generate power.

4   5   6

MOST COMMON MISTAKES

The most common error made by students throwing the Hook Kick is also the thing which causes the most injuries - using just the knee tendons to hook the leg. The hooking motion is caused by the quadriceps pushing out as well as the biceps femoris pulling in. Another very common mistake is bringing the kicking leg too wide, making the kick too much like a crescent kick. Not only will this rob the kick of a majority of its power, but it slows the kick down to the point where an opponent can now jam in on you as you try to execute the technique.

The other main mistake is leaning either too far back or standing too straight while throwing the kick. Your upper body should be leaning back around 45 degrees.

REPETITIONS

Beginners - 7 to 12 times, each leg.
Advanced - 15 to 20 times, each leg.

NOTE - If you begin to feel a little discomfort in your knees while practicing this technique, then stop. The knee tendons should be developed slowly to avoid any injury.

BREATHING

INHALE before throwing the technique, HOLD YOUR BREATH as you move forward, and then EXHALE SHARPLY as you execute the kick.

WEIGHT LIFTING

Weight training is an often overlooked addition to any martial arts training program. Besides just toning and shaping the body, it can dramatically increase both your muscular strength and endurance.

Many people are unsure how to begin a personalized weight training program, which is why I have included exercises appropriate for each technique.

To increase your muscle size, start with 2 sets of 5 repetitions using light weights, 5 sets of 5 to 6 repetitions using medium weights, and then go for the maximum weight you can handle for 2 or 3 sets of 2 or 3 repetitions. Rest between sets for 15 to 20 seconds. This type of workout should only be done every other day.

If you want to tone your muscles without drastically increasing size (also called "cutting" your muscles), pick a weight which you can work with for 10 sets of 15 to 20 repetitions, usually between 30 and 80 pounds depending on the exercise. Rest between sets for no more than 15 seconds.

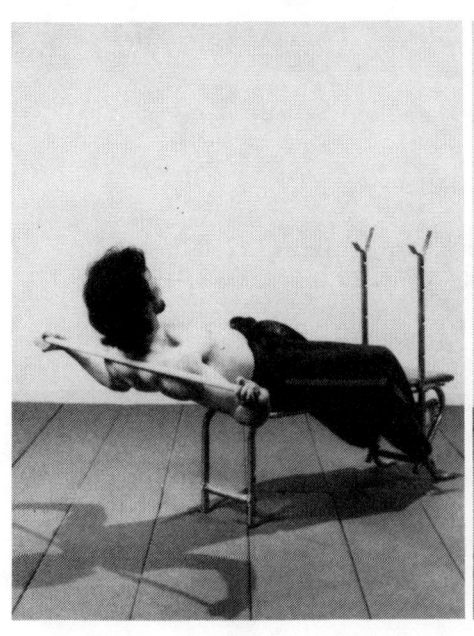

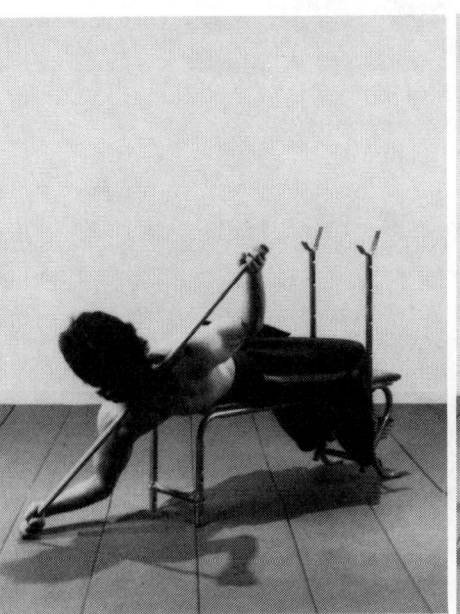

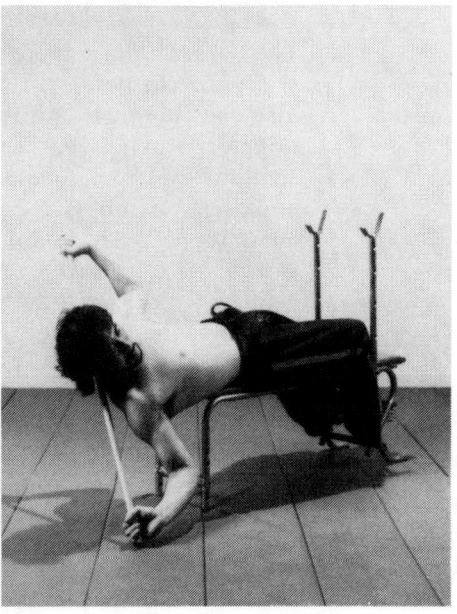

1   2   3

3. OBLIQUES I - Using a bench, lie flat on your back with the small of your spine at the edge of the bench. Holding a stick behind your neck, rotate your waist as far as you can in both directions. Try for 10 sets of 10-15 repetitions, or keep going until you feel a slight burning in the muscles.

1   2

1. QUADRICEPS & HAMSTRINGS - The best exercise for both the quadricep and biceps femoris muscle groups is bicycling - either on a regular bicycle or on a stationary "Life Cycle." If don't own a bicycle,

light ankle weights can be worn and you can "bicycle" by lying on your back and moving your legs in a pedaling motion. The faster you pedal, the better the cardiovascular workout you'll get.

1   2   3

ABDOMINALS - Because the stomach muscles play such an important role in keeping the leg raised, they must be strengthened. Using a bench, lie flat on your back with the small of your spine at the edge of the bench. Rise up to an angle of 45 degrees, and then lower yourself back down. Repeat this for 15 sets of 10-15 repetitions. Advanced students can hold a light weight or dumbell behind their heads.

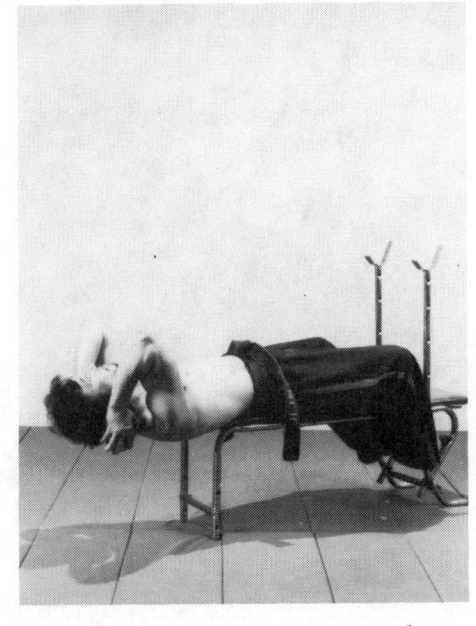

1

GLUTEUS & TENSOR FASCIA LATAE - Supporting yourself by leaning against a chair or some other stationary object, balance yourself on your left leg and raise your right leg, knee bent, keeping your foot close to your buttocks. Using short movements, raise and lower your right leg, trying to keep it parallel to the floor at the height of the swing. Do this for 10 repetitions of 10 sets, working both legs. NOTE - the movement of the leg should be very slight. Also, the leg is not being lifted behind you as in a side kick, but 90 degrees away to the side.

1   2

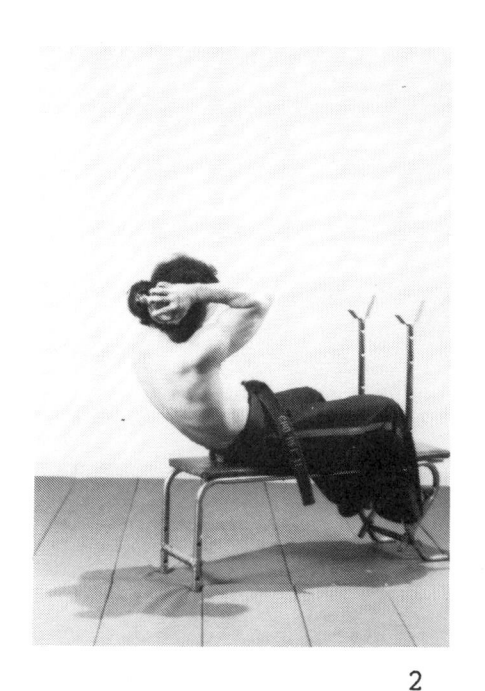

OBLIQUES II - Do the same exercise as above, except only rise up about 15 degrees, and then rotate your upper body from side to side for 10 sets of 10-15 repetitions.

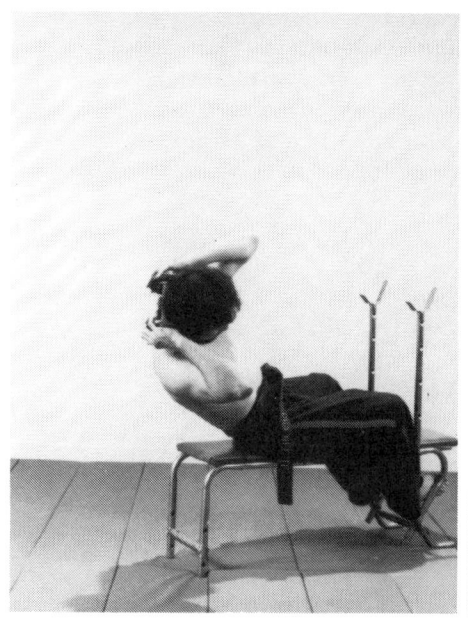

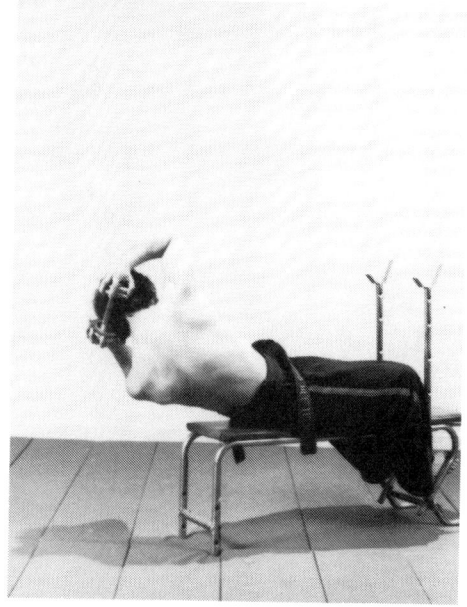

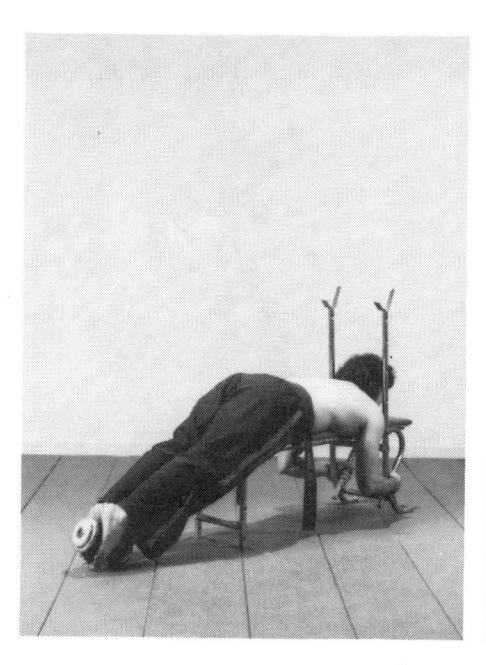

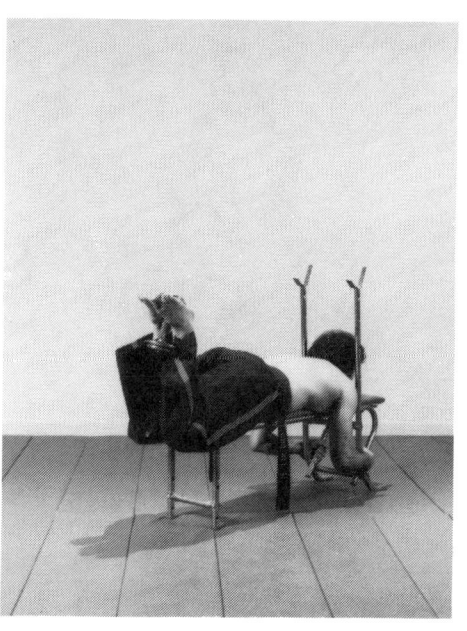

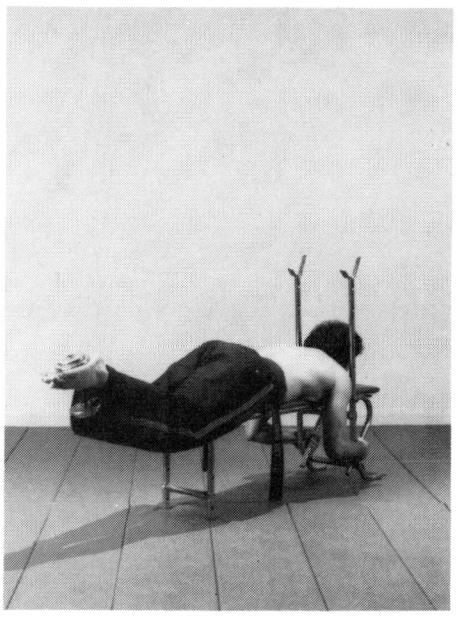

2

3

4

2. HAMSTRINGS & GLUTEUS
Exercising your hamstring muscles can be done by lying down on your stomach on a long bench and doing reverse curls with leg weights on your ankles. Do 10 repetitions for 5 sets. If you really want to build size, you should consider getting a leg machine.

1

2

3

174

STRETCHING

1. KNEE TENDON, QUADRICEPS & HAMSTRINGS - Placing a foot on a low bench or stool, lower yourself into a deep forward stance, bending your front leg as far as you can, concentrating on your front knee. After the squat, straighten the front leg for a moment and then repeat. Do this for 15 to 20 times, and then switch legs. Do this for 5 sets.

1

1    2

175

2　　　　　　　　　　　　3

3

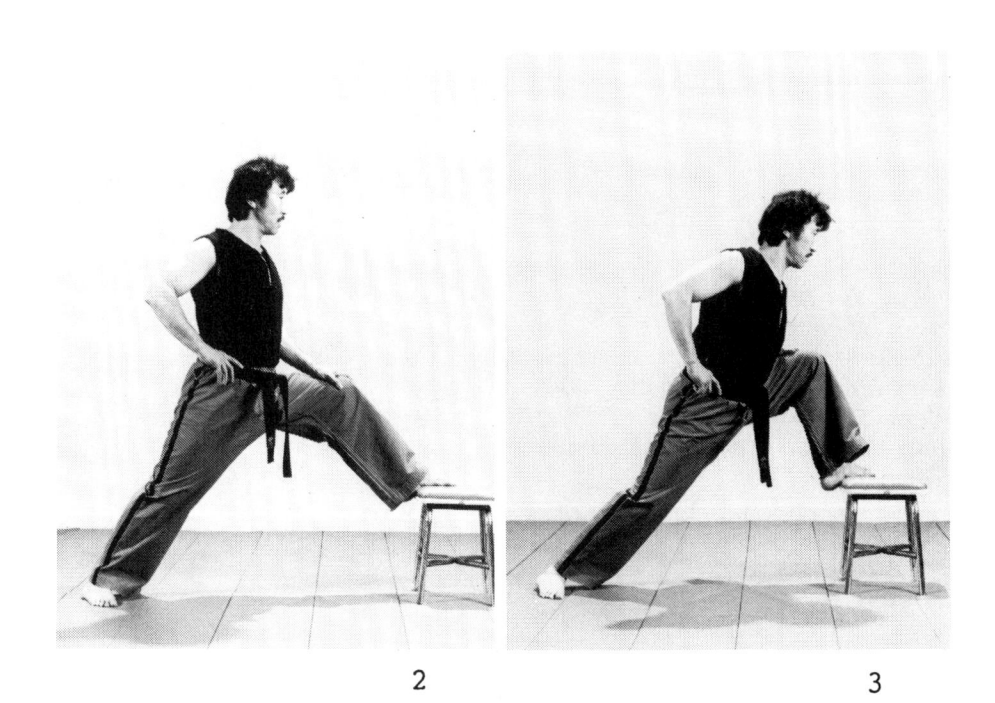

3. QUADRICEPS - Having someone help you, arch your back, trying to bring the bottom of your foot to the top of your head. Make sure not to overdo this until you are better stretched.

2. SARTORIUS I - Any high section kick depends on a well stretched sartorius muscle, and stretching the sartorius muscle requires the most discipline. Because of this, is it useful to have someone help you. Sit flat on the floor with your legs as wide apart as you can spread them, heels flat and toes pointing upward. From this position, lean yourself forward. The goal here is not to arch your back, touching your head to the floor, but to lie down directly in front of yourself, chest to the ground. You can also stretch the sartorius by kneeling on the floor with your knees as far apart as you can spread them and then bending your body straight out. Have someone help by gently pushing your pelvis down.

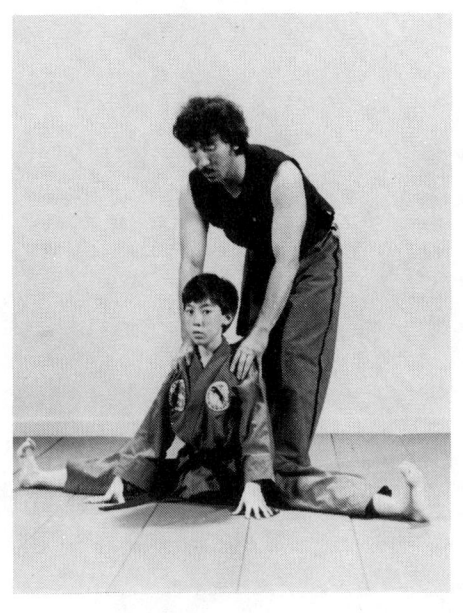

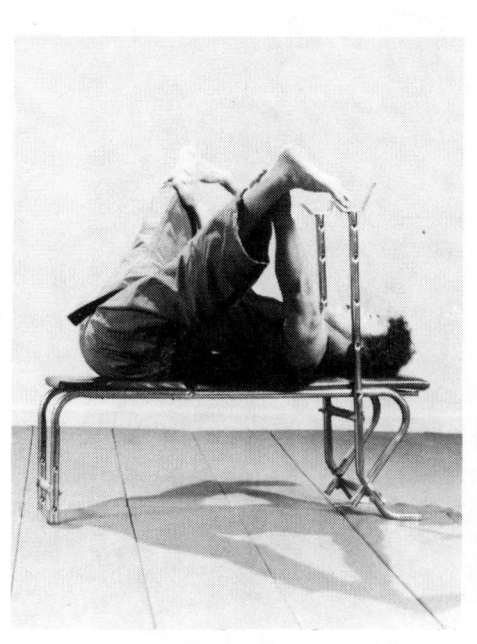

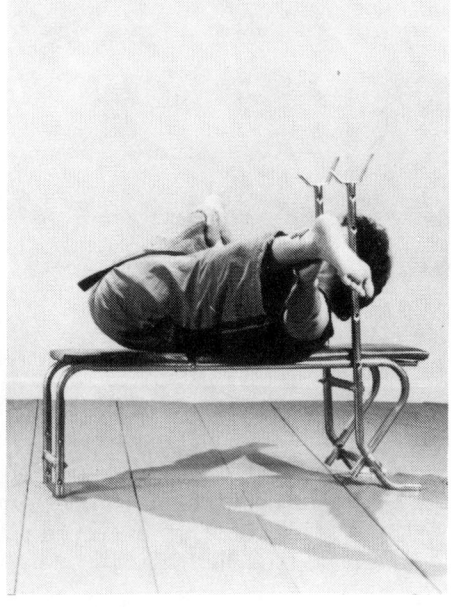

SARTORIUS II - Using a bench, lie down on your back, legs raised and as far apart as possible. Grabbing onto your ankles with your hands, pull your legs as far down as you can.

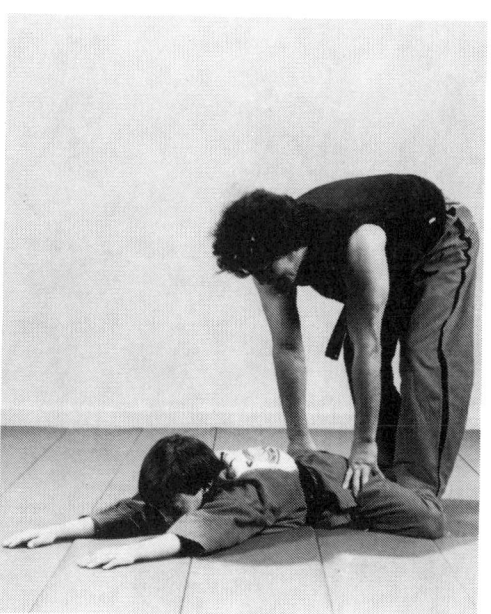

2

3

1

2

178

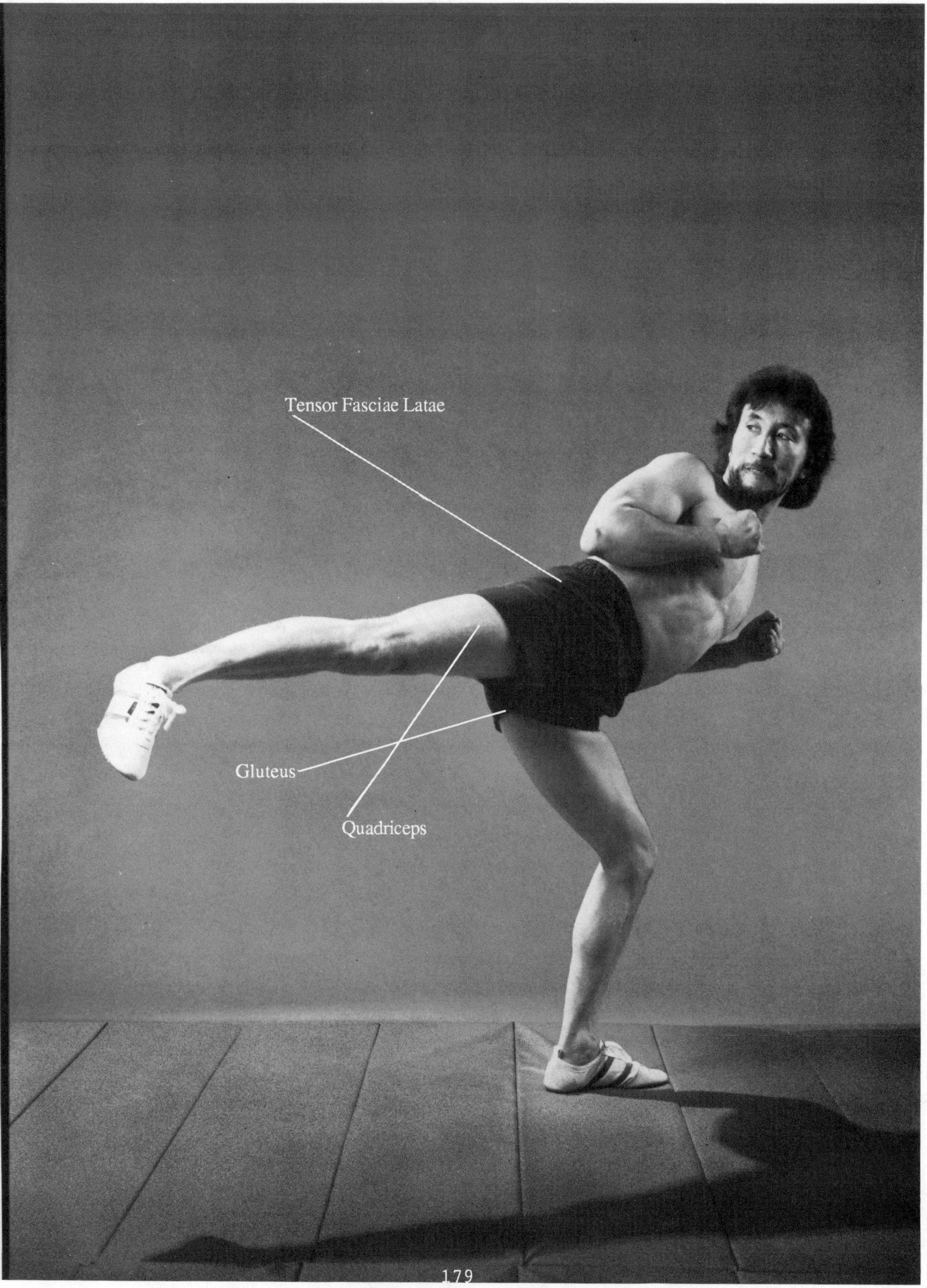
Tensor Fasciae Latae
Gluteus
Quadriceps

LOW SIDE KICK

Using the same principles as the Side Kick, the Low Side Kick is a very effective self defense technique which maintains power while delivering a potentially disabling blow. The balance is kept low for this kick, putting you in a better position to follow the kick with any one of a number of techniques. In point fighting, the Low Side Kick is a useful blocking tool, first jamming an opponents kick, and then being followed with hand techniques.

Because of the balance, this kick is easily executed with the front leg. The Low Side Kick gets a majority of its speed and power from the same muscle group as the Side Kick - the quadriceps. A little extra "oomf" can be added to this kick by hopping slightly forward and downward in the direction of the kick.

HOW TO

1. Assume a left fighting stance.

2. Moving in, step with your right foot behind your left. Leaning your body slightly back, raise your left leg, bending your knee no more than 90 degrees. Pushing with your quadriceps, thrust your left leg out and downward with very much like a stamping motion. At the moment of impact, your body should be turned sideways and the heel of your balance foot should be facing your opponent. Your left ankle should be bent back as you strike with the heel or the blade of the foot. When executing the kick you can hop in a little with the right leg to cover more distance. The best contact areas for this kick are the knee joint and lower leg.

1

APPLICATION

3. After executing the kick, follow up with a right cross to the jaw or a right ridgehand to the windpipe (self defense), or a left hand backfist attack or higher section side kick (point fighting).

2   3   4

MOST COMMON MISTAKES

The most common error made while attempting the Low Side Kick is over-cocking the kicking leg past 90 degrees. This is a speed technique, and over-cocking will slow down the kick. Also your upper body should not be bent back any further than 45 degrees. Another common error is not turning your body sideways enough. The final body position should be exactly like the Side Kick.

REPETITIONS

Beginners - 10 to 12 times, each leg.
Advanced - 20 to 27 times, each leg.

BREATHING

INHALE before throwing the technique, HOLD YOUR BREATH as you move forward, and then EXHALE SHARPLY as you execute the kick.

WEIGHT LIFTING

Weight lifting is, to me, the real "Fountain of Youth". No matter what your sport is, if you train with weights your body will keep its tone well into your later years.

Different people set different goals for themselves when weight lifting. If you want to maintain size but increase your strength, you should work with lighter weights rather than heavier ones. By experimenting, find a weight which you can comfortably work with for 10 sets of 15 to 20 repetitions. Rest between sets for 10 to 15 seconds.

If you want to increase your size, start with a lighter weight as a warmup for 2 sets of 10 repetitions, a medium weight for 5 sets of 5 to 6 repetitions, and then go for the maximum weight you can handle, 2 to 3 repetitions for 2 or 3 sets. Between each set, you should rest for 20 to 30 seconds.

If you are just maintaining size, this workout can be done every day. If you are trying to increase your size, this workout should be done every other day, concentrating on different muscle groups.

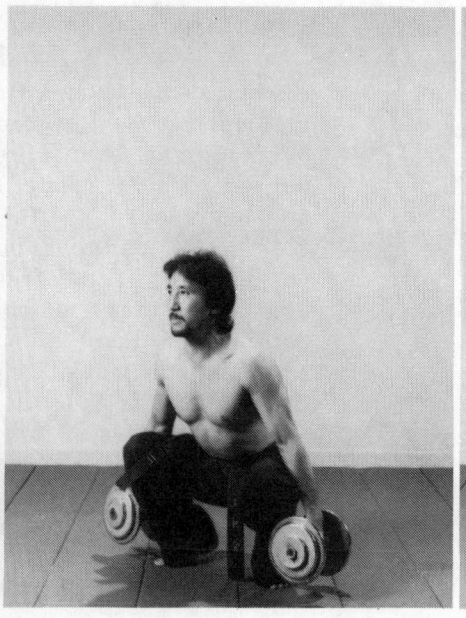

1   2   3

3. QUADRICEPS & HAMSTRINGS
Exercising your quadriceps and hamstrings can be done by holding as heavy a dumbell as you can manage in each hand and squatting all the way down. Keep your back as straight as you possibly can to prevent straining it as you squat and stand. Do ten repetitions for five sets.

OBLIQUES - Using a bench, lie flat on your back with the small of your spine at the edge of the bench. Holding a stick behind your neck, rotate your waist as far as you can in both directions. Try for 5 sets of 10 repetitions, or keep going until you feel a slight burning in the muscles.

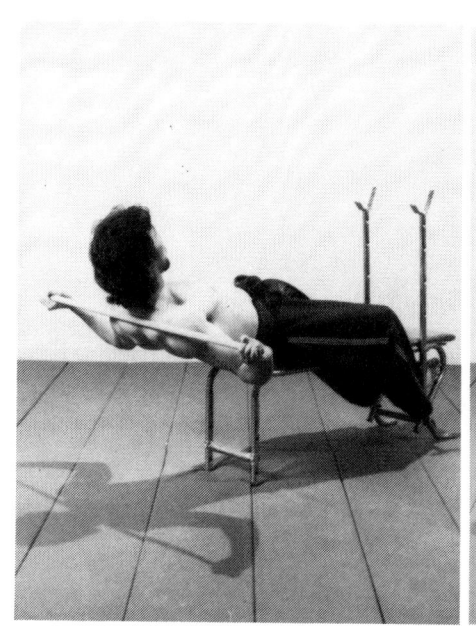

1

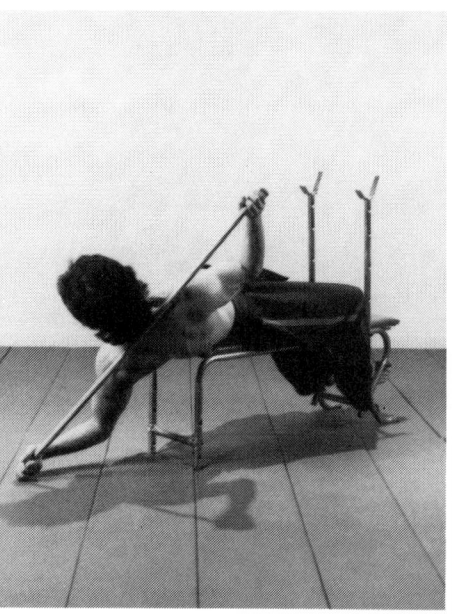

2

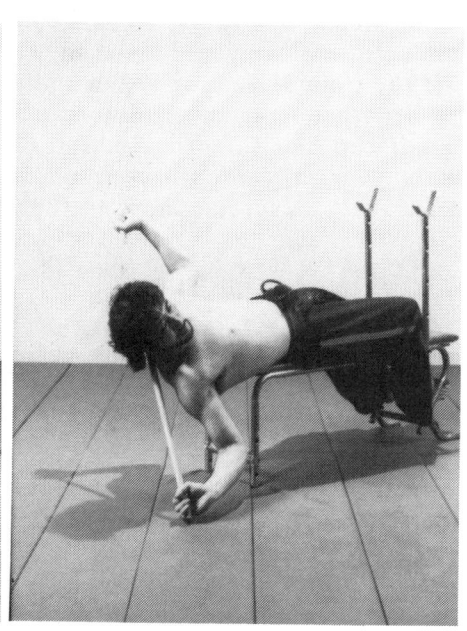

3

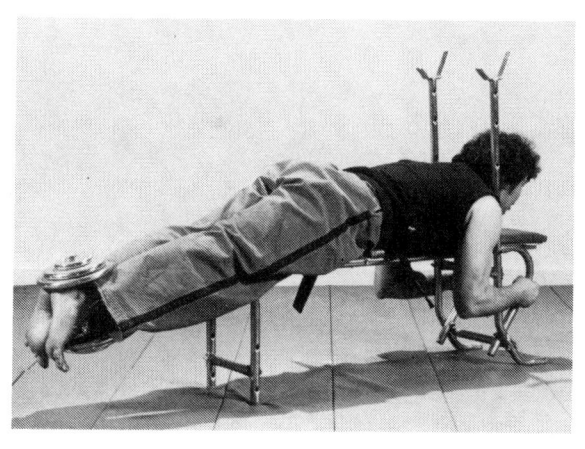

1

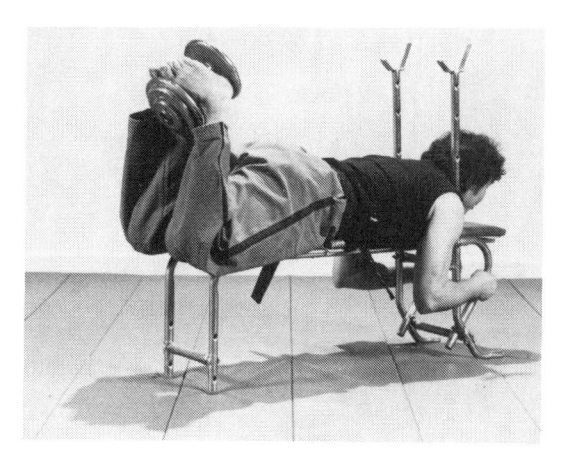

2

1. **HAMSTRINGS** - Exercising your hamstring muscles can be done by lying down on your stomach on a long bench and doing reverse curls with leg weights on your ankles. Do 10 repetitions for 5 sets. If you really want to build size, you should consider getting a leg machine.

STRETCHING

1. Quadricep - Kneel on the floor Japanese style, except keeping your knees spread out as wide as you can. Supporting your weight with your hands, lean backwards, dropping your neck and raising your hips as high off the floor as you can. Remember to breath deeply and isolate the quadricep and sartorius muscles. Hold yourself there for 20 seconds. Repeat this exercise three or four times.

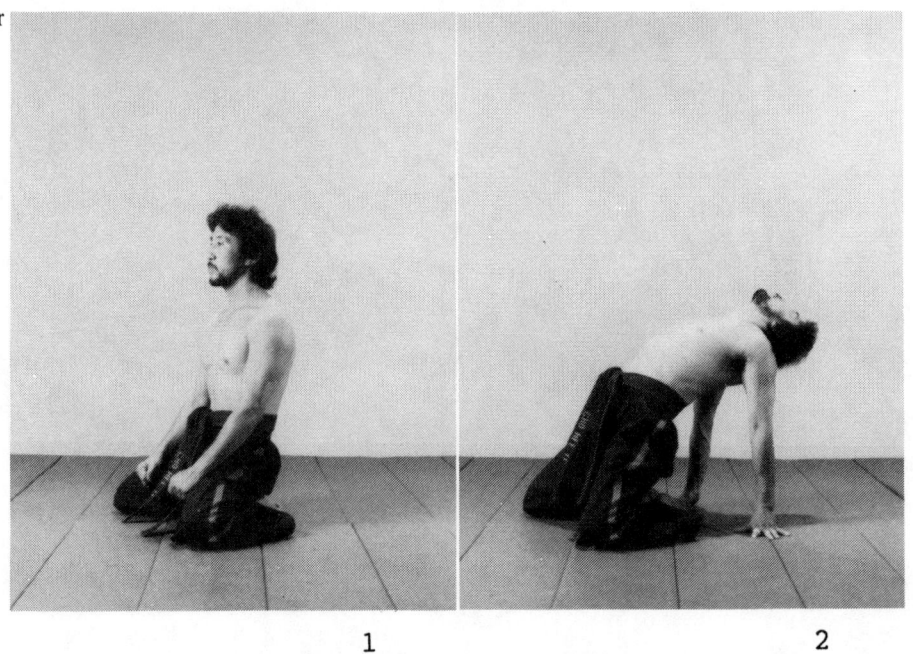

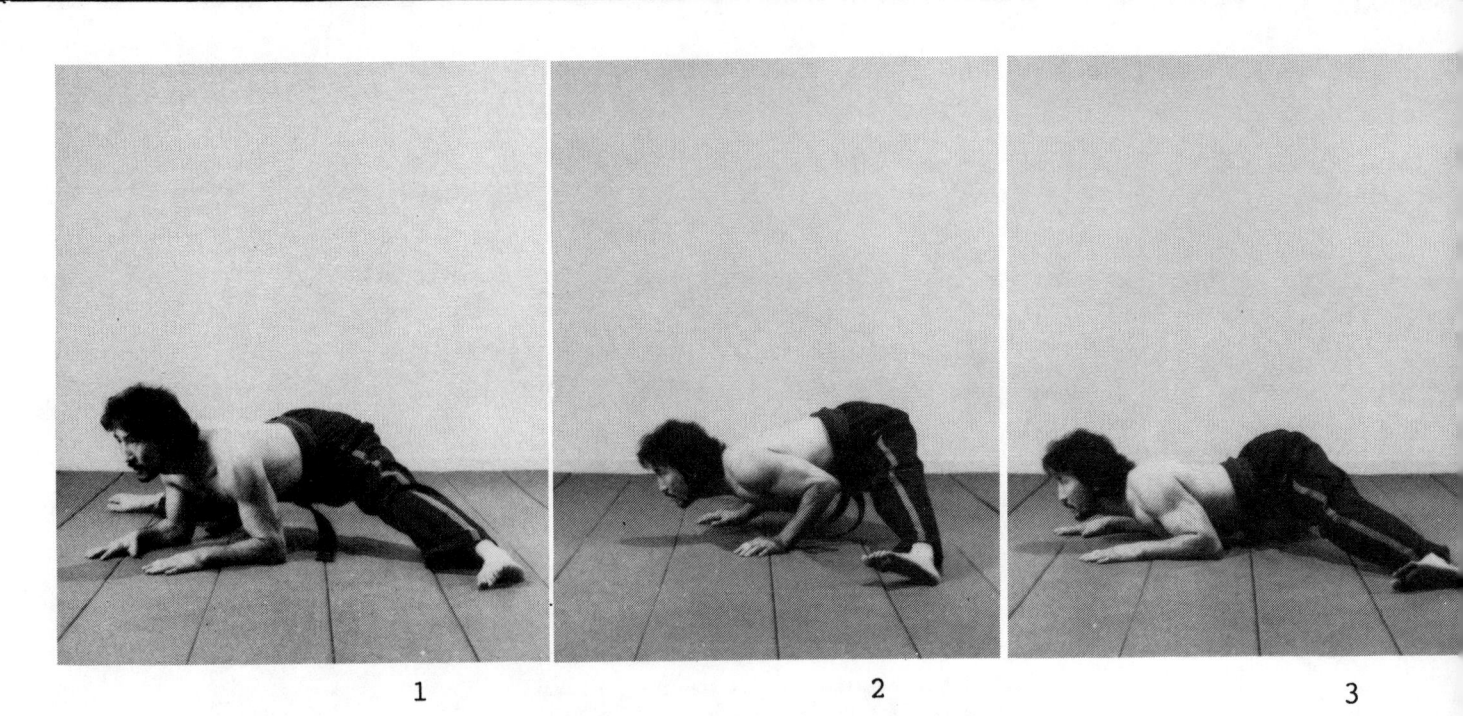

1

2

1

2

3

1. SARTORIUS - With your feet on the floor, separate your legs as wide as you can, locking your knees and keeping your legs straight. Slowly bend over, and with your hands and arms first pull yourself forward, holding for 20 seconds, and then push yourself back, also holding for 20 seconds. Rest for a few moments, and then repeat two more times.

Quadriceps

Lower Abdomen

Obliques

45 DEGREE ROUNDHOUSE KICK

The 45 Degree Roundhouse Kick is a tremendous fighting technique for either full contact or self defense fighting. Because the body is largely straight up when the kick is thrown, the position is perfect for following the kick with hand techniques. The kick gets its name from the angle the kicking leg comes up from the ground, attacking neither straight up like a Front Snap Kick, or cutting across like the Roundhouse Kick. The 45 Degree Roundhouse Kick attacks at an angle which most opponents are unprepared to defend themselves against, sneaking up through their defenses and attacking their ribcage area.

The strength of this kick is generated from the quadriceps areas as well as from the oblique muscles. The kicking leg is brought up by flexing the lower abdomen, with only a minimum snapping of the knee.

HOW TO

1. Assume a left fighting stance.

2. Shifting balance onto the left leg, simultaneously twist your waist counterclockwise as you raise your right leg at a 45 degree angle to the ground, knee bent.

1

2

3

3. Maintaining the 45 degree angle, bring your upper leg inward sharply. Right before contact extend your lower leg, locking your knee and flexing your quadricep muscles. Strike with the instep or shinbone. Your waist should be turned no more than 45 degrees counterclockwise. All of these movements must flow smoothly and continuously - be careful not to separate the moves.

7

4. After executing the technique you can drop the kicking leg forward and either follow it up with a right cross to the jaw or left ridgehand to the face. It is not recommended that this kick be followed by another kicking technique, however it can be followed with another 45 Degree Roundhouse Kick.

4 5 6

MOST COMMON MISTAKES

The most common mistakes of the 45 Degree Roundhouse Kick are overturning the body more than 45 degrees and dropping the guard. Because this kick is meant to be thrown at close distances, it is essential that you keep your arms up to protect yourself against a counter attack by your opponent.

REPETITIONS

Beginners - 7 to 12 times, each leg.
Advanced - 17 to 25 times, each leg.

BREATHING

INHALE before throwing the technique, and as you execute the kick EXHALE SHARPLY. When you return to the ready stance, INHALE again.

WEIGHT LIFTING

Weight training is the most effective way of increasing and maintaining muscle tone. The idea that it will slow a martial artist down is a myth as far as I am concerned. I've been lifting weights steadily for over 30 years, and it hasn't slowed me down in the least.

Increasing muscle mass and maintaining muscle tone require two different types of workouts. To increase size you must first warm up with light weights for 2 sets of five repetitions. Rest for no more than 30 seconds between sets. After you have done your 2 sets, move on to a medium weight for 5 sets of 5 to 6 repetitions. Finish your workout by training with the heaviest weight you can handle for 2 or 3 sets of 2 or 3 repetitions each. This type of workout should be done only every other day.

To maintain a desired muscle tone without increasing mass, work with 30 to 80 pounds and do 10 sets of 15 to 20 repetitions, resting for no more than 15 seconds between sets.

1
2
3

3. OBLIQUES - With your legs two shoulder widths apart, place a broomstick across your shoulders and hold onto the ends with your hands. Bend forward from the waist 90 degrees, keeping your back straight, and then alternating sides, rotate your waist first 90 degrees to the left, and then 90 degrees to the right. Do this for 10 sets of 10-15 repetitions, each side.

1. QUADRICEPS - Placing a weight on your shoulders and trapezius, keep your legs one shoulder width apart. Slowly bend you knees, back as straight as possible. To increase size, start with a lighter weight for 2 sets of 10 repetitions, then move on to a medium weight for 5 sets of 5 to 6 repetitions. Finish by using the maximum weight you can handle for 2 or 3 sets of 2 to 3 repetitions. Rest between sets for 20 to 30 seconds. This exercise will also help to strengthen your sartorius muscles if you open your stance to two shoulder widths.

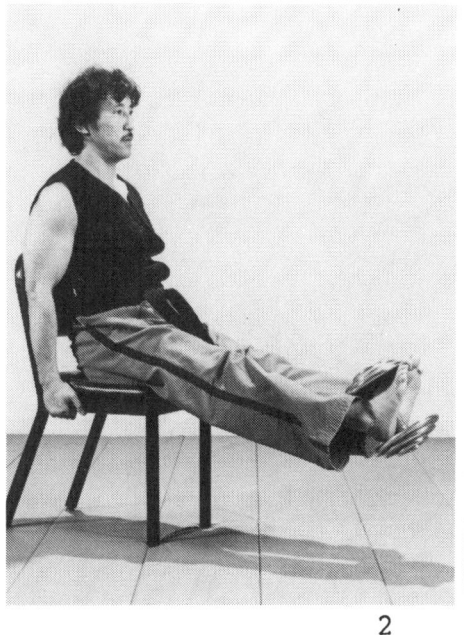

1  2

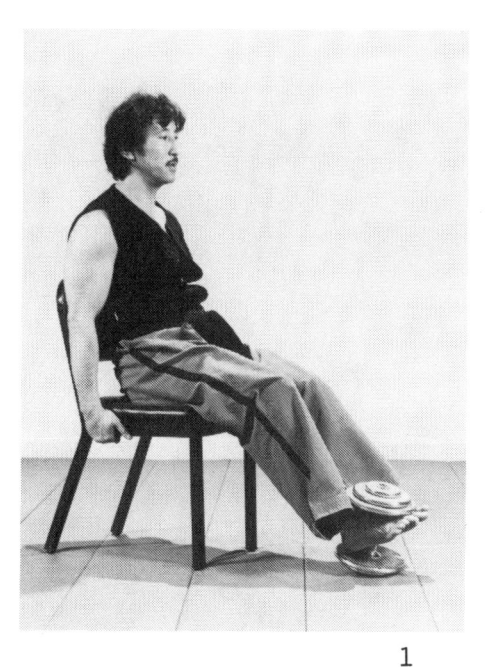

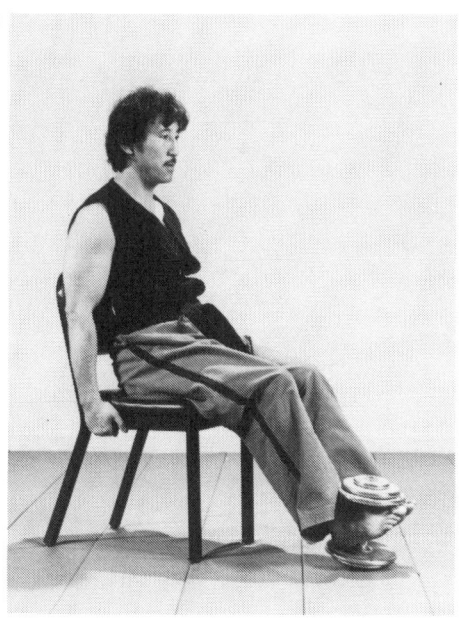

2. QUADRICEPS - If you don't have a leg rising machine to use, you can do this exercise with a chair (preferably one which is high enough to allow your legs to hang all the way down. Placing weights on your ankles (tying them down if necessary) sit with your back straight and hold onto the bottom or back of the chair with your hands. Straighten and lower your legs directly in front of you. Follow the same guide as exercise number 1 above for sets, repetitions, and recommended weight.

192

STRETCHING

1. QUADRICEPS & SARTORIUS - Kneel on the floor Japanese style, except keeping your knees spread out as wide as you can. Supporting your weight with your hands, lean backwards, dropping your neck and raising your hips as high off the floor as you can. Remember to breath deeply and isolate the quadricep and sartorius muscles. Hold yourself there for 20 seconds. Repeat this exercise three or four times.

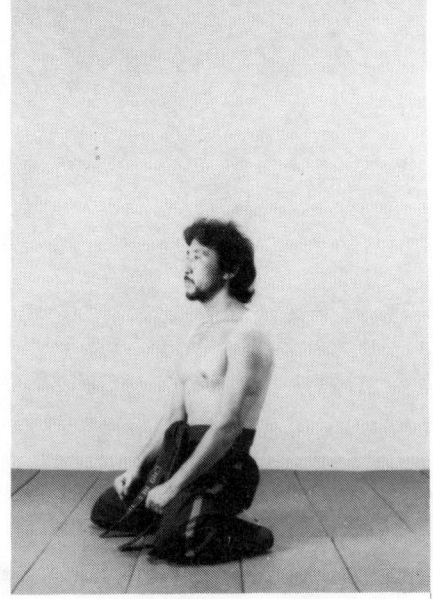

1

2

1

2

193

2. HAMSTRINGS & QUADRICEPS - Get into a front split position with the heel of your front foot flat on the floor, toes pointing upward. The instep of the rear leg should be flat on the floor. In this position, your front leg will be stretching the biceps femoris while your back leg will be stretching the quadriceps. Leaning backwards will emphasize the quadricep stretch, while leaning forward will add to the hamstring stretch. Hold yourself in both positions for 20 seconds, and then switch direction. Repeat this three or four times.

3. HAMSTRINGS - Standing with your legs a shoulder width apart, bend your body slowly forward. First reach with your hands as deep as you can in front of you and then grab your ankles, pulling yourself downward and trying to touch your head to the floor. Hold yourself in this position for 20 seconds. Rest briefly and then repeat 10 times.

Abdomen

Oblique

Biceps Femoris

Quadriceps

FRONT INWARD HOOK KICK

The Front Inward Hook Kick was developed largely by myself as a close distance offensive technique. Used for self defense, the Front Inward Hook Kick can be executed as either an attack to the groin or lower body, or as a sweeping technique. This is perhaps the most effective kick you can use when you have grabbed an opponent or when you are grappling in close distances.

The Front Inward Hook Kick gets its power from the hamstring muscles as well as from the torquing action of the obliques. These two powerful muscle groups are then coupled with one of the hardest striking surfaces, the back of the heel, to create a very effective attacking force.

HOW TO

1. Assume a left fighting stance.

2. Shifting weight to the front leg bring your right leg up 90 degrees clockwise to the outside. Your right hip should be turned 90 degrees to the outside.

1

2

3

3. Keeping your lower leg turned inward and as parallel to the floor as possible, pivot the balance foot 90 degrees or greater, and flexing the biceps femoris muscle of the right leg, hook the leg sharply inward, turning your hips and upper body counter clockwise almost 180 degrees.

APPLICATION

4. After executing the kick, drop the kicking leg back down into a fighting stance, following with a left hand reverse punch or a left hand ridge hand attack.

4 5

MOST COMMON MISTAKES

When throwing the Inward Hook Kick, the most common mistake is not to hold the lower leg parallel to the floor. Thrown this way, the kick looks more like a low Crescent Kick and is very ineffective. You must also pivot on the balance leg when you execute the kick - don't keep the balance leg forward but turn in the direction of the kick.

REPETITIONS

Beginners - 7 to 12 times, each leg.
Advanced - 15 to 20 times, each leg.

NOTE - If you notice any discomfort in your knee while throwing this technique you should slow down, taking more time to develop your knee tendon and ligament areas. This will help you to avoid a particularly painful and persistent injury.

BREATHING

INHALE before throwing the technique, **HOLD YOUR BREATH** as you move forward, and then **EXHALE SHARPLY** as you execute the kick.

WEIGHT LIFTING -

I have found weight training to be a great asset to the martial artist. If done properly, it can tremendously increase both kicking and punching power.

There are two goals that the martial artist can set for himself with weight training. One is to increase muscle mass, while the other is to maintain muscle mass and increase tone and endurance. These involve two different types of workouts.

To increase size begin with light weights for 2 sets of five repetitions taking no more than 30 second rests between sets. Next move on to a medium weight for 5 sets of 5 to 6 repetitions, and end the sessions with the maximum weight you can handle for 2 or 3 sets of 2 or 3 repetitions. This type of workout should be done only every other day.

To maintain a desired muscle tone without increasing mass, work with 30 to 80 pounds and do 10 sets of 15 to 20 repetitions, resting for no more than 15 seconds between sets.

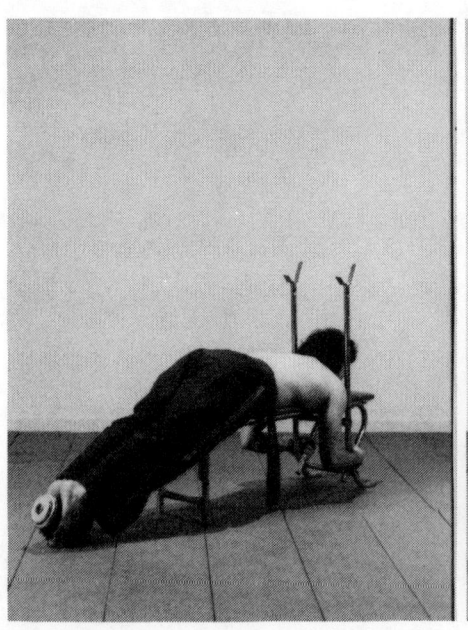

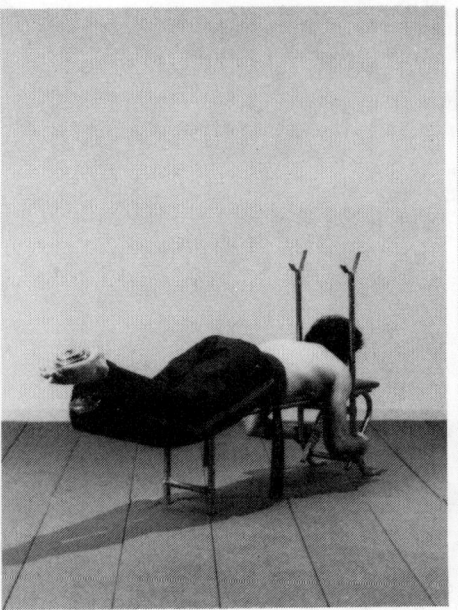

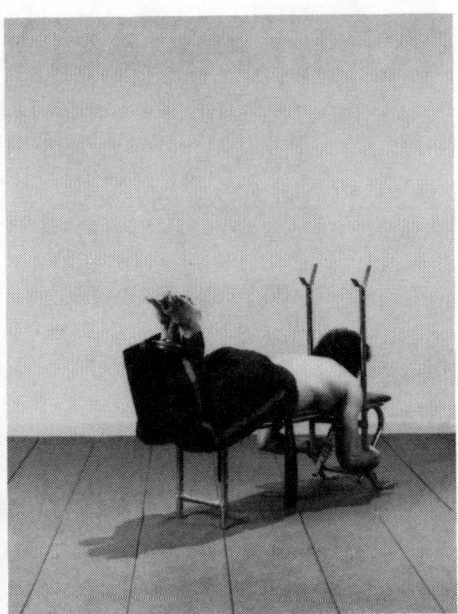

1

2

3

1. HAMSTRINGS - Exercising your hamstring muscles can be done by lying down on your stomach on a long bench and doing reverse curls with leg weights on your ankles. Do 10 repetitions for 5 sets. If you really want to build size, you should consider getting a leg machine.

1 2 3

2. QUADRICEPS & SARTORIUS - Placing a weight on your shoulders and trapezius, keep your legs two shoulder widths apart. Slowly lower yourself into a horse riding stance, knees bent, back as straight as possible. To increase size, start with a lighter weight for 2 sets of 10 repetitions, then move on to a medium weight for 5 sets of 5 to 6 repetitions. Finish by using the maximum weight you can handle for 2 or 3 sets of 2 to 3 repetitions. Rest between sets for 15 to 20 seconds. This exercise will also help to strengthen your sartorius muscles.

4. **OBLIQUES** - Using a bench, lie flat on your back with the small of your spine at the edge of the bench. Holding a stick behind your neck, rotate your waist as far as you can in both directions. Try for 10 sets of 10-15 repetitions, or keep going until you feel a slight burning in the muscles.

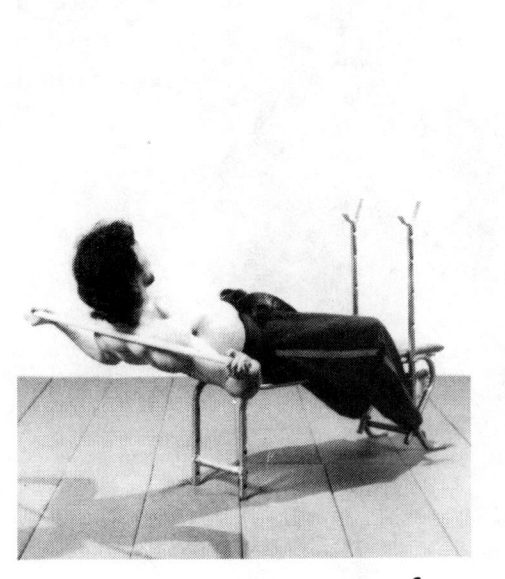

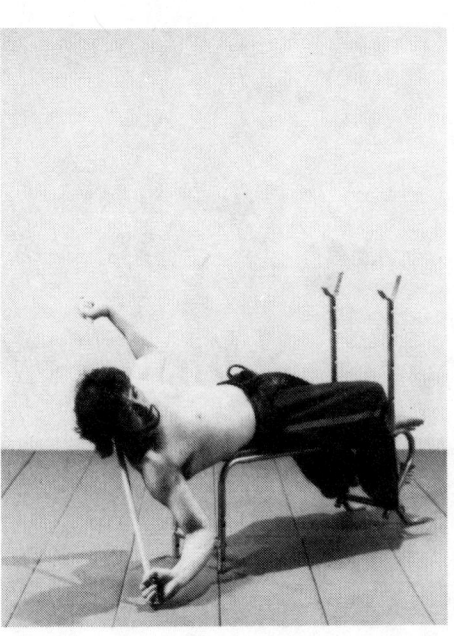

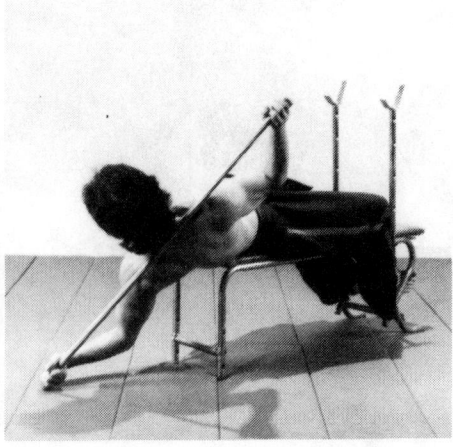

1

2

3

1   2

3. **QUADRICEPS & HAMSTRINGS** - The best exercise for both the quadricep and biceps femoris muscle groups is bicycling - either on a regular bicycle or on a stationary "Life Cycle". If don't own a bicycle, light ankle weights can be worn and you can "bicycle" by sitting in a chair and moving your legs in a pedaling motion. Keeping the pace up will help your caradiovascular system, increasing your endurance.

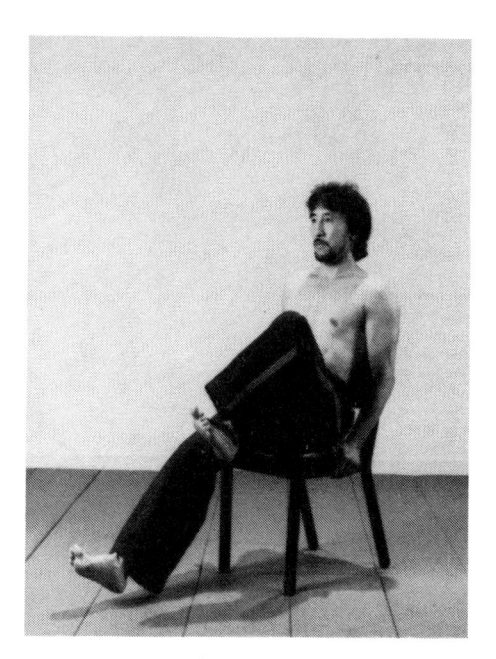

1   2

STRETCHING

1. SARTORIUS - From a standing position, spread your legs as wide as you can, keeping your feet flat on the floor. Locking your knees, lean your body as far forward as you can, hold yourself there for 20 seconds, and then push yourself back as far as you can, also holding yourself there for 20 seconds. Repeat this three or four times, resting slightly between sets. floor.

2. KNEE TENDON, QUADRICEPS & HAMSTRINGS - Getting into a deep forward stance, bend your front leg as far as you can, concentrating on your front knee. After the squat, straighten the front leg for a moment and then repeat. Do this for 15 to 20 times, and then switch legs. Do this for 5 sets.

2   3

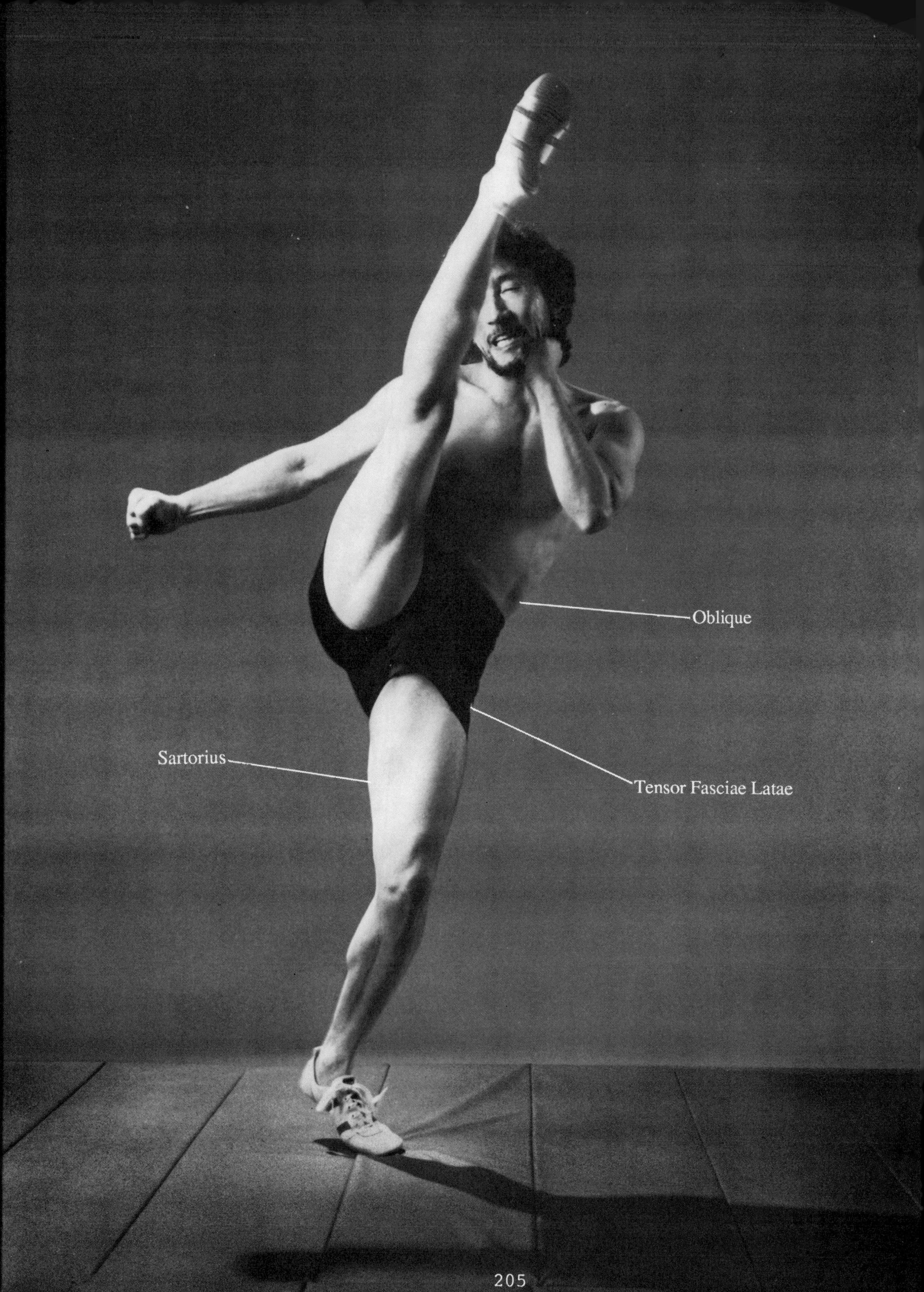
Oblique
Sartorius
Tensor Fasciae Latae

CRESCENT KICK
(Outside to Inside)

Like the Inside Crescent Kick, the Outside Crescent Kick derives its power from a rising motion coupled with torquing the hips. It is an effective high section attacking technique which gets its energy from the oblique muscles in the waist, the tensor fascia latae, gluteus and sartorius muscles.

Another good close distance technique, the Outside Crescent Kick uses either the bottom of the foot or the ankle bone as the striking surface. You can also grab your opponent by the uniform or wrist as you throw the crescent kick, providing you with additional balance. Flexibility is the key to this technique, with a good stretch enabling you to use the kick as an attack to the collarbone or side of the face.

HOW TO

1. Assume a left fighting stance.

2. Shifting balance onto your left leg, torque your waist to your right (clockwise) simultaneously raising your right leg, knee slightly bent. your left leg (the balancing leg) should also be slightly bent.

1   2   3

3. Even though the tendency will be to raise your leg directly in front of you, bring your right leg up towards the right, outside of your target area. As you raise your leg, simultaneously twist your hip to the left, bringing the kicking leg across the target. Concentrate your power at your hip and biceps femoris muscles, tensing as you pass through the target. Flex your sartorius muscle either inward or outward, depending on the position of your target. Your left foot pivots on the ball of the foot anywhere from 90 degrees to 180 degrees, depending on how much reach you are trying attain; the more reach, the greater the pivot. It is even possible to grab your opponent and use him for balance when throwing the technique if he is close enough.

7   8

4. After the kick is thrown, you can bring your leg down in one of two ways. The first way involves bringing the right leg down sharply in front of you, using it like an Axe Kick. In the second method you snap your leg across the target, bending your knee and striking with the heel, much like an Inward Hook Kick. Always keep your hands up, protecting your upper body.

4

5

6

MOST COMMON MISTAKES

The most common mistakes students make when throwing this kick include separating the motions of the kick (kicking and torquing the hips at different times), and snapping the leg down too soon. For the Outside Crescent Kick as well as any kick to be effective, it must be thrown fast and strong with both a clean strike and effective follow through.

REPETITIONS

Beginners - 3 sets of 5 to 10 times, each leg
Advanced - 4 sets of 15 to 20 times, each leg.

BREATHING

INHALE before throwing the technique, and as it is being executed, EXHALE SHARPLY. As you return to the ready stance, INHALE again.

APPLICATION

1

2

WEIGHT LIFTING

If you want to maintain size, but increase your strength, you should work with lighter weights, between 30 and 80 pounds, and do 15 to 20 repetitions for 10 sets. Rest time between sets should only be 10 to 15 seconds.

If you want to increase your size, start with a lighter weight as a warmup for 2 sets of 10 repetitions, a medium weight for 5 sets of 5 to 6 repetitions, and then go for the maximum weight you can handle, 2 to 3 repetitions for 2 or 3 sets. Between each set, you should rest for 20 to 30 seconds.

If you are just maintaining size, this workout can be done every day. If you are trying to increase your size, this workout should be done every other day, concentrating on different muscle groups.

1. SARTORIUS & QUADRICEPS - Carefully place the weight on your shoulders and trapezius muscles. With your feet two shoulder widths apart, bend your knees without leaning forward, keeping your back as straight as possible. Squat down until your legs are at 90 degree angles, like a Horse Riding Stance. An angle of 90 degrees isolates the quadriceps area, and a deeper squat will exercise the biceps femoris and hamstrings.

2. OBLIQUES - To work your oblique muscles, assume a position as if you were going to do a bent leg sit-up, but instead of laying flat on the floor, turn your upper body so that you are facing either your right or your left side. Do your sit-ups in this position, working both sides for 5 sets of 15 repetitions. If you are more advanced, do 7 sets of 30 repetitions. You can enhance this exercise by holding light weights close to your head as you sit up.

1   2

1 GLUTEUS & TENSOR FASCIA LATAE Supporting yourself by leaning against a chair or some other stationary object, balance yourself on your left leg and raise your right leg behind and away from your body 90 degrees foot parallel to the 2 floor. Using long movements, raise and lower your leg for 10 repetitions of 10 sets, working both legs. You can also do this same exercise raising your leg 90 degrees away to the side, which will benefit the tensor fascia latae muscle. 3

3. OBLIQUES & ABDOMINALS - The best exercise for developing the oblique and abdomen area is to lie on your back, having someone hold your legs as you turn your upper body greater than 90 degrees. Raise your upper body in this modified sit-up position, concentrating on the oblique muscles. Do as many repetitions as you can, turn your upper body the other direction and do as many repetitions as you can on this side. Repeat this for 10 sets. This exercise should be done every day in order to fully develop your obliques. Regular sit-ups are also highly recommended - you should actually do them every day in order to develop your abdominal strength. As you become stronger, continue these exercises, but include a light weight held by your head.

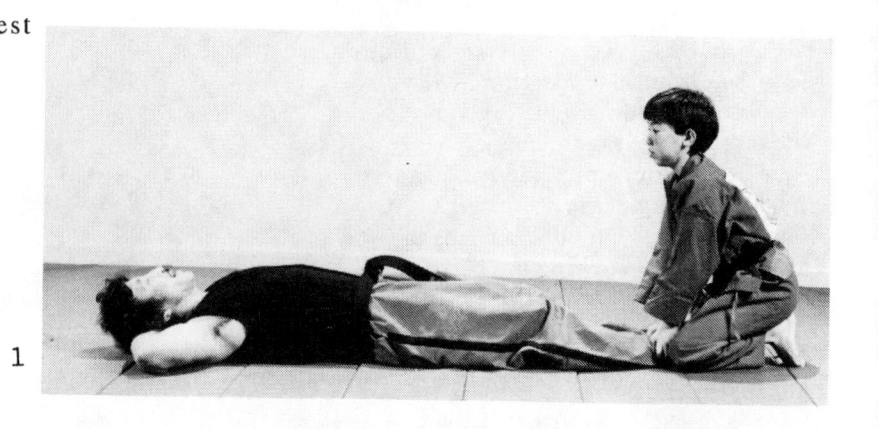

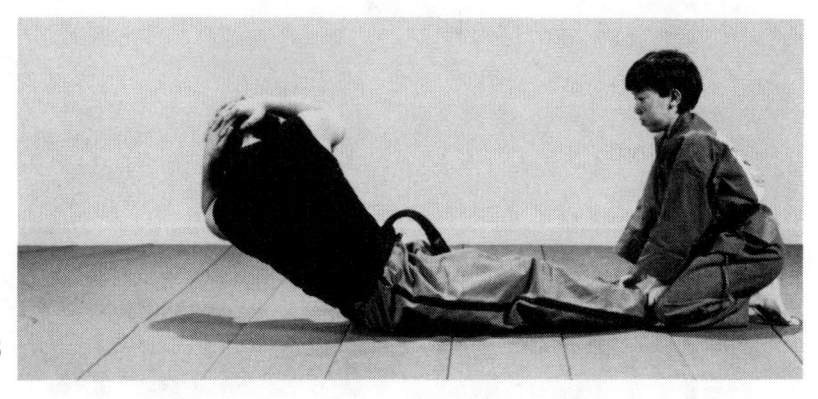

STRETCHING

1. HAMSTRINGS I - Stand on a sturdy chair or bench with your feet about shoulder width apart. Keeping your legs straight and bending from the waist, hold onto a 30 to 40 pound weight, letting it pull your upper body down. The goal of this stretch is to eventually get your head lower than the level of your feet. Hold yourself there for 10 to 20 seconds and then straighten up and rest. Keep the rest periods short - no more than ten seconds. Repeat this ten times.

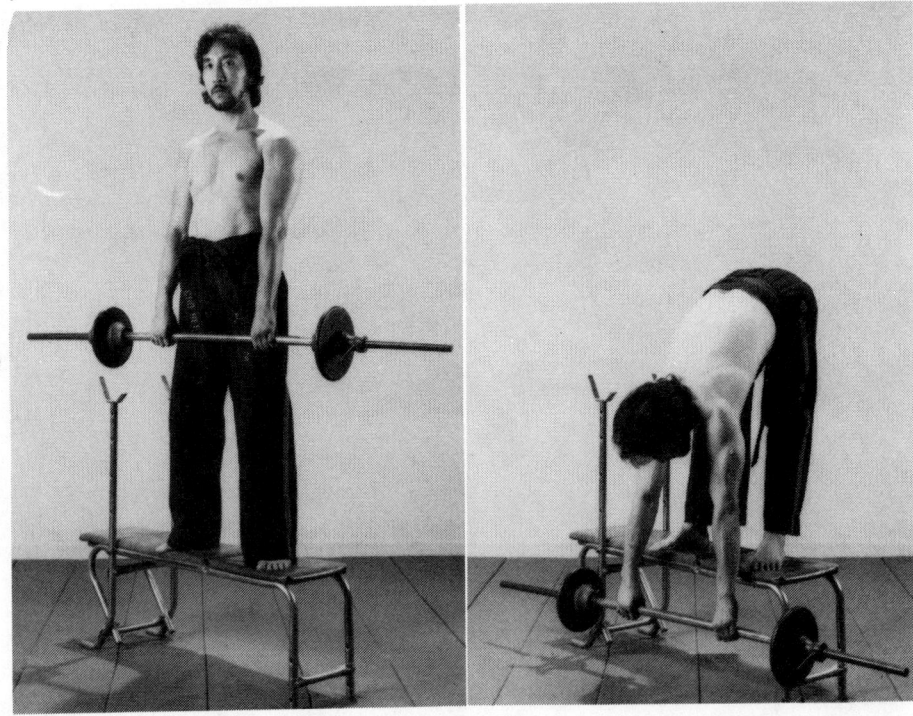

3. HAMSTRINGS III & QUADRICEPS - Get into a front split position with the heel of your front foot flat on the floor, toes pointing upward. The instep of the rear leg should be flat on the floor. In this position, your front leg will be stretching the biceps femoris while your back leg will be stretching the quadriceps. Leaning backwards will emphasize the quadricep stretch, while leaning forward will add to the biceps femoris stretch. Hold yourself in both positions for 20 seconds, and then switch legs. Repeat this three or four times.

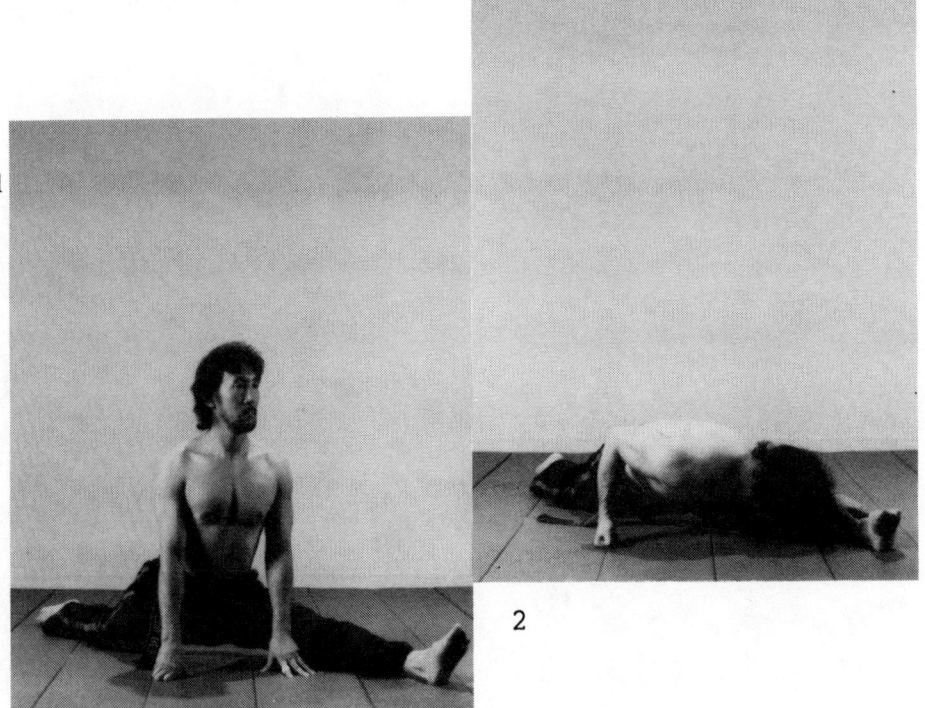

1    2

2. HAMSTRINGS II - Work one leg and then the other by extending your leg onto a chair or a ladder, heel flat and toes pointing upward. Bend your body forward towards the middle, bringing your upper body below your leg. As you stretch, it is important that you continue breathing properly as well as isolate whichever muscle group are working, giving it full attention.

Quadriceps

Obliques

Tensor Fasciae Latae

Gastrocnemius

ROUNDHOUSE KICK

There are several different ways to throw the Roundhouse Kick, perhaps the most widely used basic kick in every form of the martial arts. More of an attacking tool rather than a stretching technique, the Roundhouse Kick is very popular as a speedy, versatile assault to the knee, leg, groin, solar plexus, face...just about anywhere your flexibility will allow.

This technique generally gets most of its power from the quadriceps and gluteus muscles, as well as the oblique muscles through the torquing of the waist. The kick can be thrown in a number of ways, utilizing different muscles depending on application. Kick boxers will often throw it low, relying on their quadriceps and the torquing motion of their oblique muscle, while a point fighter might throw it higher, using the quadriceps and gastrocnemius muscles for speed and the tensor fascia latae for height. The Roundhouse Kick lends itself very easily to be followed by additional kicks or hand techniques.

HOW TO

1. Assume a left fighting stance.

2. Shifting balance onto the left leg, push your right leg forward and counter-clockwise, turning your waist counter-clockwise about 45 degrees. Bring your heel as close to your buttocks as you can, with your lower leg parallel to the floor. Your right knee should be facing slightly to the outside of your body.

1

2

3

APPLICATION

3. Swing your waist another 45 degrees counter-clockwise, simultaneously turning the upper portion of your right leg towards the target area. Shoot out your lower leg, locking it outstretched with the quadricep. You should be leaning back, watching your target over your shoulder, reaching with the kick. The striking surface for this kick can either be the instep (by pointing your toes and hitting flat with the top of the foot), or the ball of the foot (by cocking your ankle and pulling your toes back).

4. After executing the technique you can either recock the kicking leg and step forward into a fighting position, or you can recock the leg and immediately throw the kick again. Throwing the Roundhouse Kick several times without putting your leg back down is a good way to develop speed and strength, working out the quadricep muscle as you kick as well as the biceps femoris muscle as you recock the leg.

4   5   6

MOST COMMON MISTAKES

The first most common mistake of the Roundhouse Kick is to bring the kicking leg up into a Front Snap Kick position (leg perpendicular to the floor), rather than a good Roundhouse Kick position. Another very common error is to separate the motions (rising, turning, throwing) rather than keeping them all continuous. It is also very important that you reach with this kick, extending your leg as far as you can. Many people throw the kick too close to their bodies, losing both distance and speed. Try not to snap with just the knee, this is how a lot of hyper-extension injuries happen.

REPETITIONS

Beginners - 7 to 12 times, each leg.
Advanced - 17 to 25 times, each leg.

BREATHING

INHALE before throwing the technique, and as you execute the kick EXHALE SHARPLY. When you return to the ready stance, INHALE again.

WEIGHT LIFTING

To maintain the size and improve the strength of the muscles, work with lighter ankle weights, between 20 and 30 pounds. Ten sets of 15 to 20 repetitions is a good goal to set. Rest between sets for only 10 to 15 seconds.

To increase size, start with a lighter weight for 2 sets of 10 repetitions, then move on to a medium weight for 5 sets of 5 to 6 repetitions. Finish by using the maximum weight you can handle for 2 or 3 sets of 2 to 3 repetitions. Rest between sets for 15 to 25 seconds.

1

2

1. GASTROCNEMIUS - Exercising your gastrocnemius muscles can be done quite simply by quickly and repeatedly rising up on your toes. Holding dumbells in your hands or a light weight on your shoulders while doing this will increase the efficiency of this exercise. Do this for 3 sets of 20 repetitions.

3. GLUTEUS & TENSOR FASCIA LATAE - Supporting yourself by leaning against a chair or some other stationary object and keeping your leg bent at the knee, raise your right leg laterally 90 degrees away from your body. Raise and lower each leg for 10 repetitions of 5 sets. You can add to the effectiveness of this exercise by wearing light ankle weights.

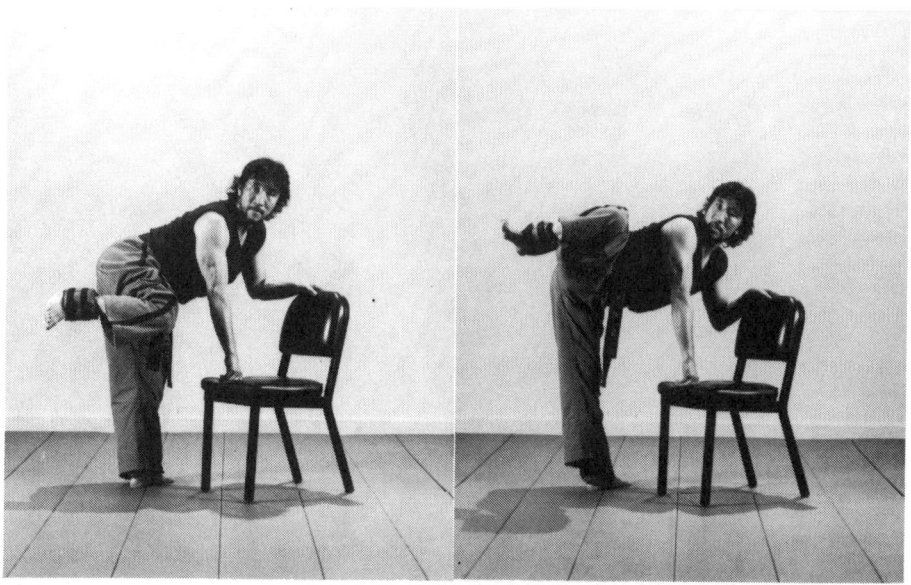

1 2

4. ABDOMEN & ILLICUS MUSCLES - Either sitting on the floor or sitting in a chair, keep both legs close together, knees straight. Raise your legs straight up in front of you, being careful not to bend your body forward. Repeat for 10 repetitions for 5 sets. This is a perfect exercise for the lower abdomen and illicus muscles.

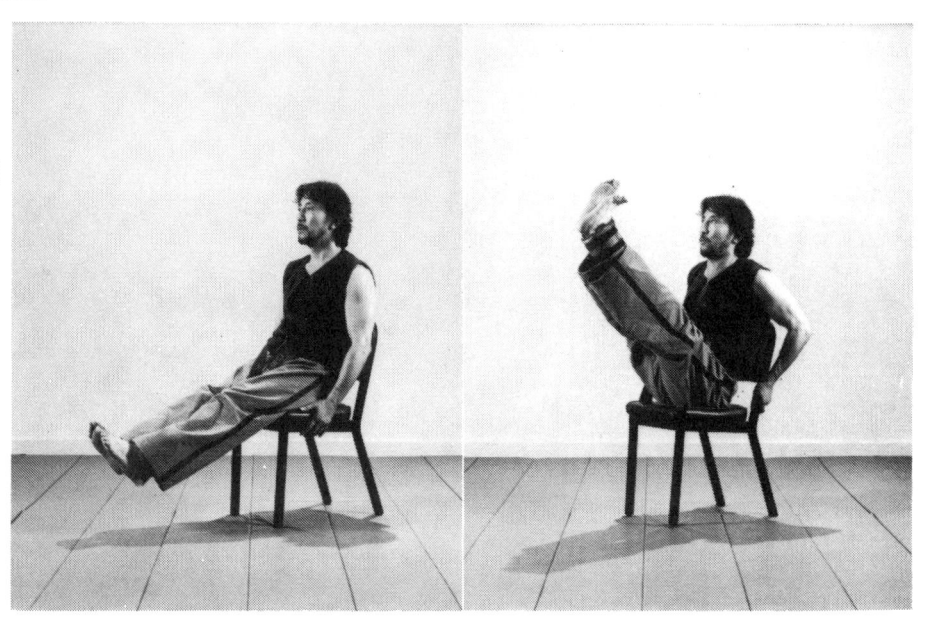

1 2

2. OBLIQUES - Getting into a sit up position, turn your body almost 90 degrees to one side. Concentrating on the oblique muscles, keep your body turned as you do 10 sets of 10 sit-ups, both sides.

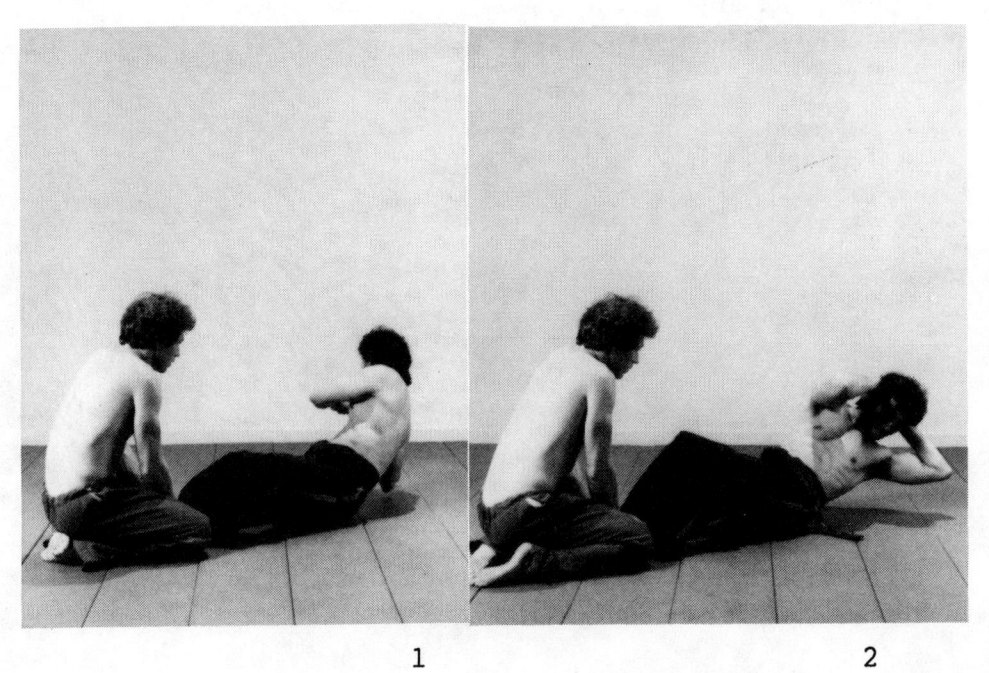

1   2

            1   2   3

2. HAMSTRINGS - Keeping your legs one shoulder width apart, place a light weight behind your head on your shoulders and trapezius muscles. Slowly bend your knees, keeping your back as straight as possible. DO NOT go any lower than 90 degrees, because with your legs this close you risk straining your back. Stand and then repeat this for 5 sets of ten repetitions.

STRETCHING

1. QUADRICEPS - Sit on the floor with one leg straight out in front of you and the other leg bent behind so that your heel is as close to your buttocks as possible. The angle between your legs should be greater than 90 degrees. Supporting your weight with your hands, lean backwards, dropping your neck and raising your hips up off the floor. Remember to breath deeply and isolate the quadricep and sartorius muscles. Hold yourself there for 20 seconds. Repeat this exercise three or four times, each leg.

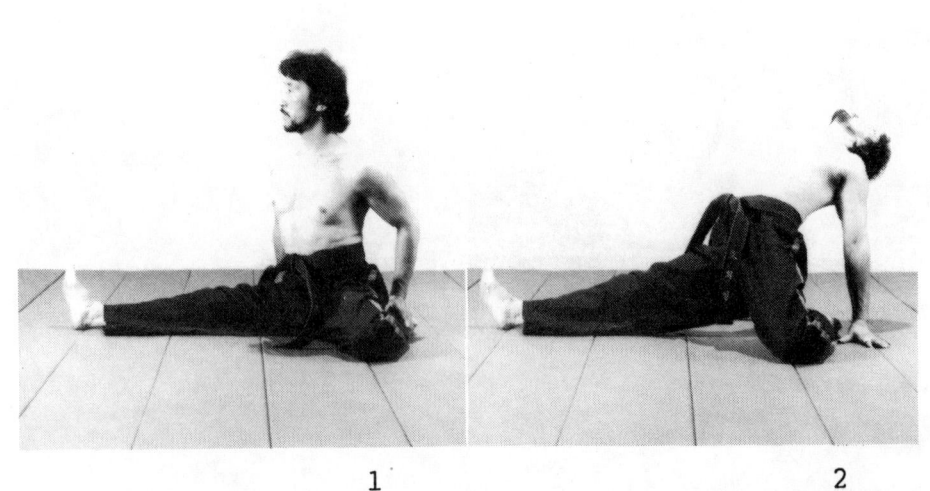

1   2

3. HAMSTRINGS - Stand on a sturdy chair or bench with your feet about shoulder width apart. Keeping your legs straight and bending from the waist, hold onto a 30 to 40 pound weight, letting it pull your upper body down. The goal of this stretch is to eventually get your head lower than the level of your feet. Hold yourself there for 10 to 20 seconds and then straighten up and rest. Keep the rest periods short - no more than ten seconds. Repeat this ten times. Also, because you're working with weights, you will actually be developing the hamstrings as you do this stretch.

1   2

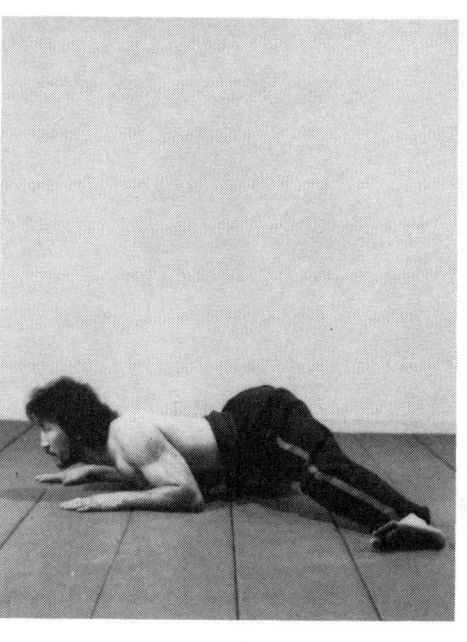

1 SARTORIUS - (In the Roundhouse Kick, used for height) Separate your legs as wide as you can, keeping your feet flat on the floor. Bending forward and balancing yourself with your hands, push yourself backwards as far as you can go for 20 seconds. Afterwards, pull yourself forward, also for 20 seconds. While doing this, it is important that you don't raise your hips and that you keep your knees straight and locked.

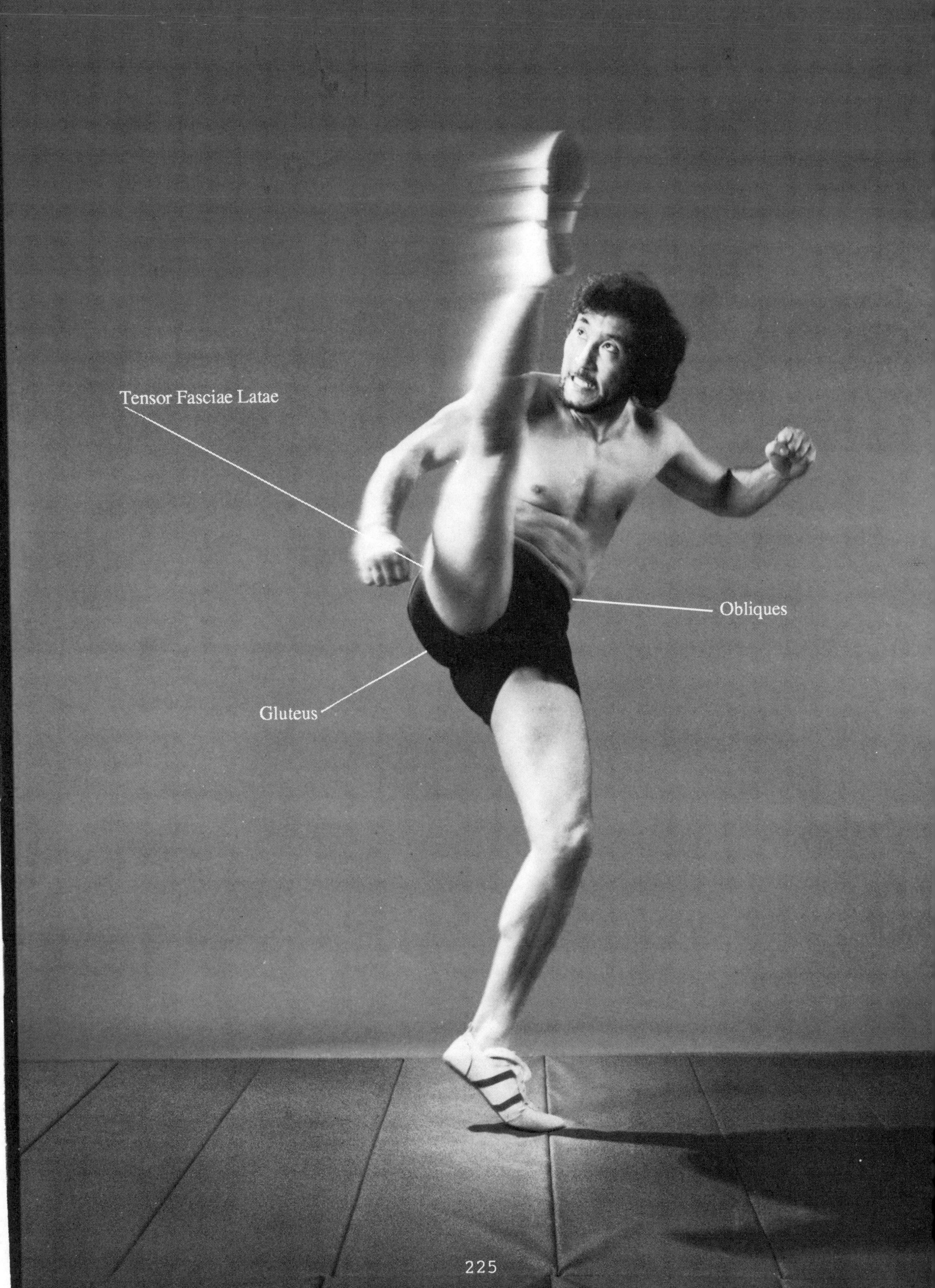
Tensor Fasciae Latae
Obliques
Gluteus

BACK SPINNING CRESCENT KICK

Even though the Back Spinning Crescent Kick is a more difficult technique to throw than some other spinning kicks, the speed and power generated by it when thrown properly make it both an effective counter attack as well as close distance offensive technique.

The kick is at its strongest when thrown face level, and because of this, flexibility is the key to executing the Back Spinning Crescent Kick effectively. Without a good stretch the kick can still be thrown to the torso, but for tighter fighting, the high section is best.

The Back Spinning Crescent Kick generates its power from the the fast spinning motion of the waist as well as the whipping motion created by the tensor fascia latae and gluteus muscles. Surprisingly, the real strength of this kick does not come from leg muscle development as much as from the speed of the torque.

HOW TO

1. Assume a left fighting stance.

2. Pushing off with your right leg, begin to rotate your upper body clockwise greater than 90 degrees as you shift your balance onto your left leg. Simultaneously bring your arms 180 degrees around, clockwise. Keeping your left leg slightly bent, continue torquing your upper body. Your head should turn quickly the entire 360 degrees, keeping your eyes on your target at all times.

1

2

3

3. Bring your right leg up as high as you can, keeping your knee slightly bent. With the balance on the ball of your left foot, your body should be in full spin now as you bring your right leg around to catch up to your body. At the point of contact, flex the biceps femoris muscle in your right leg, cutting the leg down across the target. The striking surface is the blade of the foot or the outside of the ankle bone. You can even strike with the heel if you are kicking with a greater downward cutting motion.

7

4. During practice, you should turn your body greater than 360 degrees, with the kicking leg passing through the target, not dropping at the point of contact. Unlike the Back Spinning Kick, you should keep your upper body straight; don't lean backwards. After fully executing the technique, return to a fighting stance.

4 5 6

MOST COMMON MISTAKES

The most common mistake made during the Back Spinning Crescent Kick is to rely on the leg for the kick instead of the spinning motion of the body. It is the body which is generating the majority of the power, therefore the body should start spinning before the leg. Another mistake is cutting the kick short, not reaching as high or as far as you can. Other errors include not keeping your upper body straight and dropping your hips while raising your leg. NOTE - When practicing this kick against a heavy bag, strike the target with the full side of the foot and lower leg, not just the blade of the foot or the ankle.

REPETITIONS

Beginners - 5 to 10 times, each leg.
Advanced - 10 to 15 times, each leg.

BREATHING

INHALE before you spin and as you start to spin EXHALE SHARPLY.

APPLICATION

WEIGHT LIFTING

Weight training is an often overlooked addition to any martial arts training program. Besides just toning and shaping the body, it can dramatically increase both your muscular strength and endurance.

Many people are unsure how to begin a personalized weight training program, which is why I have included exercises appropriate for each technique.

To increase your muscle size, start with 2 sets of 5 repetitions using light weights, 5 sets of 5 to 6 repetitions using medium weights, and then go for the maximum weight you can handle for 2 or 3 sets of 2 or 3 repetitions. Rest between sets for 15 to 20 seconds. This type of workout should only be done every other day.

If you want to tone your muscles without drastically increasing size (also called "cutting" your muscles), pick a weight which you can work with for 10 sets of 15 to 20 repetitions, usually between 30 and 80 pounds depending on the exercise. Rest between sets for no more than 15 seconds.

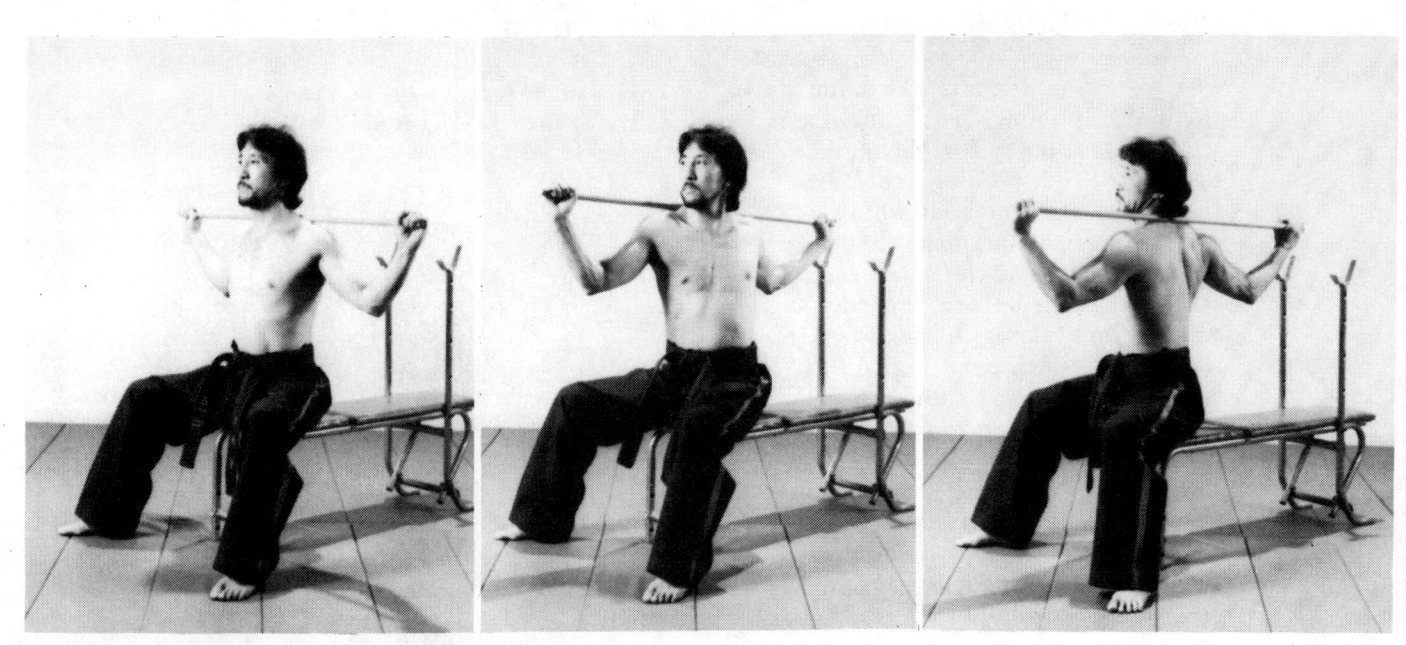

1 2 3

OBLIQUES - In a sitting position and holding a broomstick behind your head, twist your waist side to side rapidly. Do as many repetitions as you can for 5 sets. This is a very good exercise for your obliques.

3. SARTORIUS - To exercise your sartorius muscles, assume a wide horse riding stance while either holding light weights in your hands or across your trapezius muscles. Keeping your back as straight as possible to avoid injury, slowly lower yourself into a 90 degree squat. Hold yourself there for a few seconds, and then rise back up. As you go into the squat inhale, and as you rise back up exhale. Do this for 5 sets of 10 repetitions.

1. BACK & LUMBAR - This exercise is called the "Good Morning" exercise. Placing a light weight on your shoulders and trapezius muscles behind your head and keeping your legs one and a half shoulder widths apart, bend forward at the waist to an angle of 90 degrees. Make sure that you keep your legs straight, however if your back is not strong enough, you can bend your knees slightly.

4. OBLIQUES & ABDOMEN - The best exercise for developing the oblique and abdomen area is to lie on your back, having someone hold your legs as you turn your upper body greater than 90 degrees. Raise your upper body in this modified sit-up position, concentrating on the oblique muscles. Do as many repetitions as you can, turn your upper body the other direction and do as many repetitions as you can on this side. Repeat this for 10 sets. This exercise should be done every day in order to fully develop your obliques. Regular sit-ups are also highly recommended - you should actually do them every day in order to develop your abdominal strength. As you become stronger, continue these exercises, but include a light weight held by your head.

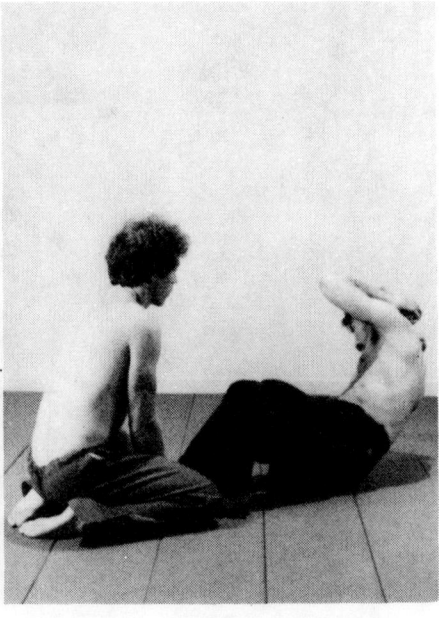

1 2

5. GLUTEUS & TENSOR FASCIA LATAE - Lying on your left side, support your upper body with your hands and arms. Using very short movements, raise and lower your right leg, keeping the knee locked and the foot in a side kick position with the edge of the foot parallel to the floor and your heel higher than your toes. Repeat this 5 times for 5 sets, and then switch sides. If you are more advanced, do this exercise 10 repetitions for 10 sets. You can also work up to adding ankle weights to increase the effectiveness of the exercise. By changing the angle that you raise your leg to a little more behind, you put more emphasis on the gluteus muscles.

3

1 2 3

STRETCHING

2. HAMSTRINGS II - Placing your heel on a low bench or chair and keeping your other leg bent inward, heel as close to your groin as possible, bend your upper body forward at the waist, trying to bring your head down below the level of your knee. Do this three or four times for each leg, holding yourself down for 20 seconds each time. You can also do this by placing both heels on the bench and bending your body forward trying to touch your head to your shin.

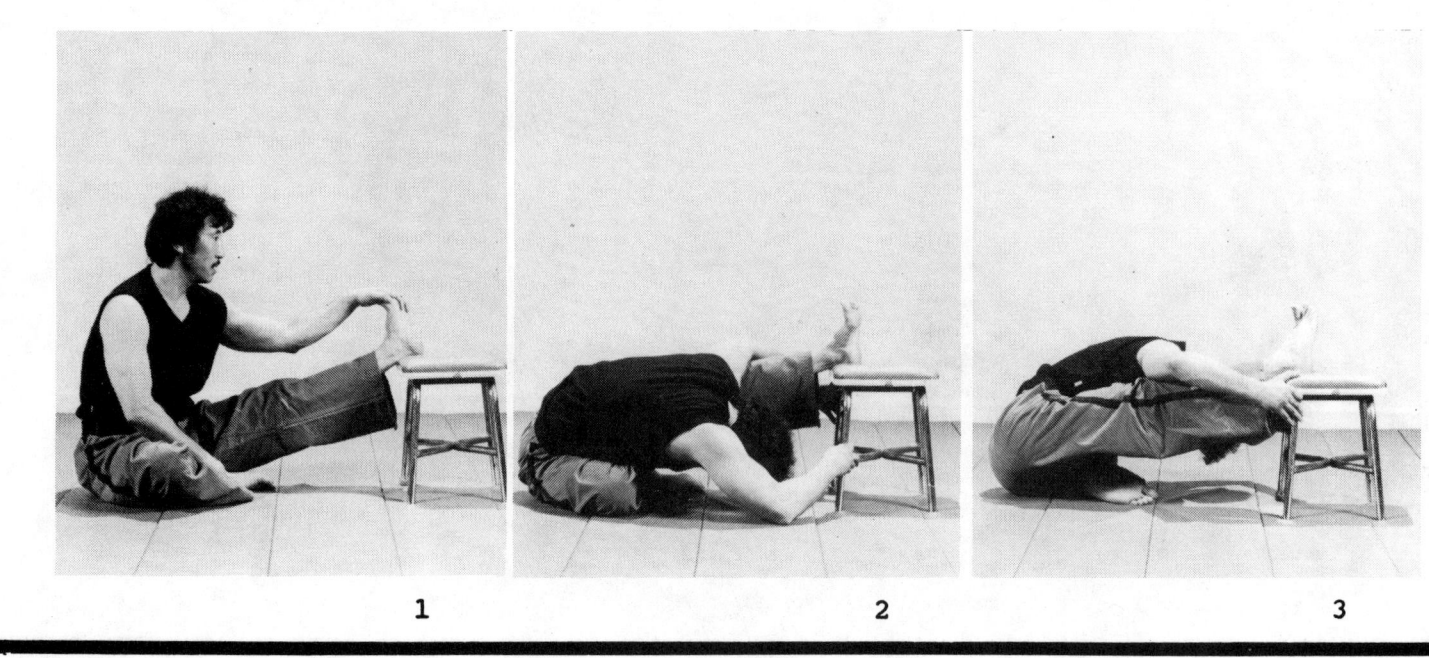

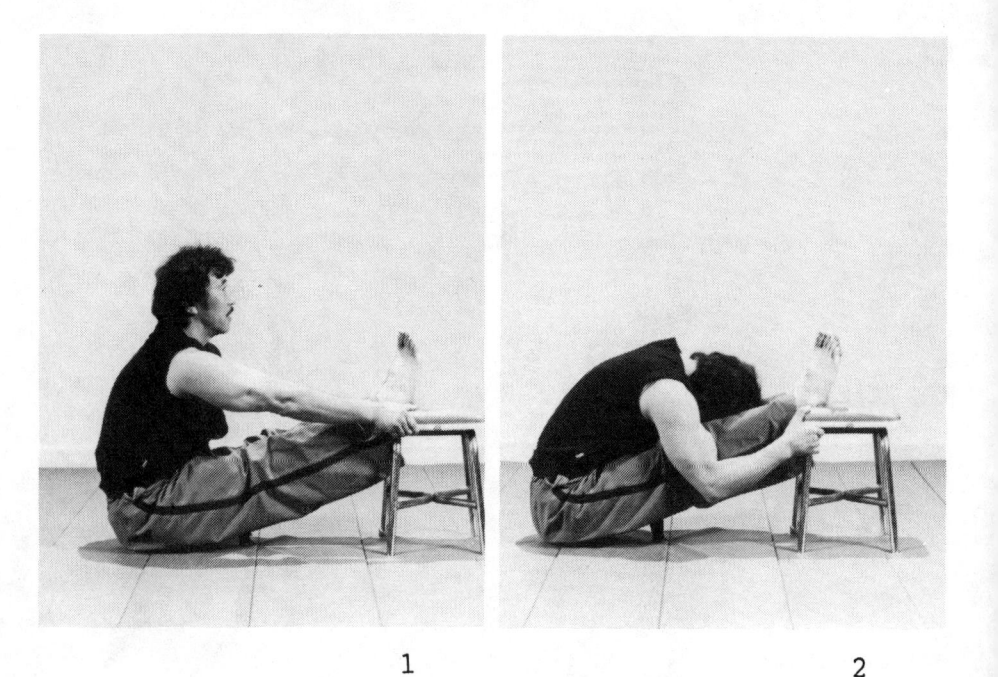

1

2

3

1

2

233

3. HAMSTRINGS & QUADRICEPS - Get into a front split position with the heel of your front foot flat on the floor, toes pointing upward. The instep of the rear leg should be flat on the floor. In this position, your front leg will be stretching the biceps femoris while your back leg will be stretching the quadriceps. Leaning backwards will emphasize the quadricep stretch, while leaning forward will add to the hamstring stretch. Hold yourself in both positions for 20 seconds, and then switch direction. Repeat this three or four times.

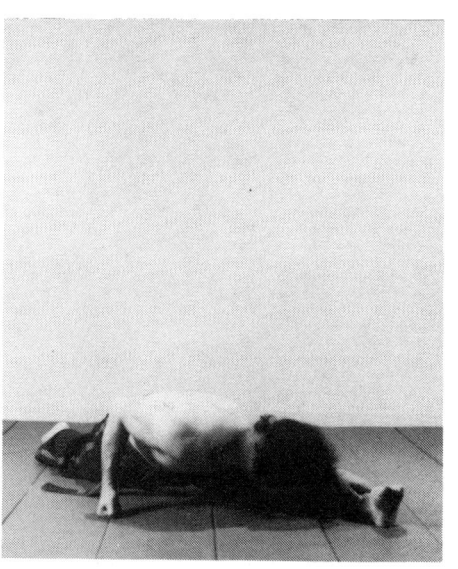

1   2   3

1. HAMSTRINGS I - Stand on a sturdy chair or bench with your feet about shoulder width apart. Keeping your legs straight and bending from the waist, hold onto a 30 to 40 pound weight, letting it pull your upper body down. The goal of this stretch is to eventually get your head lower than the level of your feet. Hold yourself there for 10 to 20 seconds and then straighten up and rest. Keep the rest periods short - no more than ten seconds. Repeat this ten times.

1   2

2. SARTORIUS- From a standing position, spread your legs as wide as you can, keeping your feet flat on the floor. Locking your knees, lean your body as far forward as you can, hold yourself there for 20 seconds, and then push yourself back as far as you can, also holding yourself there for 20 seconds. Repeat this three or four times, resting slightly between sets.

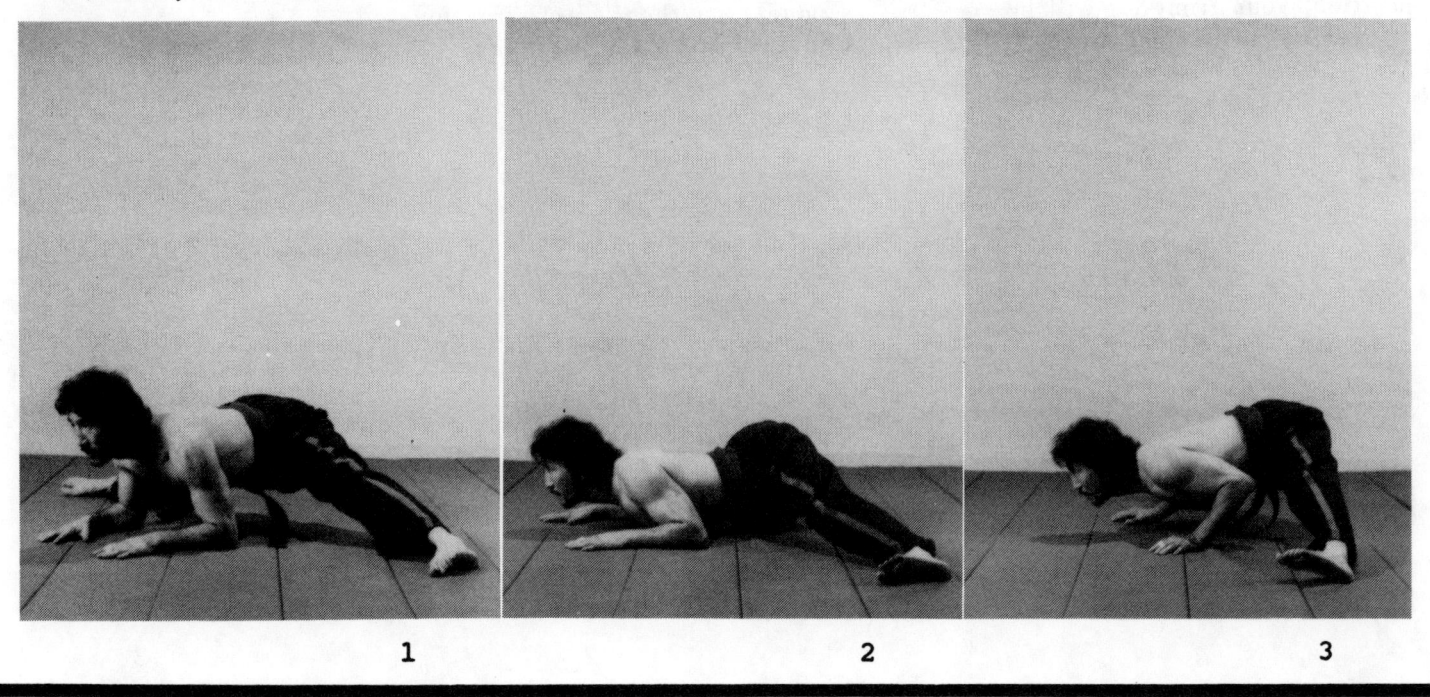

1   2   3

Quadriceps
Tensor Fasciae Latae
Gluteus
Biceps Femoris
Obliques

BACK TURNING KICK

As far as I'm concerned, the Back Turning Kick is one of the best techniques a martial artist can master. It's a perfect kick for a smaller person to use against a larger opponent as well as lending itself perfectly to be followed by a succession of other kicking or punching techniques.

This kick generates power from the simultaneous actions of both turning and kicking, a combination which capitalizes on the strength of both. Speed is essential to the Back Turning Kick because of the brief moment when you are turning, but it is the same turning motion which can confuse an unsuspecting opponent, catching him off guard. You must be careful after completing this technique that you resume to a solid fighting stance.

The turning motion is created by the oblique and waist muscles, and the kicking motion uses the quadriceps and hamstrings, as well as the tensor fascia latae and gluteus muscles to help raise the leg to chamber position.

HOW TO

1. Assume a left fighting stance.

2. Pushing off with the right leg, quickly turn your upper body clockwise almost 180 degrees, simultaneously drawing your leg up to chamber position - knee close to your chest, lower leg parallel to the floor.

3. Without snapping your knee, push your leg out with the quadriceps muscles in your upper leg. Your balance foot (the left) should pivot sharply on the ball of the foot 180 degrees, so that as you kick your left heel turns in a direct line towards the target. Keeping your ankle back, strike the target with the blade of the foot or the heel. Your upper body should be leaning back about 45 degrees and at the height of the kick you should be looking over your shoulder - your heel, hip, and shoulders should all be a perfect vertical line. If you want to reach a little deeper, lean your upper body greater than 45 degrees.

APPLICATION

4. After executing the technique, you can either draw back and throw a Side Kick, drop the kicking leg in front of you and throw another kick, or drop the kicking leg and follow up with hand techniques. The Back Turning Kick can also be thrown both while skipping in or dropping back for greater variety.

4 5 6

MOST COMMON MISTAKES

The most common error made during The Back Turning Kick is separating the techniques. All the elements of this kick - the quick turning, the raising of the kicking leg, and the actual kick itself - should happen together. Another very common mistake is not drawing the kicking leg up far enough to the chest, keeping the lower leg perpendicular to the floor rather than parallel. Other mistakes include overturning which causes the kicking leg to hook the kick rather than throw it in a straight line, and leaning your body forward rather than back.

REPETITIONS

Beginners - 10 to 15 times, each leg.
Advanced - 15 to 25 times, each leg.

BREATHING

INHALE before throwing the technique, HOLD YOUR BREATH as you turn, then EXHALE SHARPLY as you throw out the kicking leg.

WEIGHT LIFTING

I have found weight training to be a great asset to the martial artist. If done properly, it can tremendously increase both kicking and punching power.

There are two goals that the martial artist can set for himself with weight training. One is to increase muscle mass, while the other is to maintain muscle mass and increase tone and endurance. These involve two different types of workouts.

To increase size begin with light weights for 2 sets of five repetitions taking no more than 30 second rests between sets. Next move on to a medium weight for 5 sets of 5 to 6 repetitions, and end the sessions with the maximum weight you can handle for 2 or 3 sets of 2 or 3 repetitions. This type of workout should be done only every other day.

To maintain a desired muscle tone without increasing mass, work with 30 to 80 pounds and do 10 sets of 15 to 20 repetitions, resting for no more than 15 seconds between sets.

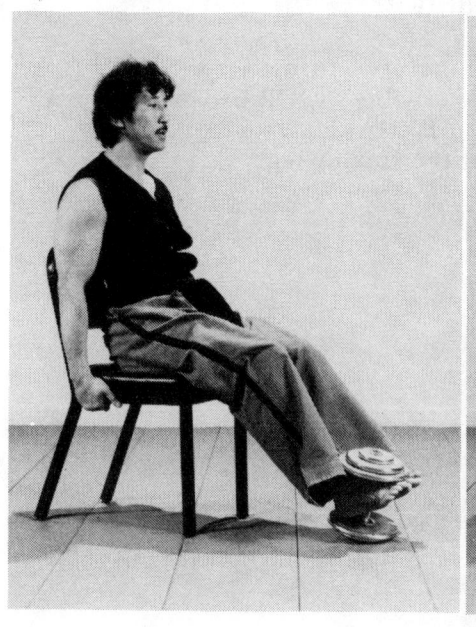

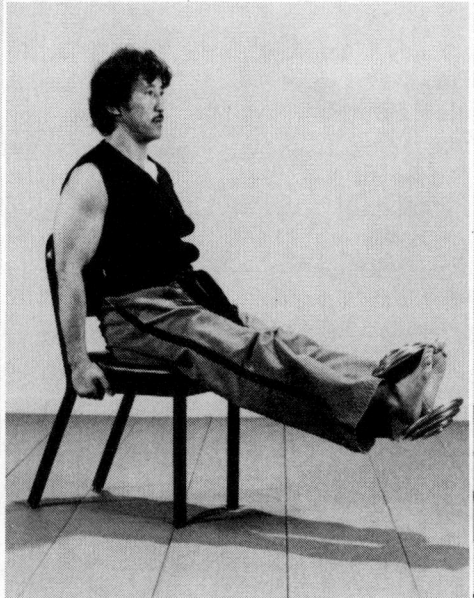

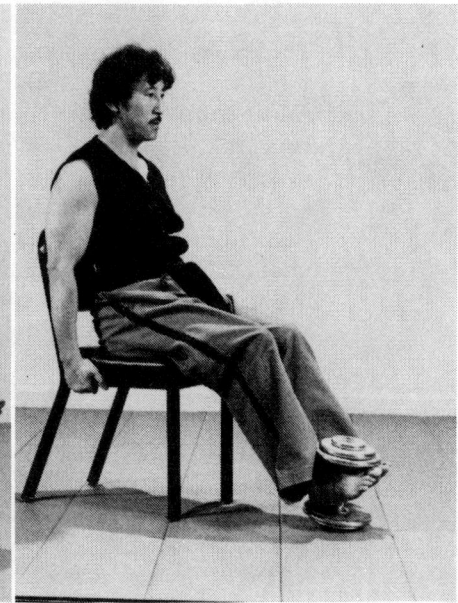

1
2
3

2. QUADRICEPS -

If you don't have a leg rising machine to use, you can do this exercise with a chair. Placing weights on your ankles (tying them down if necessary) sit with your back straight and hold onto the bottom or back of the chair with your hands. Straighten and lower your legs directly in front of you.

1. **HAMSTRINGS & QUADRICEPS** - An excellent exercise for the hamstrings involves placing a small lift beneath your heels (in this case, a piece of wood). This gives you a little balance and allows the quadriceps to get some extra workout. Holding light weights across the top of your chest, squat down until your legs are at a slightly greater angle than 90 degrees. Repeat this ten times for five sets.

1  2  3

1

4. **TENSOR FASCIA LATAE** - Assume a squat position on the floor, supporting yourself on your hands by leaning forward. Keeping your leg bent at the knee, raise your right leg laterally 90 degrees away from your body. Raise and lower each leg for 10 repetitions of 5 sets, making sure to keep your knee from touching the floor between repetitions. You can add to the effectiveness of this exercise by wearing light ankle weights.

3. **OBLIQUES & LUMBAR** - Using a bench, lie flat on your back with the small of your spine at the edge of the bench. Holding a stick behind your neck, rotate your waist as far as you can in both directions. Try for 5 sets of 10 repetitions, or keep going until you feel a slight burning in the muscles.

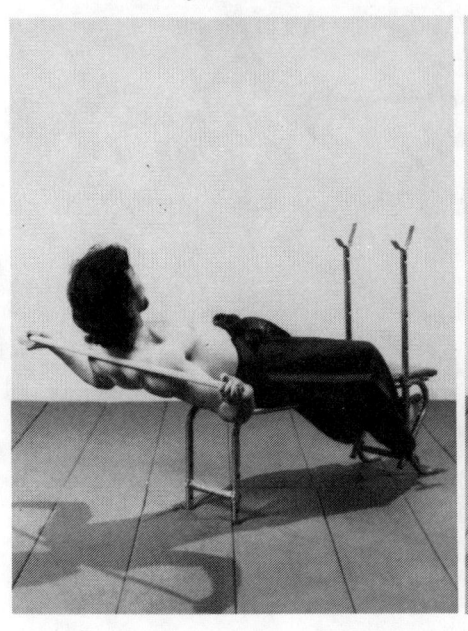

1 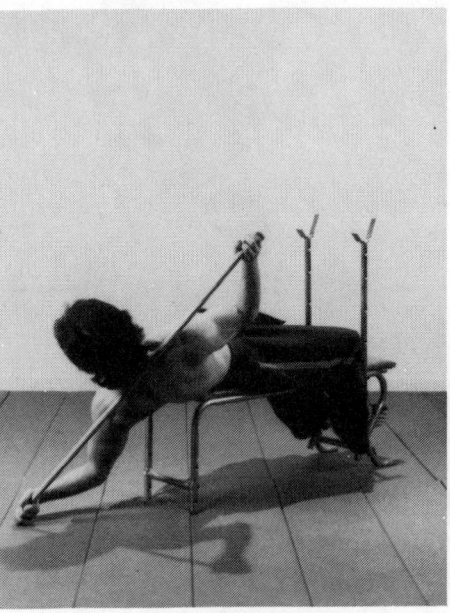 2 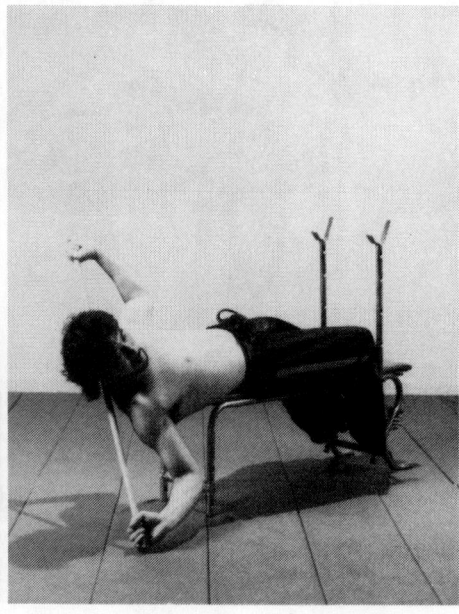 3

1   **TENSOR FASCIA LATAE** - Supporting yourself by leaning against a chair or some other stationary object, balance yourself on your left leg, toes pointing forward. Bending your right leg at the knee to concentrate this exercise in the tensor fascia latae muscle, raise your right leg to your right side at an angle of 90 degrees away from your body. Using short motions, raise and lower your leg for 10 repetitions of 10 sets. NOTE - the movement of the leg is very slight. You can also add to the effectiveness of this exercise by wearing ankle weights.

2

243

TENSOR FASCIA LATAE & OBLIQUES - Supporting yourself by holding onto some stationary object (in this instance a "roman" bench), raise and lower your leg behind you in a side kick position with your toes parallel to the ground using a long, swinging motion. The higher you bring the leg, the better will be the workout that your oblique muscles get. Repeat this for 10 sets of 10 repetitions.

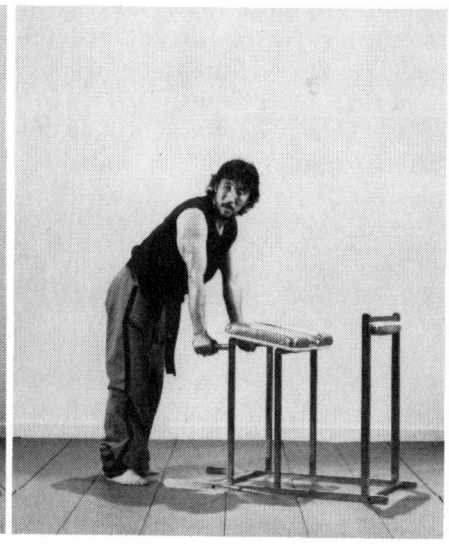

1   3   3

STRETCHING

1. **KNEE TENDON, QUADRICEPS & HAMSTRINGS** - Placing a foot on a low bench or stool, lower yourself into a deep forward stance, bending your front leg as far as you can, concentrating on your front knee. After the squat, straighten the front leg for a moment and then repeat. Do this for 15 to 20 times, and then switch legs. Do this for 5 sets. This stretch can also be done using a higher stool or a ladder.

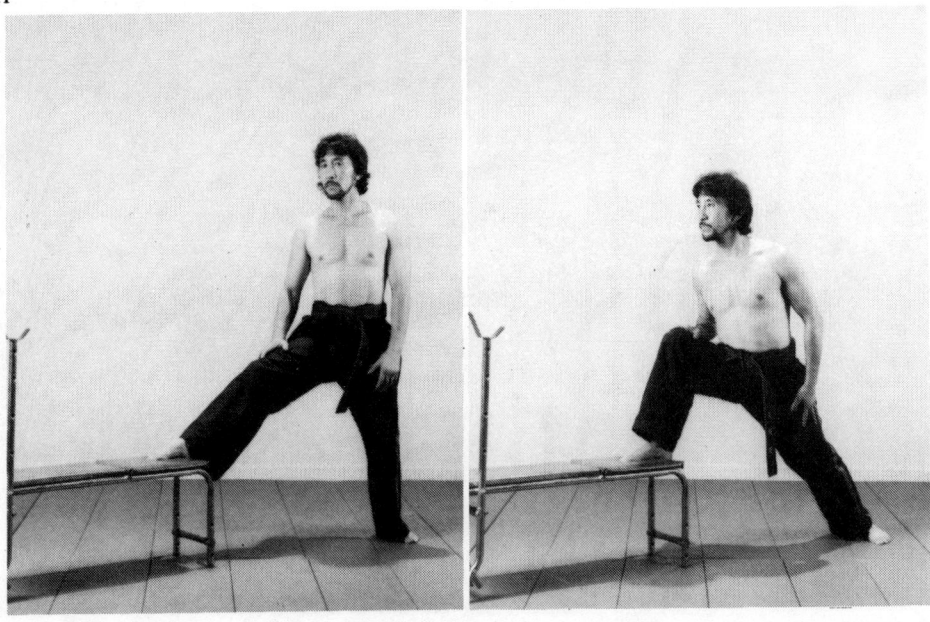

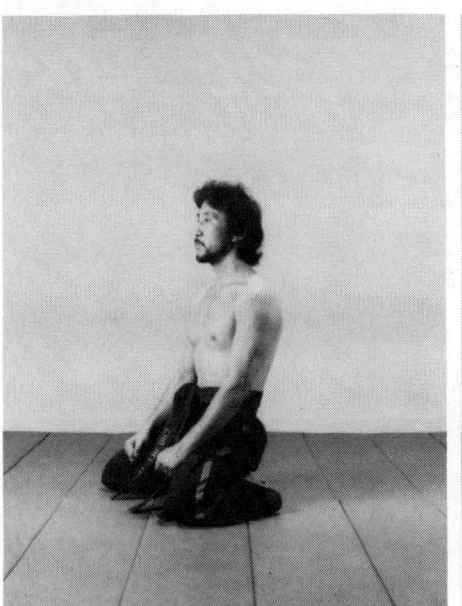

1 2

3. **QUADRICEPS & SARTORIUS II** - Kneel on the floor Japanese style, except keeping your knees spread out as wide as you can. Supporting your weight with your hands, lean backwards, dropping your neck and raising your hips as high off the floor as you can. Remember to breath deeply and isolate the quadricep and sartorius muscles. Hold yourself there for 20 seconds. Repeat this exercise three or four times.

1 2

1 2

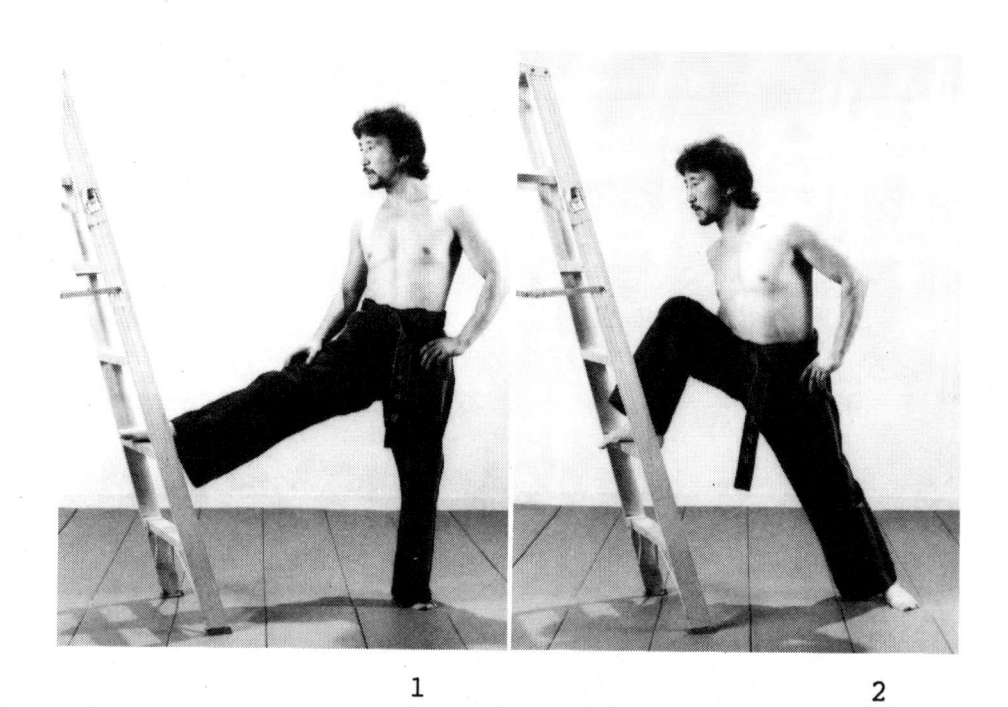

2. QUADRICEPS & SARTORIUS I - Sitting on the floor with one leg straight out in front of you and the other bent behind, heel as close to the buttocks as you can get it, lean backwards and support your weight with your arms. Pushing forward towards the middle, raise your body off the floor, concentrating the stretch in the quadricep muscle of the bent leg. Hold yourself in this position for 20 seconds, rest for a few moments, and then repeat three or four times.

1 2

Quadriceps
Oblique
Gastrocnemius
Gluteus
Hamstrings
Abdomen

BACK SPINNING HOOK KICK

The Back Spinning Hook Kick is really a less difficult version of the Back Spinning Kick. It can be thrown effectively at very close distances and it can also be thrown very powerfully at face level. It is a perfect kick to use in combination with other techniques such as The Side Kick, Roundhouse Kick, or even other Spinning Kicks.

Like the Back Spinning Kick, this kick also gets its power from the spinning motion of the upper body, but differs from the Back Spinning Kick in that it also generates a great deal of power from the pulling in motion of the hamstring and gluteus muscles as well as the snapping action of the lower leg. The tensor fascia latae muscle helps to keep the leg raised in a solid chamber position.

During sparring, the Back Spinning Hook Kick can be used as a faking technique, setting up your opponent for a second kick. There is also less spinning involved in throwing this kick, therefore it is very possible to flick the kicking leg out a second or even third time in quick succession.

HOW TO

1. Assume a left fighting stance.

2. Pushing off with your right leg, begin to rotate your upper body clockwise greater than 90 degrees as you shift your balance onto your left leg. Simultaneously bring your arms 180 degrees around, clockwise. Keeping your left leg slightly bent, continue torquing your upper body, leaning it 45 degrees back away from your target. Your head should turn quickly the entire 360 degrees, keeping your eyes on your target at all times.

1   2   3

APPLICATION

3. Bring your right leg up to at least waist level, bending your knee slightly. At about 270 degrees from the starting point, push your right leg out with the quadricep muscle. Your body should be fully spinning now as you bring your leg around to catch up to your body. The balance leg should be spinning on the ball of the foot, not the heel. Just before the point of impact, hook your lower leg towards the target by flexing your biceps femoris. The striking surface can be the back of the heel, or for a little extra reach, the bottom of the foot. It is very important to realize that the hooking motion does not occur after the body stops turning, but <u>while</u> the body continues to spin.

4. It is a bit easier to maintain balance while throwing this kick than with other spinning kicks. Keep in mind that your guard should always be up, covering your jaw. After executing this kick, return to a fighting stance.

4   5   6

MOST COMMON MISTAKES

Like the Back Spinning Kick, the most common mistake made during this kick is to pivot on the balance leg first, bringing the kicking leg up afterwards. These motions must happen simultaneously if the kick is to be powerful. A variation of this mistake is bringing the kicking leg around first, followed by the body. Everything must be fluid. Along with this is the error of stopping the spinning motion when the hook is thrown, rather than allowing the leg to pass completely through the target. Another very common error is to rely on the lower leg solely as the source of the hooking power. In order to get the most out of this kick, the upper leg should also be used to generate speed for the hooking motion.

REPETITIONS

Beginners - 5 to 10 times, each leg.
Advanced - 10 to 15 times, each leg.

BREATHING

INHALE before you spin and as you start to spin EXHALE SHARPLY.

WEIGHT LIFTING

Weight lifting is, to me, the real "Fountain of Youth". No matter what your sport is, if you train with weights your body will keep its tone well into your later years.

Different people set different goals for themselves when weight lifting. If you want to maintain size but increase your strength, you should work with lighter weights rather than heavier ones. By experimenting, find a weight which you can comfortably work with for 10 sets of 15 to 20 repetitions. Rest between sets for 10 to 15 seconds.

If you want to increase your size, start with a lighter weight as a warmup for 2 sets of 10 repetitions, a medium weight for 5 sets of 5 to 6 repetitions, and then go for the maximum weight you can handle, 2 to 3 repetitions for 2 or 3 sets. Between each set, you should rest for 20 to 30 seconds.

If you are just maintaining size, this workout can be done every day. If you are trying to increase your size, this workout should be done every other day, concentrating on different muscle groups.

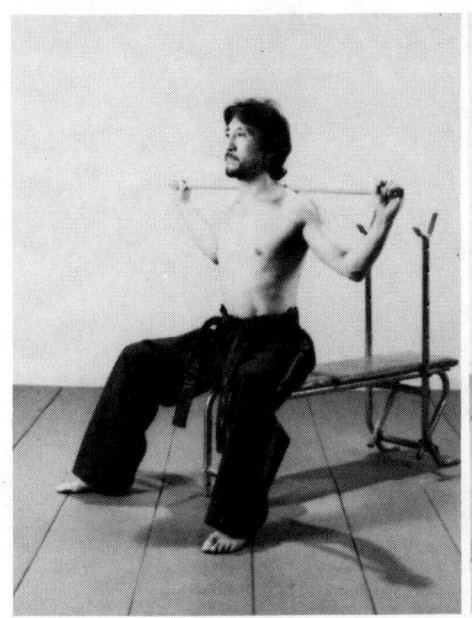

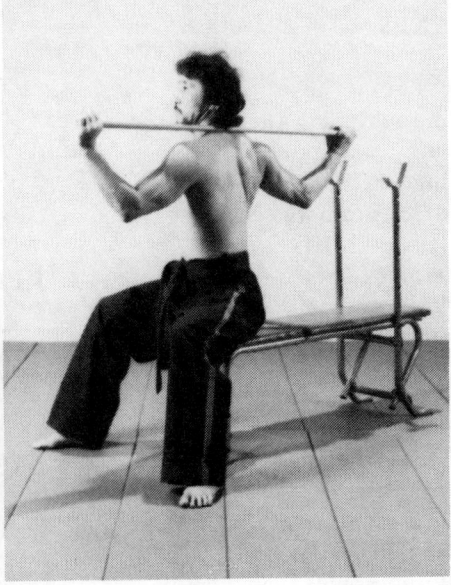

1   2   3

OBLIQUES II - In a sitting position and holding a broomstick behind your head, twist your waist side to side rapidly. Do as many repetitions as you can for 5 sets. This is a very good exercise

3. OBLIQUES I - A good exercise for the obliques is to place a light weight on your shoulders and trapezius muscles, and keeping your legs one to one and a half shoulder widths apart torque your waist slowly side to side. Do 5 sets of ten repetitions in each direction.

1

2

3

5. TENSOR FASCIA LATAE & OBLIQUES - Supporting yourself by leaning against a chair or some other stationary object, balance yourself on your left leg and looking over your right shoulder, raise your right leg behind and away from your body 90 degrees, foot parallel to the floor. Using long movements, raise and lower your leg for 10 repetitions of 10 sets, working both legs. You can also do this same exercise raising your leg to 90 degrees and the lowering your leg only slightly, putting a little more stress on the active muscles.

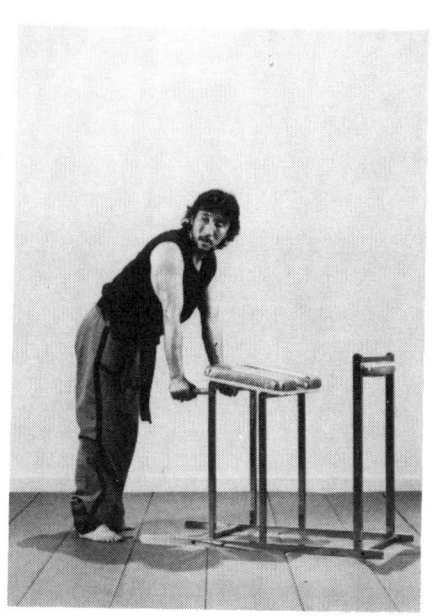

1

2

1. HAMSTRINGS - Exercising your hamstring muscles can be done by lying down on your stomach on a long bench and doing reverse curls with leg weights on your ankles. Do 10 repetitions for 5 sets. If you really want to build size, you should consider getting a leg machine.

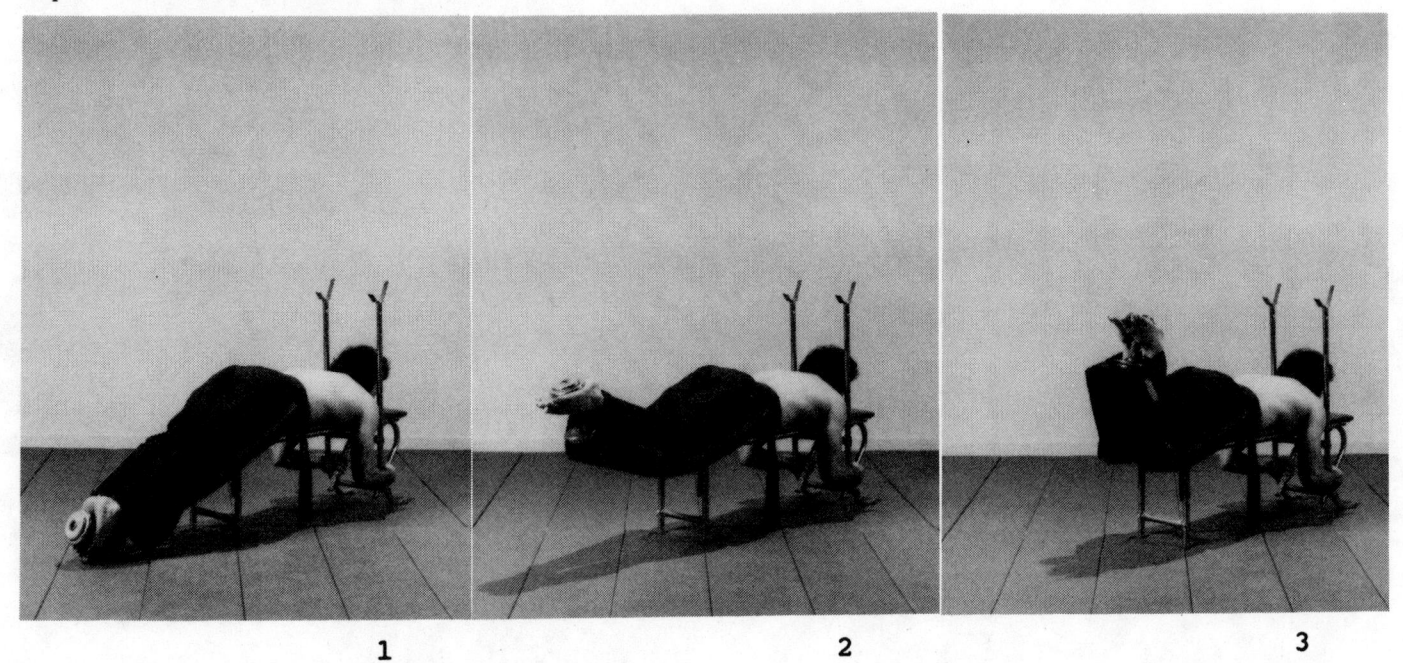

1   2   3

1   2   3

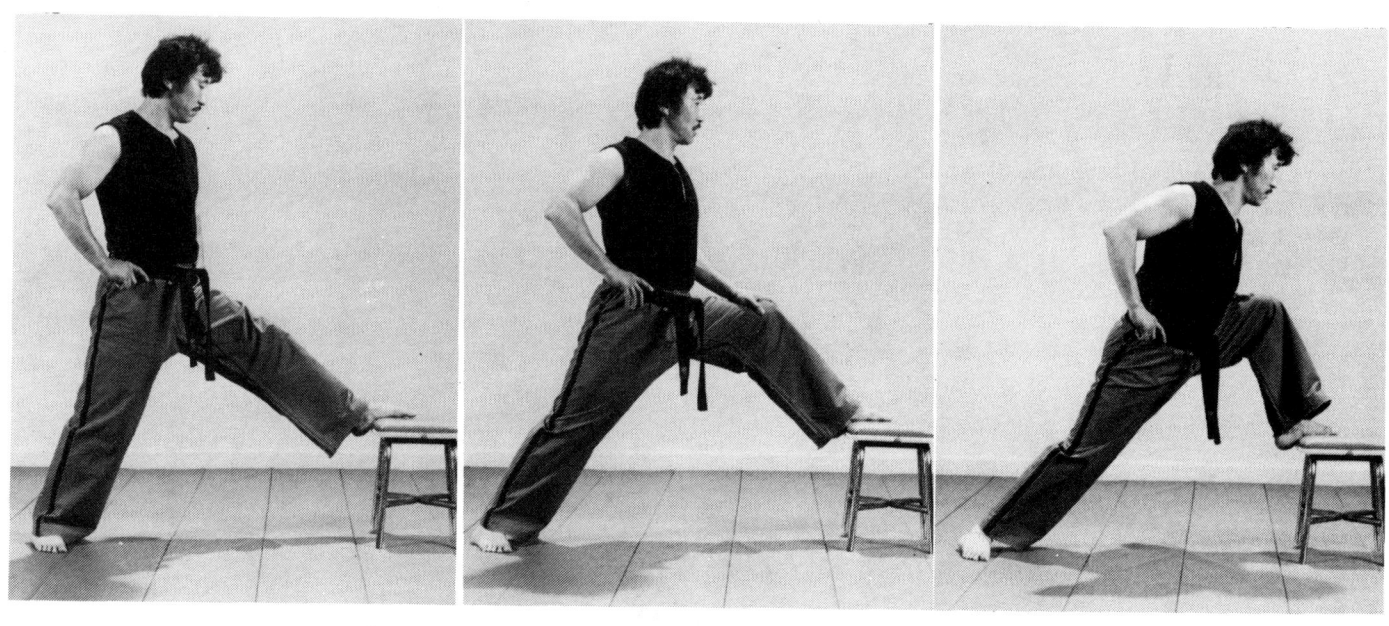

KNEE TENDON, HAMSTRINGS & QUADRICEPS - Placing a foot on a low bench or stool, lower yourself into a deep forward stance, bending your front leg as far as you can, concentrating on your front knee. After the squat, straighten the front leg for a moment and then repeat. Do this for 15 to 20 times, and then switch legs. Do this for 5 sets.

STRETCHING

1. SARTORIUS & QUADRICEPS - Place a foot on a low stool, bottom of the foot touching the top of the stool. Bend your rear leg, lowering yourself down and placing pressure on your outstretched leg. When you do this stretch, make sure that the balance leg is turned outward, knees opened out. Hold yourself in the lowered position for 15 seconds and then rise back up. Repeat this three or four sets of 10-15 repetitions.

2. SARTORIUS I - Spreading your legs as wide as possible and keeping your knees locked, lower yourself down and try to touch the inside of your legs to the floor. You can use a low bench or stool to support yourself. Hold yourself there for 15 seconds. Repeat for 10-15 repetitions.

2

3

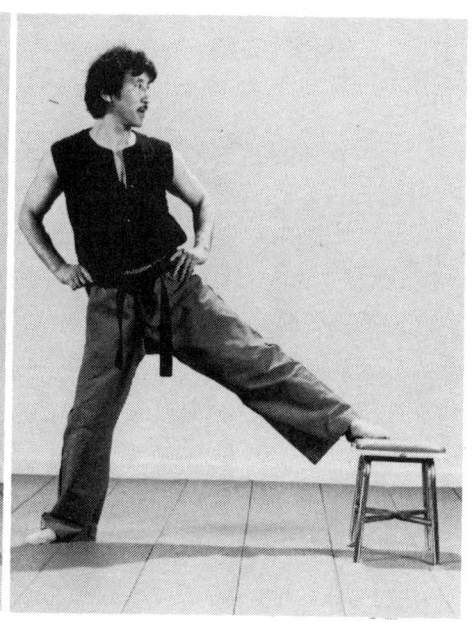

3. HAMSTRINGS - Enlisting the help of a partner, slowly have raise your leg straight up in front of you. Some people find it useful to keep a wall to their back for support, while in the case of a larger and stronger partner, it is possible to have the partner pin your balance foot down to the floor with his foot while lifting your leg. In this way, your partner does all the work and you get all the stretch!

2

1

256

4. QUADRICEPS - Kneel on the floor "Japanese style" with your knees close together. Leaning backwards, grab onto your ankles and raise your hips upwards as high off the floor as possible. Make sure to drop your head back as far as you can. Hold yourself in this position for 20 seconds, repeating for three or four times. Another very good stretch for the quadriceps is simply kneeling "Japanese style" with your knees together, and then slowly lying backwards until your back is on the floor.

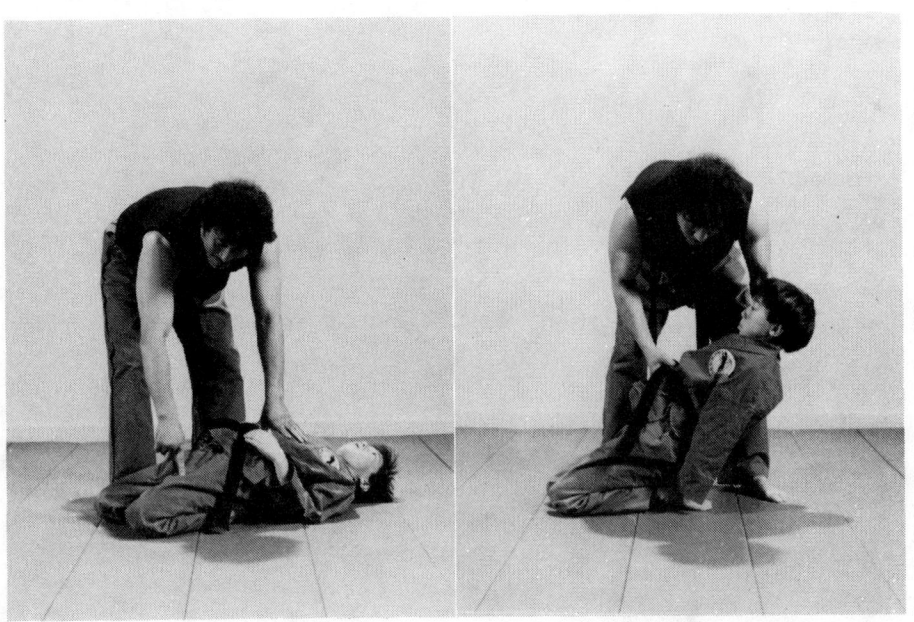

1

2

5. SARTORIUS II - Using a partner, lie on your back, knees bent, bottoms of your feet touching. Separate your knees as wide as you can, having your partner place firm but even pressure on the insides of your knees. Stay in this position for 20 seconds, rest for a few moments, and then repeat three or four times. You can do the same type of stretch with your legs straight, or with your knees bent slightly to take some of the pressure off of your knee tendons.

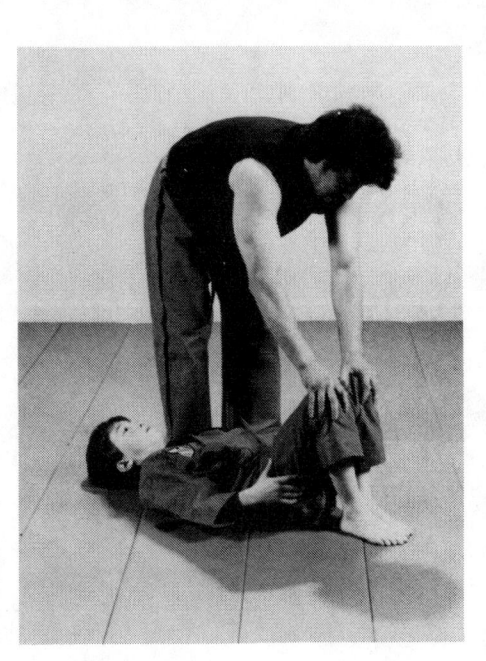

1

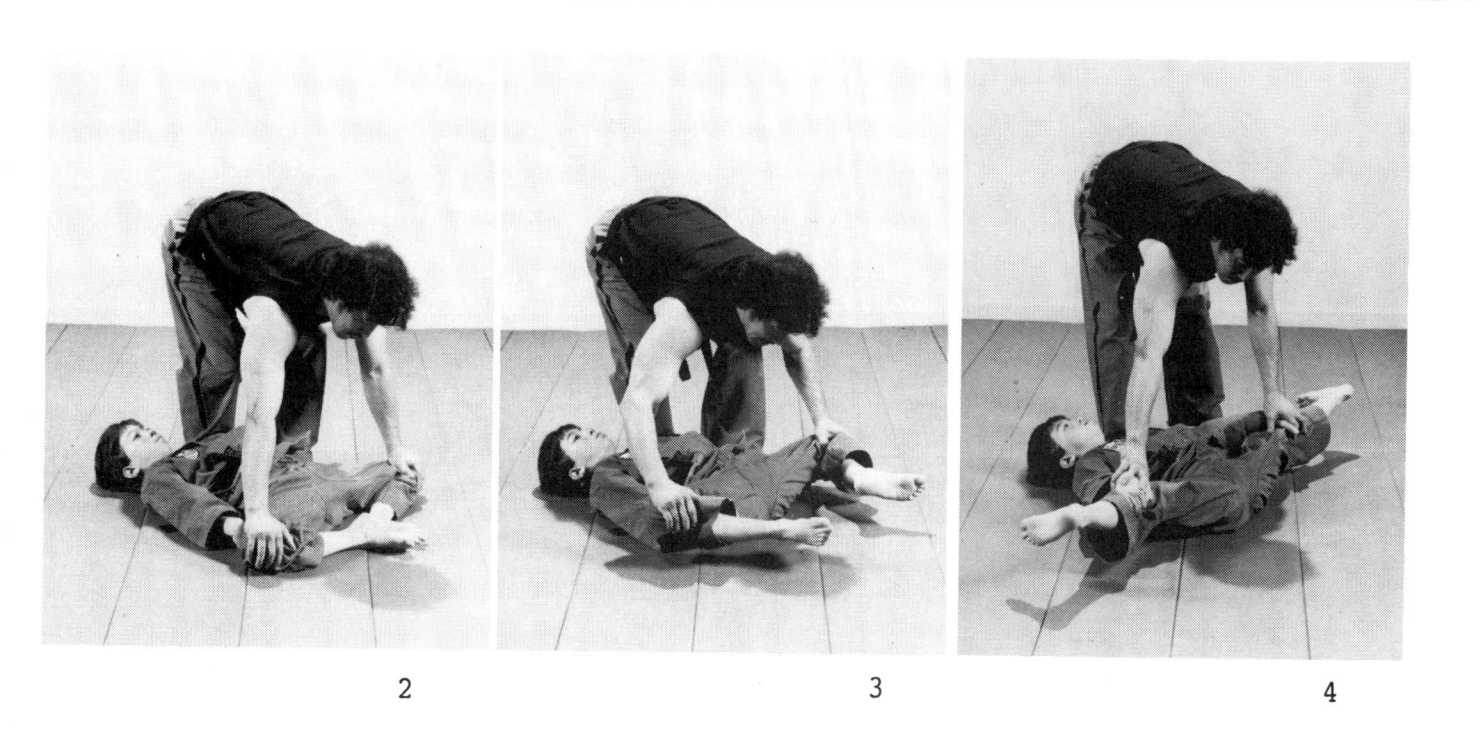

3

2

3

4

Tensor Fasciae Latae

Oblique

Gluteus

Abdomen

BACK SPINNING KICK

Thrown properly, The Back Spinning Kick can be one of the most powerful as well as artistic kicks in your arsenal. When people think about martial arts kicking, they think of the Back Spinning Kick. It can open an opponent up at the same time it breaks through his defenses. The most effective attacking area is the torso and even the face, depending on your flexibility.

Many people think that the strength of this kick comes from the legs, but in my experience I've found that the real power comes from the spinning motion - from the oblique muscles. Because of this, special attention should be paid to the development of the abdomen, gluteus and tensor fascia latae muscles which hold the leg up as well as the biceps femoris muscles which controls the kicking leg as this technique is thrown.

Equally important with the ability to throw the Back Spinning Kick is the ability to effectively defend yourself after the kick is executed. Any spinning kick demands great balance in order to recover properly, and this kick is certainly no exception.

HOW TO

1. Assume a left fighting stance.

2. Pushing off with your right leg, begin to rotate your upper body clockwise greater than 90 degrees as you shift your balance onto your left leg. Simultaneously bring your arms 180 degrees around, clockwise. Keeping your left leg slightly bent, continue torquing your upper body, leaning it 45 degrees back away from your target. Your head should turn quickly the entire 360 degrees, keeping your eyes on your target at all times.

1

2

3

3. Bring your right leg up to waist level, keeping your knee as straight as you can. Your body should be in full spin now as you bring your leg around to catch up to your body. The balance leg should be spinning on the ball of the foot, not the heel (this is true for all spinning kicks). The striking surface is the back of the heel, and at the point of impact, flex the biceps femoris muscles in the kicking leg.

7

8

REPETITIONS

Beginners - 5 to 10 times, each leg.
Advanced - 10 to 15 times, each leg.

BREATHING

INHALE before you spin and as you start to spin EXHALE SHARPLY.

4. During practice, you should turn your body greater than 360 degrees, with the kicking leg passing through the target, not dropping at the point of contact. Also, your upper body should be leaning slightly forward after the kicking leg has passed through the target - this is the only way you can maintain your balance. After fully executing the technique, return to a fighting stance.

MOST COMMON MISTAKES

The most common mistake made during this kick is to pivot on the balance leg prior to bringing the kicking leg up. All the parts of this technique should happen simultaneously - pivoting and raising the kicking leg followed by executing the kick. In the same light, many people also do the kick wrong by trying to bring the kicking leg around first, followed by the body. It is the body which is generating the majority of the power through the spinning motion, therefore the body should start spinning before the leg. Another common mistake is striking the target with the side of the foot rather than with the back of the heel. This gives the kick the appearance of a Crescent Kick, rather than a heel kick. Other errors include not leaning your body back enough, not keeping the kicking leg at the same height during the technique, and hooking the leg at the last moment.

APPLICATION

WEIGHT LIFTING

Weight training is the most effective way of increasing and maintaining muscle tone. The idea that it will slow a martial artist down is a myth as far as I am concerned. I've been lifting weights steadily for over 30 years, and it hasn't slowed me down in the least.

Increasing muscle mass and maintaining muscle tone require two different types of workouts. To increase size you must first warm up with light weights for 2 sets of five repetitions. Rest for no more than 30 seconds between sets. After you have done your 2 sets, move on to a medium weight for 5 sets of 5 to 6 repetitions. Finish your workout by training with the heaviest weight you can handle for 2 or 3 sets of 2 or 3 repetitions each. This type of workout should be done only every other day.

To maintain a desired muscle tone without increasing mass, work with 30 to 80 pounds and do 10 sets of 15 to 20 repetitions, resting for no more than 15 seconds between sets.

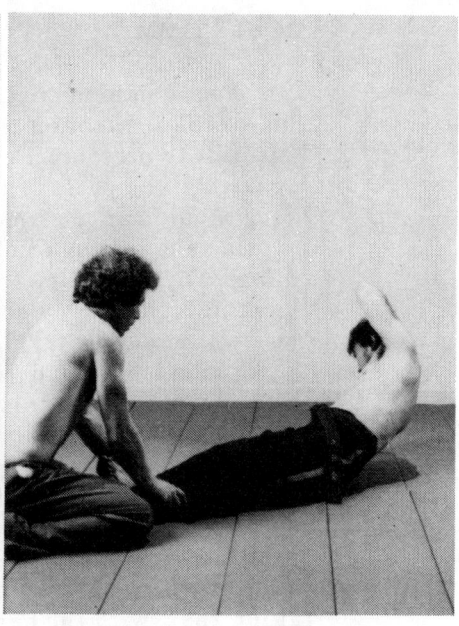

1. OBLIQUES - Exercising the oblique muscles in your waist is essential for this and any spinning kick. The best exercise is to lie on your back, having someone hold your legs as you turn your upper body greater than 90 degrees. Raise your upper body in this modified sit-up position, concentrating on the oblique muscles. Do as many

repetitions as you can, turn your upper body the other direction and do as many repetition as you can on this side. Repeat this for 10 sets. This exercise should be done every day in order to fully develop your obliques. You should also do regular sit-ups - it is your abdominal strength which helps to keep your leg steady while executing the Back Spinning Kick.

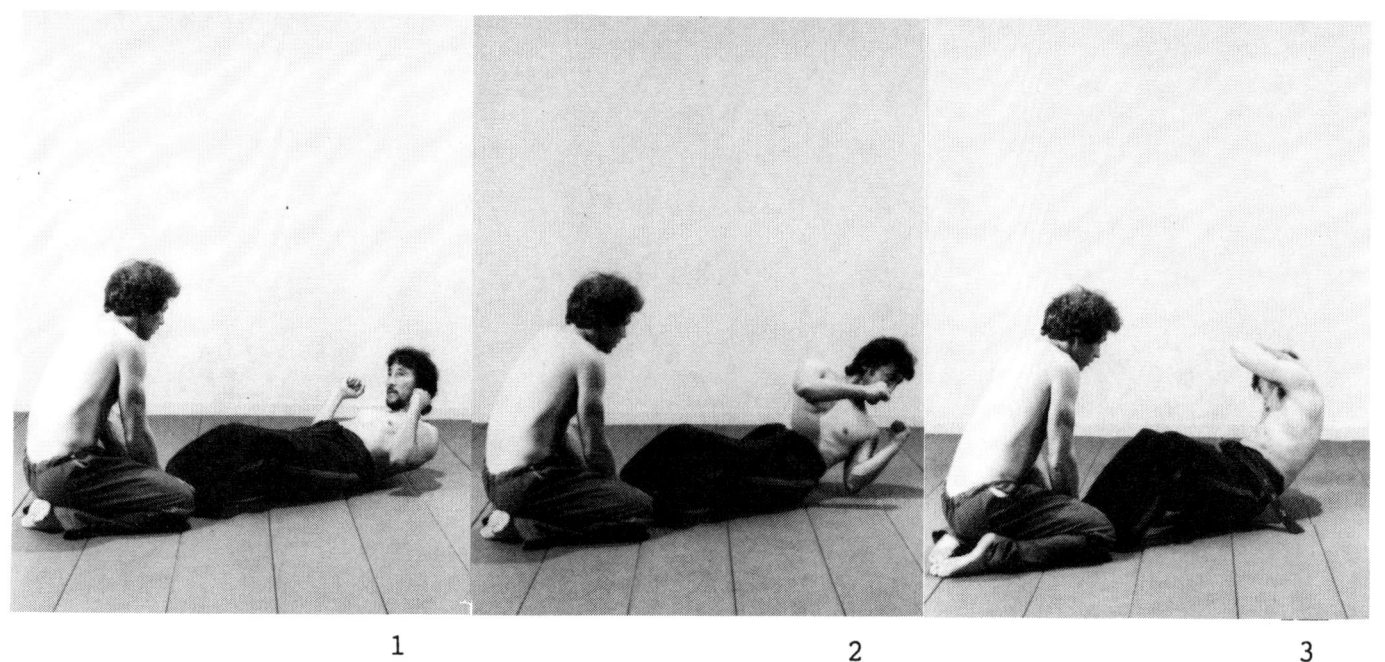

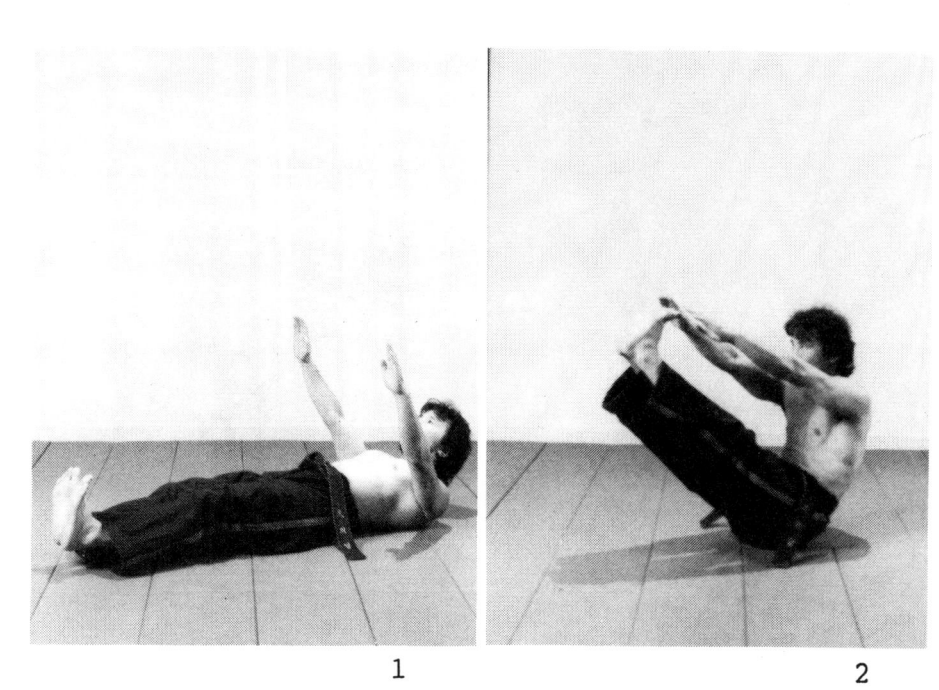

1 2 3

1 2

2. OBLIQUES & ABDOMINALS - Lying flat on your back with your arms raised in front of you, simultaneously lift your legs straight kneed and raise your upper body, trying to touch your toes with your finger tips. Do as many repetitions as you can, 10 sets worth.

264

3. HAMSTRINGS - Exercising your hamstring muscles can be done by lying down on your stomach on a long bench and doing reverse curls with leg weights on your ankles. Do 10 repetitions for 5 sets. If you really want to build size, you should consider getting a leg machine.

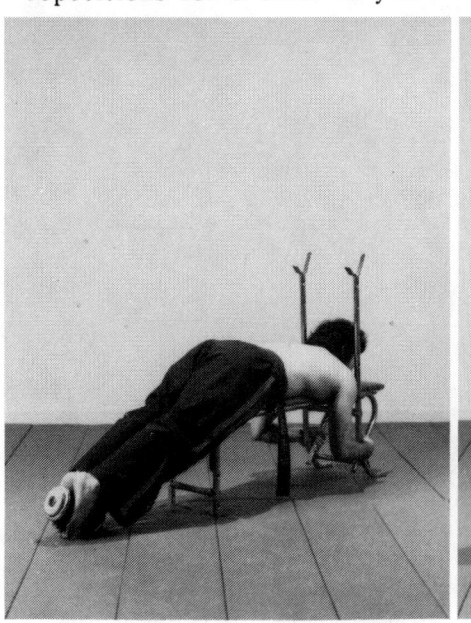

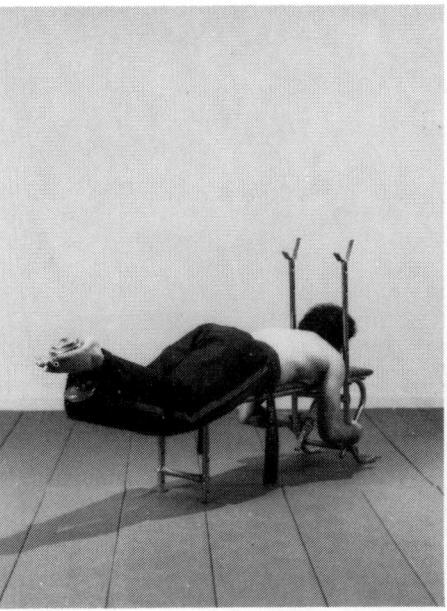

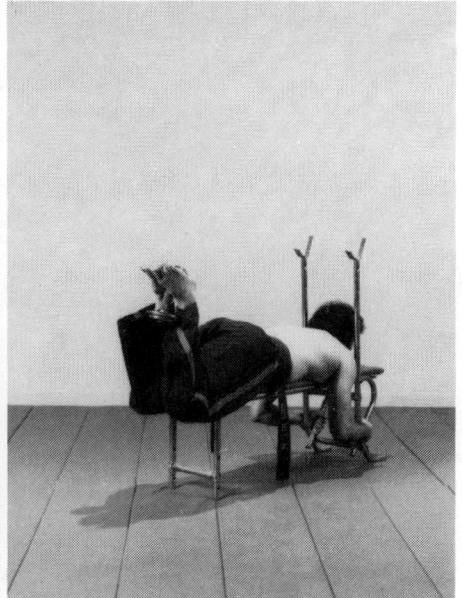

1

2

3

1

5. GLUTEUS & TENSOR FASCIA LATAE -
Supporting yourself by leaning against a chair or some other stationary object, balance yourself on your left leg and raise your right leg behind and away from your

2

body 90 degrees foot parallel to the floor. Using long movements, raise and lower your leg for 10 repetitions of 10 sets, working both

4. QUADRICEPS - Exercising your quadriceps can be done by holding as heavy a dumbell as you can manage in each hand and squatting all the way down. Keep your back as straight as you possibly can to prevent straining it as you squat and stand. Do ten repetitions for five sets.

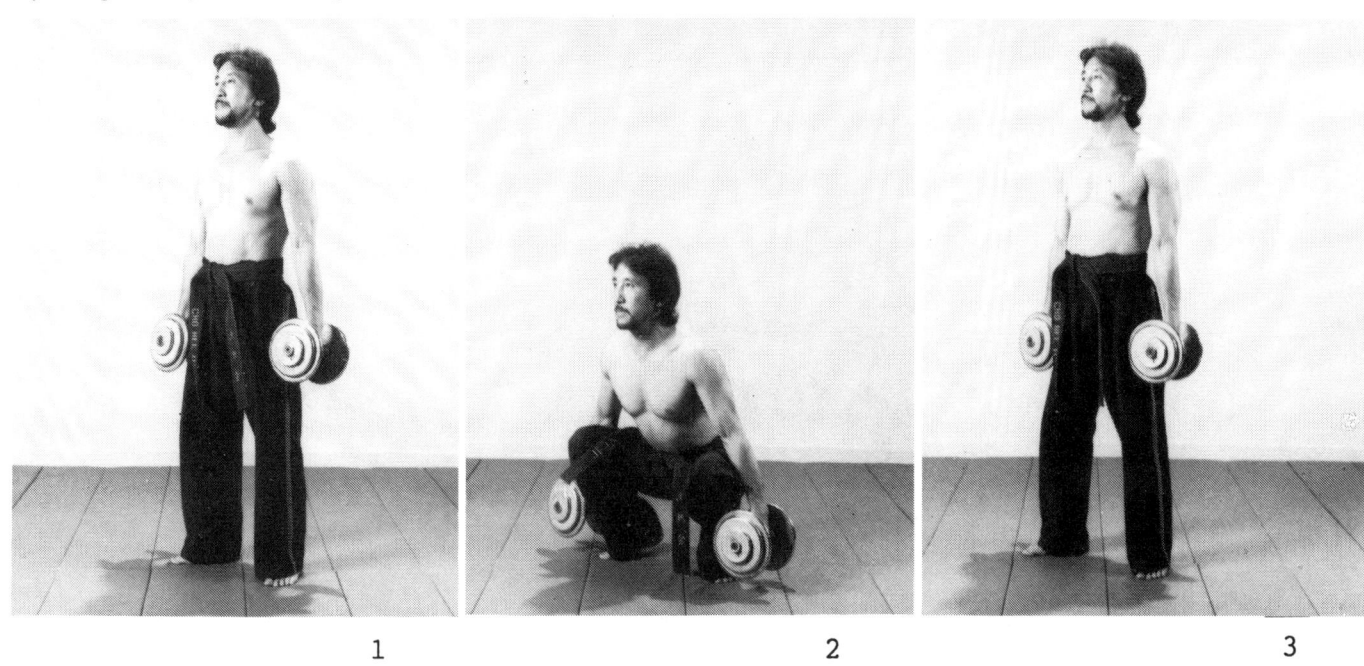

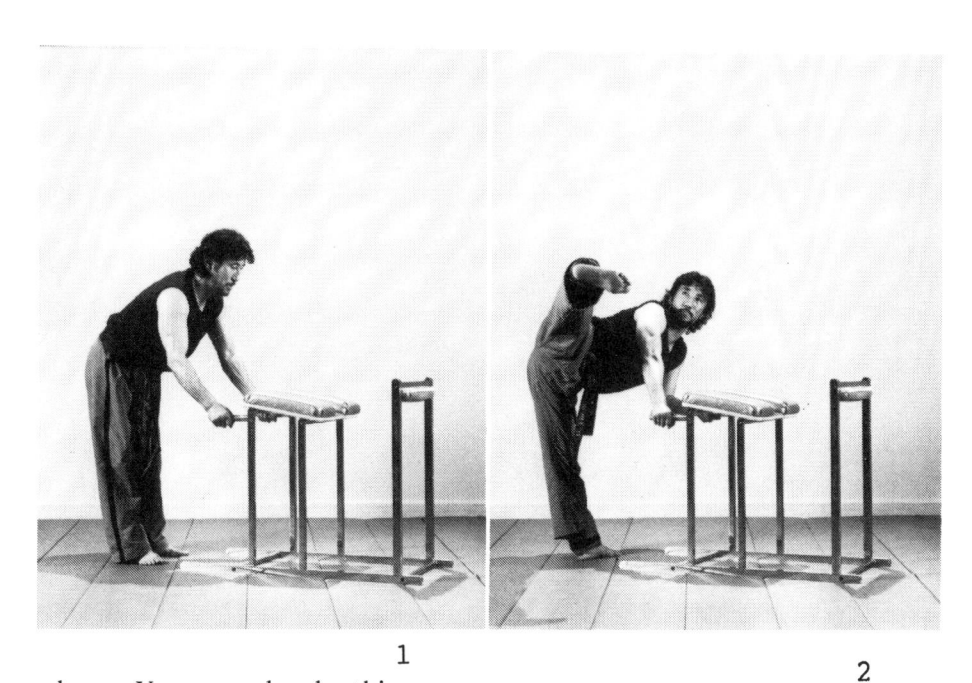

1

2

3

1

2

legs. You can also do this same exercise raising your leg 90 degrees away to the side, which will benefit the tensor fascia latae muscle.

STRETCHING

1. QUADRICEPS I - To stretch your quadriceps, lie on a bench, grab your ankles with both hands and pull your legs back and below the level of your body. The more you pull, the better your stretch will be. Hold yourself there for 20 seconds, repeating three or four times.

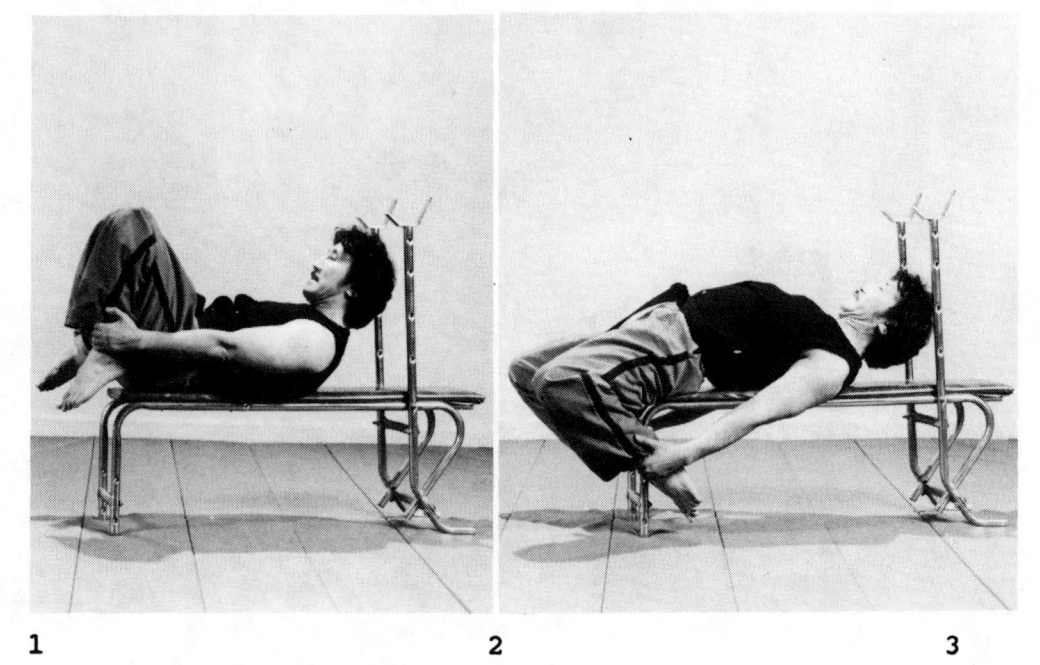

1   2   3

2. QUADRICEPS II - Another good quadricep stretch is to lie on the floor face down, reach behind and grab an ankle in each hand, and then pull your legs towards your head as you arch your back. Hold yourself for about 20 seconds, rest a moment, and then repeat. Do this stretch three or four times.

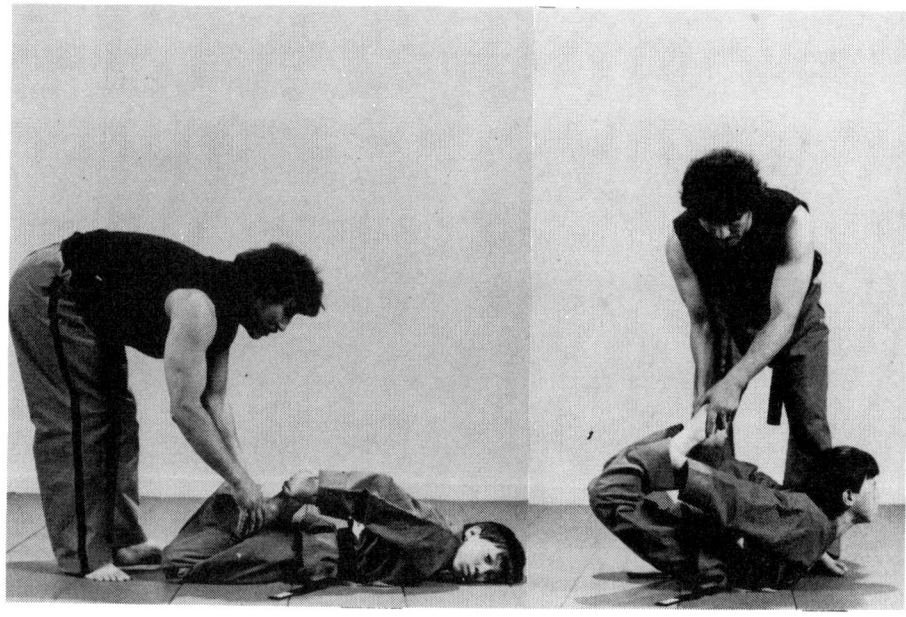

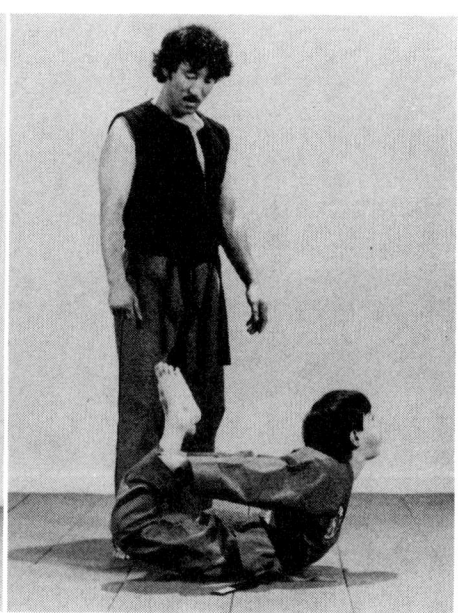

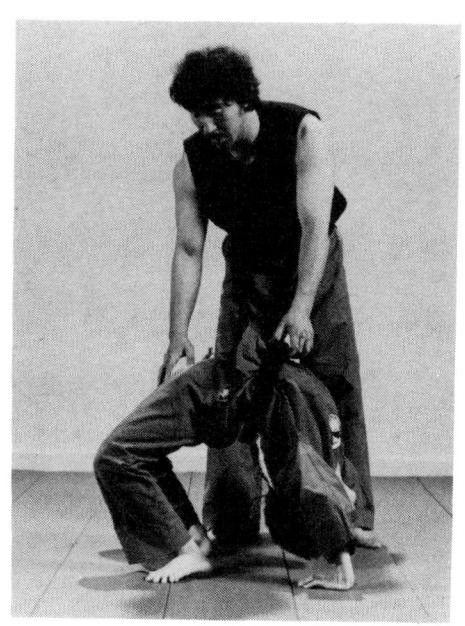

3. BACK & LUMBAR - This stretch is called the "Bear Bridge." Lying on the floor with your feet as close to your buttocks as possible and your hands turned over and palm down by your shoulders, push yourself up, raising your stomach high off the floor and arching your back. Hold yourself like this for 20 seconds, and then slowly lower yourself. Rest for a few moments and then repeat. Do this three or four times.

4. SARTORIUS, OBLIQUES, BACK & LUMBAR - Sit on the floor with your legs spread as wide as you can. You are going to bend side to side in two different ways - first by bringing your outside arm high over

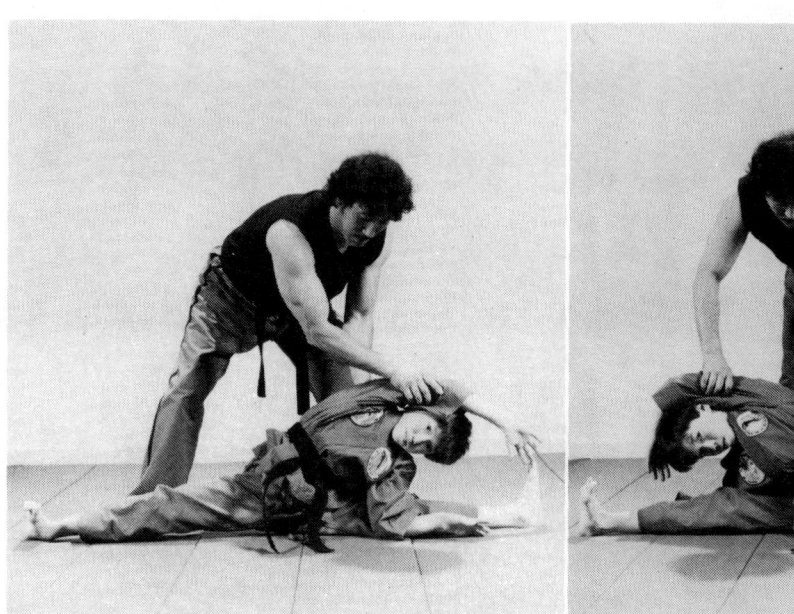

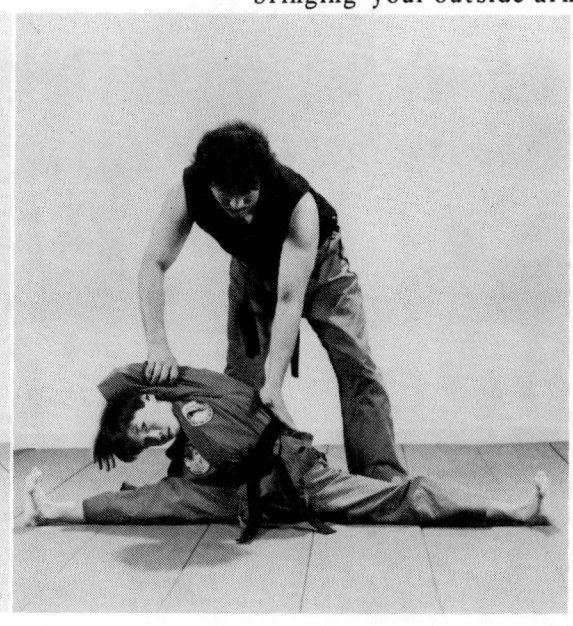

1   2

your head and trying to touch your toes, and then by turning your waist and trying to bring your chin down to your knee. Hold yourself in each position for moments and then switch sides. Repeat the entire cycle three or four times.

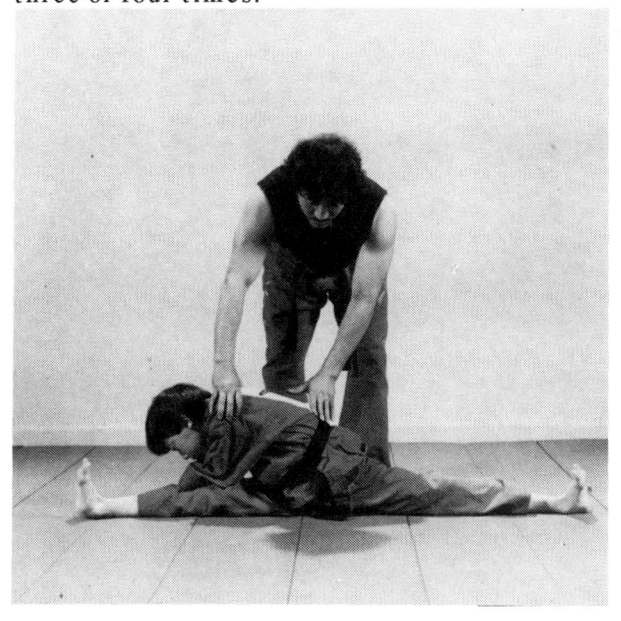

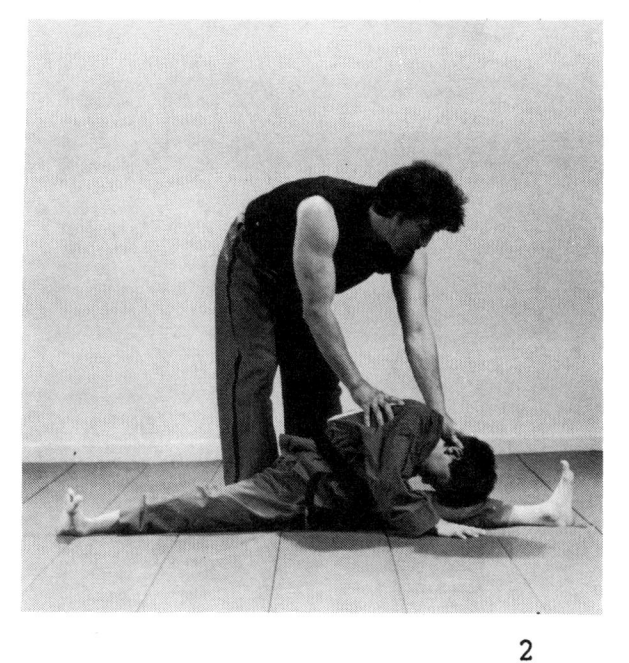

1

2

1988 World Open Tae Kwon Do Championships in England, Women's winners.

A.I.T.K.D. members after a December, 1988 seminar taught by Master Cho.

From left to right: Master Bong Soo Han, Mr. Chuck Norris, Master Hee Il Cho and Mr. Bob Wall at Las Vegas,

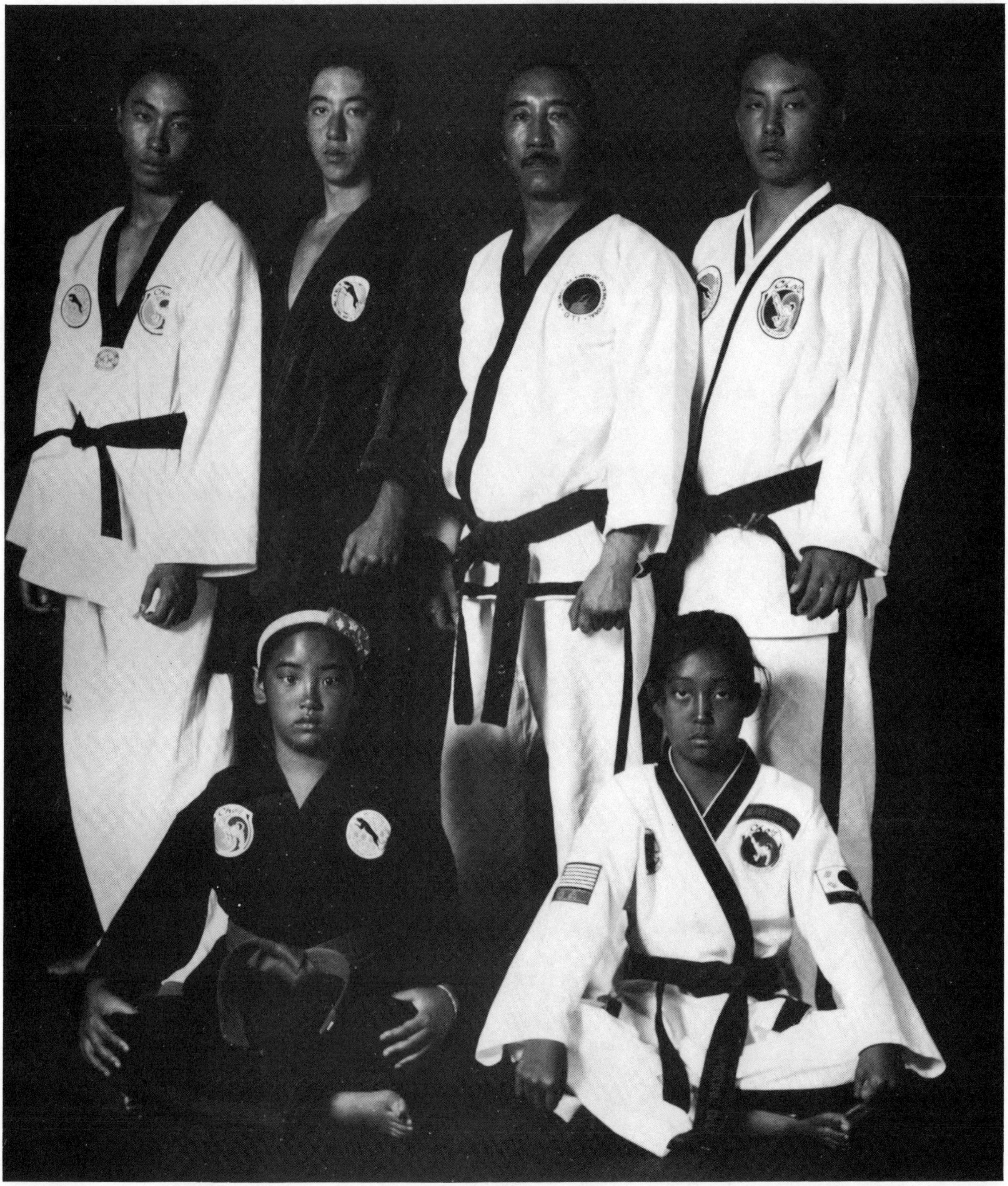

Full contact champion Dennis Alexio, Master Cho and Philip Ameris.

AIMAA Technical Director, Mr. Rick Kenton.

AIMAA Technical Director, Mr. Phillip Ameris.

Master Cho leading an advanced in class in meditation, helping to relax and focus his student's minds before training.

Woman's Forms Champion Cynthia Rothrock with Master Cho.

Intense training at the AIMAA World Headquarters in Los Angeles, California.

A typical adult class at AIMAA World Headquarters in Los Angeles, California.

On location for Sybervision.

Demonstration, 1984.

Appreciation award from England, 1984.

Calligraphy demonstration, Los Angeles "Open", 1984

English Championship, 1984.

Los Angeles "OPEN", 1984.

Master Cho as a member of the winning team, Rhode Island Championship, 1972.

ACTION INTERNATIONAL MARTIAL ARTS ASSOCIATION
국제무도협회

World Headquarters, U.S.A.
10587 Pico Boulevard
Los Angeles, CA., 90064
Phone: (310) 470-2467
Fax: (310) 441-8379

President of A.I.M.A.A
Master Hee Il Cho
9th Degree Black Belt

Thank you for your recent inquiry regarding the Action International Martial Artist Association (AIMAA), the leading and most innovative martial arts organization today. AIMAA was founded in 1980 by Master Hee Il Cho to serve as a unifying body for martial artists of all styles and disciplines. Master Cho adopted his personal philosophy for the charter of the AIMAA, adapting the best from all sources to make a stronger whole. It is for this reason that the AIMAA can provide the powerful exchange of information to further the growth of the martial arts.

Because of Master Cho's tireless efforts, AIMAA has affiliated school members all around the globe. As an affilated member, you will receive all of the following benifits:

1.) ***DIRECT COMMUNICATION WITH MASTER CHO.*** You have the privilege of an open line communication with Master Cho, a Black Belt Hall of Fame member. Master Cho will answer any questions you might have in the realm of martial arts.

2. ***INTERNATIONAL RANK RECOGNITION!*** Official AIMAA rank can be given to all Korean stylists currently holding a black belt certificate from the International Tae Kwon Do Federation and World Tae Kwon Do Federation, as well as the governing bodies of Tang Soo Do, Mu Duck Kwon and others. If you are presently **not** training in a Korean style, don't be despair! Even though AIMAA cannot ethically issue a belt certificate in a style which Master Cho does not personally know, AIMAA will honor both your rank and your students' ranks, while at the same time giving you the opportunity to earn a certification in Tae Kwon Do. To make this as easy as possible for you, with your approved school affiliation you will receive, **free of charge, 2 VIDEO TAPES FROM MASTER CHO'S COMPLETE MARTIAL ARTISTS VIDEO LIBRARY!** You may choose the tapes that cover either the 20 ITF (AIMAA) Tae Kwon Do patterns or the 20 WTF Tae Geuk patterns, both up to 9th Dan Black Belt. **THIS IS AN $80.00 VALUE ABSOLUTELY FREE!** By following Master Cho's training and teaching system, you will be able to test at AIMAA World Headquarters for your black belt in Tae Kwon Do. You will also be able to test your students at your own school up to 1st degree black belt with belt certifcates issue from AIMAA headquarter and signed by Master Cho. This gives both you and your students the chance to be certified in more than one style-your present one and Tae Kwon Do! You will be eligible to test 6 months after becoming a member. There is a $10 fee for each belt certificate and $70 fee for the 1st degree Black Belt certificate. W.T.F. Black Belt certificates are available upon request with an additional fee.

3. ***DELUXE INSTRUCTOR'S KIT!*** Expand your school enrollment with the Deluxe Instructor's Kit which includes a comphrensive instructor manual, student handbook and all the forms necessary for establishing and maintaining a successful school. The instructor manual contains detail information for the following topics: AIMAA ranking system; student curriculum guidlines; testing procedures; criteria for achieving a rank; how to conduct proper public relations; how to double your income with a special black belt program sales techniques; Master Cho's business philosophy, training principles, conduting class methods and much, much more. **Everything you need and want to know** about running an AIMAA afiliated school are in this kit.

4. ***PERSONALIZED SCHOOL CHARTER!*** Affiliated school members will receive

a personal AIMAA school charter. This handsome certificate serves as your international recognition as a member of a worldwide organization. In addition, once all of your present students are enrolled as student members of AIMAA, you will also receive your personal **INSTRUCTOR CERTIFICATE**.

5. *TRAINING WITH MASTER CHO, FREE OF CHARGE!* One of the most exciting benefits of joining AIMAA is that you may train with Master Cho at AIMAA headquarter for 20 days per year **without charge**. In addition, also without charge, you may train for 10 days per year in any AIMAA affiliated school around the world--allowing you to meet and train with martial artists of other styles and disciplines to expand your knowledge.

6. *DISCOUNT ON BOOKS AND VIDEOS*! Master Cho's video library has a total of 43 different videos and 11 books that cover all aspects of the martial arts. With Master Cho's **Scientific Class Tapes**, you can add new motivation in your students training as well as broaden you and your students martial arts knowledge. Affiliated members can purchase all of Master Cho's books and video tapes at an incredible volume discounts--a minimum order of three copies per titles: **40% off** of retail on Master Cho's books and **$30.00** per tape; or at a member discount--no minimum: **25% off** on books and **$40.00** per tape.

7. *INCREDIBLE STUDENT BENEFITS!* Your students benefit as well through your affiliation with AIMAA. Once they join AIMAA through your school (for $30.00 per year--$20.00 for AIMAA and $10.00 for your school) they receive a personalized membership card, a 25% discount on individual title of both books and tapes, an annual AIMAA newsletter, an exciting poster of Master Cho in action, a beautiful membership patch, and the chance to train at any AIMAA affiliated school worldwide for 10 days per year. Add all of this to the international rank recognition and belt certificate that they receive every time they test and you will have some very satisfied, proud students.

8. *LOTS MORE!* In addition to everything already mentioned, you will receive a **complete set of Master Cho's action posters plus 2 complete sets of AIMAA patches; a value of $120.00 at no extra cost**. AIMAA also offers newsletters, training seminars, equipment, tournaments, championship sanctioning for your own tournaments...the list goes on and on!

Because of your expressed interest, you now have an opportunity to join one of the most progressive martial arts associations in the world. You will be part of an elite group of individuals who practice the martial arts for the development of mind, body, and spirit. AIMAA has worldwide recognition, and so can you as an affiliated member. Qualifying for AIMAA affiliation is simple--all you need is your 1st Dan Black Belt from a recognized system and a valid business license.

All of the benefits of being an AIMAA affiliate are available to you for a **ONE TIME FEE of $300.00** which includes shipping in the U.S. (Foreign countries add $40.00 for shipping). If you have any questions, please contact AIMAA headquarter.

Looking forward to having you as an affiliated member.

Sincerely,

Action International Martial Arts Association

Membership Office

MASTER HEE IL CHO
"SEE WHATS MISSING IN YOU TRAINING"
VIDEO LIBRARY

FOR OVER FORTY YEARS, MASTER HEE IL CHO HAS BEEN THE LEADING VOICE IN TAE KWON DO, 9TH DAN BLACK BELT, MEMBER OF THE HALL OF FAME AND FOUNDER OF ACTION INTERNATIONAL MARTIAL ARTS ASSOCIATION

Tape 1- TAE KWON DO BASIC TECHNIQUES & STANCES 60min
Step-by-step demonstrating all basics.

Tape 2- THE COMPLETE STRETCH 60min
Master-Cho's proven stretching techniques, designed for excellence.

Tape 3- ONE & THREE STEP SPARRING 60min
Take-downs, arm-locks and jumping techniques, improve fighting and defensive skills.

Tape 4- I.T.F. HYUNG (1-10) 60min
Chun-Ji, Dan Gun, Do San, Won Hyo, Yul Kok, Joong Gun, Toi Gye, Haw Rang, Choong Moo and Gwang Gae.

Tape 5- I.T.F. HYUNG (11-20) 90min
Ge Back, Po Eun, Choong Jang, Yoo Sin, Ko Dong, Ui-Ji, Choi Youn, Sam Il, Se Jong, and Tong Il.

Tape 6- DYNAMIC KICKING 80min
Ground kicking, the awesome master Cho way.

Tape 7- DYNAMIC JUMP KICK 90min
Advanced kicking, Master Cho's secrets.

Tape 8- CHO'S WORKOUT SYSTEM 60min
For "the Complete Martial Artist" only! Weights, bag, boxing...the works.

Tape 9- DYNAMIC BREAKING 90min
Not magic, but technique and focus. Techniques include mid-air, spinning, blindfolded and combinations.

Tape 10- SELF DEFENSE & FALLING 120min
Falling, dropping techniques self-defense against weapons, ground fighting and controlling assailants.

Tape 11- FREE SPARRING- AMATEUR 90min
Amateur Tae Kwon Do and American One Point

Tape 12- FREE SPARRING PROFESSIONAL FULL CONTACT 60min
Full contact fighting skills. Sharpen your technique and confidence.

Tape 13– DYNAMIC BAG WORKOUT 60min
Learn balance, timing and precision, speed and power, both hand and foot techniques are covered.

Tape 14- INSTRUCTOR TRAINING-ADULT 60min
Complete Adult's Class. Learn how to motivate your students and develop their self-awareness & self-confidence.

Tape 15- INSTRUCTOR TRAINING-CHILDREN 60min
Follow Master Cho step-by-step. Learn how to instruct, control and inspire children.

Tape 16- DYNAMIC WEIGHT LIFTING 120min
Master Cho teaches different exercises to develop individual muscle groups, making you nothing less than awesome.

Tape 17-COMPLETE TESTING GUIDE 120min
White belt through 3rd Dan Black, The physical as well as the philosophical aspects of a belt test.

Tape 18- EIGHTH ANNUAL L.A. OPEN CHAMPIONSHIP, VOL. 1 60min
Black Belt competition and team fighting.

Tape 18- EIGHTH ANNUAL L.A. OPEN CHAMPIONSHIP, VOL. 2 60min
Children's events, weapons competition, Master's demonstrations, American Freestyle, 9 musical patterns & forms.

Tape 19- A COMPLETE LOOK AT MASTER CHO'S TAPE LIBRARY 60min
What it takes to be : The Complete Martial Artist Entertaining as well as enthralling.(Tapes1-18)

Tape 20- BOXING BEGINNERS & ADVANCED 80min
Boxing Techniques, stances and movements in slow-motion and full-speed.

Tape 21- ADULT'S DEFENSE WORKOUT 60min
For the non-martial artist! Easy effective self defense techniques linked to an intensive workout.

Tape 22- ADULT'S SELF DEFENSE 60min
For both the martial artist and non-martial artist. Practical techniques involving joint locking and counter attack.

Tape 23A- TENTH ANNUAL L.A. OPEN CHAMPIONSHIPS, VOL.1 60min
Junior and adult sparring, black belt sparring, Grand Championship match and more.

Tape 23B- TENTH ANNUAL L.A. OPEN CHAMPIONSHIPS, VOL.2 60min
Forms competition, women's sparring, master's demonstration.

Tape 24- W.T.F. TAE GEUK HYUNG 60min
The official Patterns of the WTF Tae Geuk 1-8 as well as Koryo, the first black belt pattern.

Tape 25- CHILDREN'S MARTIAL ARTS TRAINING- BEGINNERS 60min
Basics include meditation, warm-up, stretching, stances, blocks, attacks, and kicks.

Tape 26- CHILDREN'S MARTIAL ARTS TRAINING- INTERMEDIATE 60min
Combination techniques including block/punching, fighting, intermediate kicking and stick exercises.

Tape 27- CHILDREN'S MARTIAL ARTS TRAINING- ADVANCED 60min
Hand techniques, advanced kicking, kicking combinations, and target training.

Tape 28- CHILDREN'S MARTIAL ARTS TRAINING- SELF DEFENSE 60min
A must! Escaping from bear hugs, wrist grabs, shoulder grabs, head locks, and restraining holds.

Tape 29- CHILDREN'S MARTIAL ARTS TRAINING- SPARRING & BREAKING 60min
Sparring, arranged sparring, sparring training, jumping and board breaking.

Tape 30- HIGHLIGHTS OF TAPES 20-29 60min
A collection of the most exciting moments from Master Cho's library, tapes 20-29

Tape 31- W.T.F. BLACK BELT HYUNG 60min
2ND DAN to 9TH DAN WTF black belt patterns including Geum-Gang, Tae-Baek, Pyeong-Won, Sip-Jin, Ji-Tae, Cheon-Kwon, Han-Soo, and Il-Yeo.

NEW 1993 TAPES
$ 70.00 each

Tape 32– THE SCIENTIFIC STRETCH 90min
Learn Isometric, Plyometric, and static stretching.

Tape 33- W.T.F. BEGINNERS 90min
The defensive/offensive foot work and all the basic kicks.

Tape 34- W.T.F. INTERMEDIATE 90min
All foot work and kicks combined to form an effective method of training.

Tape 35- W.T.F. ADVANCED 90min
Learn accuracy, distance, and timing of kicks/jump kicks with the use of targets.

Tape 36- W.T.F. SPARRING 90min
Counterattacks, enticing, faints, and tournaments. Master Cho also discusses a weakness in the W.T.F. style.

Tape 37- SCIENTIFIC CLASSES- BEGINNERS & INTERMEDIATE 90min
Instructors and students learn a new scientific class for all styles.

Tape 38- SCIENTIFIC CLASSES- ADVANCED 90min
Instructors and students learn a new scientific class for all styles.

Tape 39- PRACTICAL INFORMATION & MASTER CHO BIOGRAPHY 90min
An interview with Master Cho, his life and practical information for students and instructors.

Tape 40- SYBERVISION-DEFEND YOURSELF 60min
10 Master's moves.

Tape 41-AIMAA INTERNATIONAL TESTING 1992 120min
Unique guide to all martial artists, white to 5th degree black belt.

BOOK LIBRARY

THE COMPLETE MASTER'S KICK	$16.95
THE COMPLETE MASTER'S JUMPING KICK	$16.95
THE COMPLETE ONE & THREE STEP SPARRING	$16.95
THE COMPLETE TAE GEUK HYUNG, W.T.F.	$15.95
THE COMPLETE BLACK BELT HYUNG, W.T.F.	$15.95
THE COMPLETE TAE KWON DO HYUNG VOL. 1	$13.95
THE COMPLETE TAE KWON DO HYUNG VOL. 2	$13.95
THE COMPLETE TAE KWON DO HYUNG VOL. 3	$13.95
THE COMPLETE MARTIAL ARTIST VOL. 1	$19.95
THE COMPLETE MARTIAL ARTIST VOL. 2	$19.95
MAN OF CONTRASTS	$16.95

Book's Shipping fee $5.00 each additional book add $2.00 no C.O.D. Foreign country $20.00 each additional book add

ACTION POSTER COLLECTION

A) 22 1/2" x 18" $10.00
B) 22 1/2" x 18" $10.00
C) 22 1/2" x 18" $10.00
D) 22 1/2" x 18" $10.00
E) 27" x 35" $15.00
F) 27" x 35" $15.00
G) 22 1/2" x 18" B/W $7.00
H) 22 1/2" x 18" B/W $7.00
J) 22 1/2" x 18" B/W $7.00

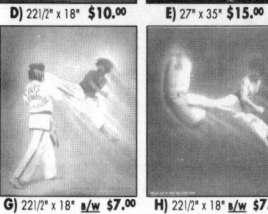

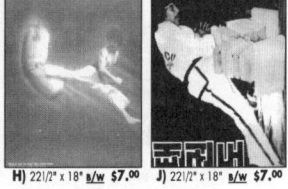

(SHIPPING FEE: U.S. INCLUDED - FOREIGN COUNTRY $10.00)

VISA & MASTERCHARGE ACCEPTED
PAY IN U.S. DOLLARS ONLY
CARD NO.
EXPIRATION DATE ____ DATE ____
SIGNATURE ____

NAME ____
ADDRESS ____
CITY ____
COUNTRY ____ STATE ____ ZIP ____

( ) VHS
( ) BETA
( ) NTSC-USA
( ) PAL-EUROPE

TO ORDER - CALL TOLL FREE 1-800-527-4833

MAKE CHECK PAYABLE TO
CHO'S TAE KWON DO CENTER
10587 Pico Blvd. Los Angeles CA 90064
TEL 310/ 470-2467 FAX 310/ 441-8379

NEW '93 TAPE	$ 70.00
REG TAPE	$ 59.00
TWO REG TAPES	$ 80.00
FOUR REG TAPES	$ 150.00

DEALER INQUIRIES ACCEPTED

TAPES SHIPPING FEE	$ 5.00
EACH ADD. TAPE ADD	$ 2.00
FOREIGN COUNTRY	$12.00
EACH ADD. TAPE ADD	$10.00
NO C.O.D.	

California residents 8.5% TAX Catalog (45 pages) $2.00

TAPE 1 - Tae Kwon Do Basic Techniques and Stances
Follow a step-by-step in-depth demonstration in slow-motion and full speed of all basic and advanced techniques and stances.

TAPE 2 - The Complete Stretch
Become one of those artists you've admired who are capable of throwing kicks high and hard. This tape leads you through Master Cho's proven stretching techniques by isolating and working each particular muscle group.

TAPE 3 - One Step & Three Step Sparring
Learn essential preparation for free-fighting activities. Develop rapid and accurate combinations of blocking and counter attacking techniques against your opponents.

TAPE 4 - Tae Kwon Do Hyung (1 - 10)
Detailed explanation of techniques, stances and movements in slow-motion and full-speed. Chun Ji, Dan Gun, Do San, Won Hyo, Yul Kok, Joong Gun, Toi Gye, Haw Rang, Choong Moo, Gwang Gae.

TAPE 5 - Tae Kwon Do Hyung (11 - 20)
Detailed explanation of techniques, stances and movements in slow-motion and full-speed. Ge Back, Po Eun, Choong Jang, Ul ji, Yoo Sin, Ko Dong, Choi Youn, Sam Il, Se Jong, Tong Il

TAPE 6 - Dynamic Kicking - Complete!
Follow step-by-step through 9 series of kicking techniques, Each exercise and kick is demonstrated and explained for your individual workout.

TAPE 7 - Dynamic Jump Kick - Complete!
Follow step-by-step through a series of jumping techniques. Each exercise and jumping kick is demonstrated and explained for your individual workout.

TAPE 8 - Master Cho's Unique Workout System
Follow Master Cho step-by-step through a series of full-body exercises. Proper use of weight training, bag workout, boxing techniques and other necessary exercises for the development of the complete martial artist.

TAPE 9 - Dynamic Breaking - Complete!
Improve your speed, power and precision with step-by-step illustrations which guide you through a progressive training program in breaking techniques. Filmed at 500 frames per second.

TAPE 10 - Self Defense & Falling
Learn how to fall and select good defensive stances incorporating hand positions that minimize target areas accessible to the opponent. All techniques are explained and demonstrated.

TAPE 11 - Free Sparring - Amateur
Amateur Tae Kwon Do and American One Point sparring. Develop winning techniques and strategies for point fighting. Master Cho teaches you in slow motion and full-speed.

TAPE 12 - Free Sparring - Professional Full Contact
The skills of a martial artist with the stamina of a boxer. If this sounds like something you wish to achieve, then this tape is it. Develop full contact fighting skills. Learn effective boxing techniques to include in your martial arts training.

TAPE 13 - Dynamic Bag Workout - Complete!
Follow step-by-step through a series of special bag workouts to develop hand speed and punching ability as well as powerful kicks including counter attacks and jumping kicks.

TAPE 14 - Instructor - The Complete Adult Class
Follow Master Cho step-by-step through a series of training exercises for adult students. Learn how to teach and motivate your students, and develop their self-awareness and self-confidence.

TAPE 15 - Instructor - The Complete Children's Class
Follow Master Cho step-by-step through a series of training exercises for young students. Learn how to control and inspire, children and develop their character through the martial arts.

TAPE 16 - Dynamic Weight Lifting - Complete!
Follow Master Cho step-by-step through a series of 30 years of experience-proven weight training workouts. Learn how to build muscle groups for effective and faster techniques and explosive power.

TAPE 17 - Complete Testing Guide
White to high Black Belt Promotions. In this unique guide to promotions, Master Cho covers both the physical as well as the philosophical aspects of a belt test.

TAPE 18 - Eighth Annual L.A. Open Championship VOL. 1
TAPE 18 - Eighth Annual L.A. Open Championship VOL. 2
TAPE 19 - Highlights of The 18 Tapes
TAPE 20 - TAPE 20 - Boxing (Beginners & Advanced)
Dalailed explanation of techniques, stances and movements in slow-motion and full-speed.

TAPE 21 - Adult's Defense Workout
A complete martial arts workout for the non-martial artist including Flexability Training, Endurance Training, Cardiovascular and Muscular Conditioning as well as the most practical of MASTER CHO'S moves to both condition as well as to develop your own personal Defense System.

TAPE 22 - Adult's Self Defense
A sensible system of self defense for both the martial artist as well as the non-martial artist. MASTER CHO covers how to escape from an attacker's grasp, how to control an attacker through the use of joint locking techniques, and when necessary, how to take away an attacker's ability to cause further harm through a devastating counter attack.

TAPE 23A - Tenth Annual L.A. Open Championships
All the action from the Tenth Annual Los Angeles OPEN Martial Arts Championships, held on May 17, 1987 in Beverly Hills and hosted by MASTER HEE IL CHO. Edited from over eight hours of non-stop action, included are junior and adult sparring, black belt sparring, Grand Champion match and more.

TAPE 23B - The Tenth Annual L.A. Open Championships
This second volume includes forms competition, women's sparring, master's demonstrations and more.

TAPE 24 - The Complete Tae Geuk Hyung 1 to 8 - & Koryo
MASTER HEE IL CHO teaches and demonstrates and new patterns as sanctioned by the World Tae Kwon Do Federation (WTF), from White belt through 1st Dan Black belt. Tae Geuk 1-8 as well as the Koryo pattern are shown at different speeds and different angles to make learning as easy as possible.

TAPE 25 - Children's Martial Arts Training, Beginners
All the basics that the younger martial artist needs to begin his or her training including Meditation, Warm-up Exercises and Stretching, Basic Stances, Blocks, Attacking Techniques and Kicks.

TAPE 26 - Children's Martial Arts Training, Intermediate
Children's intermediate techniques are explained in a follow along fashion, including combinations of Blocks, Block/Punch Techniques, Fighting Techniques and Intermediate Kicking Techniques as well as Stick Exercises to help develop balance.

TAPE 27 - Children's Martial Arts Training, Advanced
A young person's guide to advanced techniques. Covered in detail are intricate Hand Techniques, Advanced Kicking and Kicking Combination Techniques, and how to train using a variety of hand held targets.

TAPE 28 - Children's Martial Arts Training, Self-Defense
Unfortunately, a must in today's world. Children's Self-Defense training is covered in detail including how to attempt to escape from Bear Hugs, Wrist Grabs, Shoulder Grabs, Head Locks and other restraining holds, as well as what to do once free. How and when Children should defend themselves is also discussed.

TAPE 29 - Children's Martial Arts Training, Sparring & Breaking
Children's Sparring and Demonstrations, including Arrangement Sparring, Free Sparring, working out using a hanging bag, and a demonstration of children's Jumping and Board Breaking Techniques.

TAPE 30 - Highlights of Tapes 20 to 29

TAPE 31 - THE COMPLETE TAEKWONDO HYUNG (WTF)
Geum-Gahg, Tae-Baek, Pyeong-Won, Sip-Jin, Ji Tae, Cheon-Kwon, Han-Soo, Il-Yeo. MASTER HEE IL CHO teaches and demonstrates and new patterns, as sanctioned by the world Tae Kwon Do Federation (WTF), from 2nd Dan to 9th black belt pattern are shown dat different speeds and different angles to make learning as easy as possible.

Master Hee Il Cho - Early Years of Competition

Master Hee Il Cho - Early Years of Competition

Scene from "The Best of the Best"

In 1989, Master Cho was asked to portray the coach of the Korean martial arts Team in the movie "The Best of the Best." Eric Roberts stars as a member of the American team and James Earl Jones plays his coach. This movie is about the bond that forms between people and will touch your heart. The competition scenes include some of the most dynamic kicking techniques ever captured on film, and it is this type of movie which portrays the "right" image of the martial arts that will help all students, regardless of system or style.

"The Best of the Best" is scheduled to open in the Winter of 1989, and Master Cho would like to see the entire martial arts community support the film.

Actor Eric Roberts with Master Cho.

Master Cho and world famous actor James Earl Jones. Actor and teacher Simon Rhee with his father,

Master Cho, film producer and actor Philip Rhee, and Eric Roberts.

Master Cho with members of the "Korean Team"

Actor Christopher Penn with Master Cho.

Scene from "The Best of the Best"

Korean Special Forces Unit with Master Cho,

Simon Rhee and Philip Rhee.

Location filming in the snow and cold in Korea.

James Earl Jones as the American Coach with Master Cho and Sally Kirkland